BARCODE ON
NEXT PAGE

W9-BTP-758

THE MERTON ANNUAL

Studies in Culture, Spirituality, and Social Concerns

Volume 21	2008

Edited by

David Belcastro   Gray Matthews

THE MERTON ANNUAL
Studies in Culture, Spirituality, and Social Concerns

THE MERTON ANNUAL publishes articles about Thomas Merton and about related matters of major concern to his life and work. Its purpose is to enhance Merton's reputation as a writer and monk, to continue to develop his message for our times, and to provide a regular outlet for substantial Merton-related scholarship. *THE MERTON ANNUAL* includes as regular features reviews, review-essays, a bibliographic survey, interviews, and first appearances of unpublished, or obscurely published Merton materials, photographs, and art. Essays about related literary and spiritual matters will also be considered. Manuscripts and books for review may be sent to the editors.

EDITORS

David J. Belcastro	Gray Matthews
818 Montrose Ave.	Department of Communication
Bexley, Ohio 43209	University of Memphis
dbelcast@capital.edu	Memphis, TN 38152
	matthews@memphis.edu

Grateful acknowledgement is expressed to The Merton Legacy Trust and the Thomas Merton Center at Bellarmine University for permission to print *Some Points from the Birmingham Nonviolence Movement* and the calligraphy by Thomas Merton for the cover artwork. We wish to thank The University of Mississippi Press for permission to reprint the interview with Walker Percy and the *Journal of Catholic Social Thought* for their kind permission to reprint the essay by Albert Raboteau.

PUBLISHED BY:	SPONSORED BY:
Fons Vitae	International Thomas Merton Society
49 Mockingbird Valley Drive	Thomas Merton Center
Louisville KY 40207	Bellarmine University
502.897.3641	2001 Newburg Road
Fonsvitaeky@aol.com	Louisville KY 40205
http://www.fonsvitae.com	502.452.8187 or 8177
	merton@bellarmine.edu
	http://www.merton.org/ITMS/

Further details about membership and subscribing to *The Merton Seasonal* and *The Merton Annual* are available at http://www.merton.org/ITMS/membership. htm or by contacting the Thomas Merton Center at the above address.

For members of the International Thomas Merton Society, available for $15.00, plus shipping and handling. Individual copes are available through bookstores and directly from the publisher for $19.95. Institutions $39.95. *Copyright:* All rights reserved.

Library of Congress Control Number: 2009927313

ISBN 9781891785351

Printed in Canada

The Merton Annual

Volume 21	2008

Introduction: Wide Open to Marveling, Fearing, Burning and Enduring

Gray Matthews

Everything depends on a red wheel barrow. I think of that line quite regularly; it is from William Carlos Williams' short yet immeasurable poem, "The Red Wheelbarrow." Actually, he said "so much depends," but I sometimes think "everything depends" on that red wheelbarrow "glazed with rainwater / beside the white chickens."[1] To simply see that wheelbarrow next to the chickens—or to take a walk, a pure walk, or to write a sentence, completely—can raise an unshakeable intuition of how much reality can be present to our awareness at any moment. Before I move to the next paragraph, and before you finish reading this one, consider how we are in a kind of conversational awareness right now, a very fluid moment that never stops. So much depends upon this seeing, this realizing, this being in this eternal moment. So often, we miss seeing something because we are doing something else. As Simone Weil put it, "the great trouble with human life is that looking and eating are two different operations."[2]

So, it is not amazing how violent a telephone can appear to ring all of the sudden. Interruptions are constant. How quickly we lose sight of the red wheel barrow and become focused on any number of dizzying tasks, responsibilities, concerns, news, horns, voices, images that constantly form a haggard environment in which we are daily shred and divided. How quickly we are infused and then bereft of contemplation. Almost literally, to survive in this world, we feel compelled to find a moment to stop, shake our head and remind ourselves that everything is crazy all around us as we gasp for air. We look for help, for signs of sanity, and every now and then we suddenly see a red wheel barrow. Or maybe someone simply reminds us, red wheelbarrow-like: Hey! look, see, behold! And we are revived. Sometimes we do not even need to see the wheel barrow itself; it is enough that someone has brought us back, with compassion, to attention.

I cannot help but think that this is the purpose of *The Merton Annual*: To help remind us of our need to be attentive, watchful, aware. Each volume seems steeped in compassionate awareness of our communal need for genuine contemplation and thus authentic action. Sursoro much depends on our seeing what is real, such as our real lives, our real weaknesses, our real illusions. We cannot forget that arresting line spoken by Thomas Beckett in T.S. Eliot's play, *Murder in the Cathedral*: "Human kind cannot bear very much reality."[3] Recognition of that seeming fact, however, does not settle the matter, for many of us cannot bear very many illusions, certainly not the endless variety manufactured daily by a culture of noise. We yearn to hear, to see, to remember the Source of reality. Like John Ruusbroec, we seek "the living life."[4]

How does *The Merton Annual* help us with this situation? Thomas Merton could have been writing about the *Annual* when he described his own attempt to wrestle with the relationship between reality and the writing of books:

> These pages do not attempt to convey any special information, or to answer deep philosophical questions about life. True, they do concern themselves with questions about life. But they certainly do not pretend to do the reader's thinking for him. On the contrary, they invite him to listen for himself. They do not merely speak to him, they remind him that he is a Hearer.[5]

If we have learned anything from Merton's counsel over the years, we have learned that we do not *read* in order to *see words*. Nor do we read in order to merely know what others have to say. Like visiting one of the desert fathers and mothers, we read good books and works such as *The Merton Annual* in order to hear a Word. We are hungry beggars.

I raise such matters here because of my initial experience as a new co-editor of *The Merton Annual*. I became so busy at times, so impatient with computers, so annoyed by my weaknesses in organization, so irritated with my inability to return messages in a timely manner, that I feared losing sight of the purpose of the *Annual* and ruining something I loved. Worst of all, though, was the realization that I was losing my balance as sheer activity and competing workloads threatened to overtake the prospects of my living contemplatively. The irony was mind-numbing at times. How can I work on everything, handle all my conflicting obligations, all at once?

I found some relief from St. Bernard in his counsel to Pope Eugenius III, a one-time monk who sat under the teachings of Bernard, his abbot, who now feared he was losing all capacity for contemplation by trying to meet the great multitude of his responsibilities. I have never compared myself to popes, and certainly am not now, but I sensed his trouble; it is the trouble of Everyman. Bernard suggested Eugenius practice "consideration," which should help return him to contemplation if he had, indeed, lost his way.[6] Bernard asked him to *consider* himself in relation to four attributes of God: His breadth, depth, length and height. He presented the consideration of breadth as leading to the contemplation of God's love. Considering depth should lead to contemplating His wisdom, considering length as flowing into the contemplation of eternity, and considering height as moving one to contemplate His majesty.

And then Bernard drew this set of parallels: Upon consideration we *marvel* at the majesty of God; we *fear* looking into the depths of wisdom; we *burn* when meditating on God's love; we *endure* by a perseverance that emulates eternity. Bernard helped Eugenius realize that, lo and behold, these four means of consideration become transformed into four kinds of contemplation! Reading this snapped me back to attention, and I would wager it did the same for Eugenius. Bernard's concluding remark, though, is what helped me reexamine the true value of *The Merton Annual*; Bernard said simply: "So let this be the end of the book but not of the search."[7]

Thus I came to realize three things that I think are important to note here. First, the *Annual* is not an end in itself, but a means to further every reader's search, a search in which we marvel and fear, burn and endure. Next, the *Annual* is filled with insightful *considerations* that serve to encourage and support contemplative living. Finally, the *Annual* functions like a red wheel barrow—it helps bring us to attention, helps us notice rainwater, chickens and other hidden realities amidst the wholeness of life.

Therefore, consider the following essays and book reviews as Merton himself would have, as seeds of contemplation in a world of action. Let what is written here help you marvel, burn, fear and by all means endure. So much depends on, not what you see in the *Annual*, but on what the *Annual* helps you see. Read to see.

All of the essays in this volume were presented in some form or fashion at the 10th General Meeting of the ITMS, June 2007, in Memphis, TN. As you may recall, the theme of the conference was: "Wide Open to Heaven and Earth." The title was taken from the same essay by Merton, "Love and Solitude," that was quoted above, This theme also spurred a subtitle, which will be helpful to remember, too, as you read through these works and consider the interrelationships between: "Contemplation, Community, Culture."

The essay by Albert Raboteau served as a basis for his moving address on Merton, race and the struggle for civil rights. Those who attended the conference were just as moved by Dr. Raboteau's presence, sincerity and participation throughout the conference. Merton would surely have enjoyed dinner discussions with him! Because the conference was held in Memphis, Dr. Raboteau's words were even more halting and helpful for reflection on the past and present moment. Who would have imagined then, however, that Americans would elect the first African-American president the following year? Dr. Raboteau's essay is insightful, and particularly significant in highlighting the role of contemplation in Merton's life, as well as ours now, as it inevitably bears on social issues. William Apel follows with a focused essay on the ill-fated meeting between Merton and Dr. Martin Luther King, Jr. Apel illuminates the correspondence between Quaker June Yungblut and Merton around the time of King's assassination and leads us to ponder the real possibilities of peace and reconciliation.

From the hope of reconciliation to the work of dialogue, John Dadosky presents Merton as a model of inter-religious engagement. Daniel Horan provides more support for the argument as he connects Merton to Franciscan interreligious dialogue. Timothy Shaffer opens the subject further by tracing Franciscan influences in Merton's life such that they provided a lens through which Merton extended his wide open gaze toward heaven and earth. Roger Lipsey's photo essay complements these three papers as he reminds us of the dialogical relationship between heaven and earth through Merton's Zen garden and the Buddhist-Christian teachings on impermanence. The mystery of relation permeates all five of these works, further commending readers to persevere in true dialogue with reality.

Pam Proietti's essay furthers such concerns by inviting readers to consider the role of the Christian artist in dialogue with reality. She explores the influence of Jacques Maritain on Merton's understanding of art and the task of the artist. Patrick O'Connell follows with an in depth exploration of Merton's poetic art in *Emblems of a Season of Fury*. O'Connell illuminates the heightened need for contemplative awareness that permeates this significant collection of Merton's poetry. John P. Collins follows with and examination of the work of Merton and Walker Percy on the myth of the Fall from Paradise. An interview with Walker Percy, conducted by Victor and Dewey Kramer a few years ago, has been included in this volume for its value in relaying further insights into the art of Percy and his thoughts about Merton's work.

The two final essays from the conference are lively forays into connections between community and culture in regard to the transformation of lives on fire. As Fred Herron explores Merton's approach to transformative education, and Nass Cannon examines parallels between Merton and John of the Cross, we begin to see more clearly a kind of dynamism at work in Merton's life and writings that illuminates and celebrates the integral relationship between contemplation and action.

Before closing, I would like to call special attention to co-editor David Belcastro's bibliographic essay, for it much more than a mere survey of recently published works on Merton. For the past few years, the bibliographic essay has increasingly become less of a report and more of a creative and substantial essay in its own right. In this year's essay, David highlights the metaphor and reality of authentic conversation in such a way that it not only ties this volume, the Memphis conference and recent publications about Merton together, but offers a glimpse into the role and future of Merton scholarship. There is no old news in the essay, but many fresh ideas to consider.

Finally, David and I wish to extend our appreciation, and that of the readership of *The Merton Annual*, to all of the past editors and co-editors for their hard, unflagging work in building the *Annual* and expanding the base of Merton scholarship. In particular, we wish to thank Victor Kramer for his endurance as editor and his love for contemplative scholarship. We also wish to humbly express our gratitude to the ITMS publications committee for the honor in being appointed co-editors. As newly appointed co-editors, David and I recognize the twin, paradoxical responsibilities of "following" past editors. In following, one must not only stay behind the leader but move ahead in the sense of succession; one follows *to* as well as *from*. We hope to do both in honoring a legacy that continues to sustain a readership that remains wide open to marveling, fearing, burning and enduring. There is still so much to consider, so much to contemplate, so much more to realize.

Endnotes

1. William Carlos Williams, "The Red Wheelbarrow," *Norton Anthology of Modern Poetry*, eds. Richard Ellmann and Robert O'Clair (NY: Norton, 1973) p. 292.

2. Simone Weil, *Waiting for God* (NY: Perennial, 1951), p. 166.

3. T.S. Eliot. "Murder in the Cathedral," *The Complete Poems and Plays, 1909-1950* (NY: Harcourt, Brace & World, 1971), p. 209

4. John Ruusbroec, "A Mirror of Eternal Blessedness," *The Spiritual Espousals and Other Works*. James A. Wiseman, Trans. (NY: Paulist, 1985) p. 235.

5. Thomas Merton. "Love and Solitude," *Love and Living*. (NY: Harcourt Brace Jovanovich, 1979), p. 15.

6. Bernard of Clairvaux. "On Consideration," *Bernard of Clairvaux: Selected Works* (NY: Paulist, 1987), pp. 170-171.

7. Bernard, "On Consideration," p. 172.

Thomas Merton and Racial Reconciliaton

Albert Raboteau

April 4th 1968—For Martin Luther King

On a rainy night
On a rainy night in April
When everybody ran
Said the minister

On a balcony
Of a hotel in Tennessee
"We came at once
Upstairs"

On a night
On a rainy night in April
When the shot was fired
Said the minister

"We came at once upstairs
And found him lying
After the tornado
On the balcony
We came at once upstairs"

On a rainy night
He was our hope
And we found a tornado
Said the minister.

And a well-dressed white man
Said the minister.
Dropped the telescopic storm

And he ran
(The well-dressed minister of death)
He ran
He ran away

And on the balcony
Said the minister
We found
Everybody dying

This Merton poem came to my mind when I first visited the Lorraine Motel, the site of King's assassination in Memphis. The motel, now remodeled as a museum, was much smaller than I expected for such a massive event. Yet, it keeps the event in memory, holds it in our memory, as does Merton's poem, waiting to be mourned.

*

Merton's reflections on the nation's racial problem dated back at least to 1941, when he volunteered to work in central Harlem at Friendship House, a recreation program, clothing center, and library, founded by the Baroness Catherine DeHueck. Impressed by her dedication to serving the poor, Merton seriously considered giving up his teaching position at St. Bonaventure's College to join the staff at Friendship House full-time. However, a retreat at the Cistercian monastery of Our Lady of Gethsemani in Kentucky had left Merton with a strong attraction for the monastic life. During the fall of 1941, three years after his conversion to Catholicism, he faced a difficult choice between the active life of serving the poor in Harlem and the ascetic life of contemplative solitude at Gethsemani. In his journal entry for 30 November Merton attempted to clarify what attracted him to Harlem:

> "A saintly woman in the tenements, was dying of cancer... but she was very holy and her holiness was in this suffering, and the Blessed Virgin has appeared to her...There is no doubt that the Blessed Virgin Mary, when she appears to people in this country, appears in places like Harlem—or Gethsemani, Harlem—or Gethsemani—are the stables of Bethlehem where Christ is born among the outcast and the poor. And where He is, we must also be. I know He is in Harlem, no doubt, and would gladly live where He is and serve Him there.[1]

Merton was impressed not only by the poverty of Harlem, but also by the mute judgment of its oppressed citizens against the degradation of the larger white society whose vices Harlem mirrored. He viewed both Harlem and Gethsemani as symbols of judgment and sites of holiness forestalling God's wrath against an evil society. On November 23, 1941 he attended a retreat for Friendship House volunteers led by Fr. Paul Hanley Furfey, a professor of sociology and social justice advocate from Catholic University. Furfey focused his reflections on the Mystical Body of Christ, "the one infinite source of life," as Merton put it, "that nourishes both Friendship

House and the Trappists." Merton claimed that he returned from the retreat "all on fire with it."[2] Perhaps we can get a hint of Fr. Furfey's message from his book *Fire on the Earth*, published a few years before the retreat. Emphasizing the social implications of the doctrine of the Mystical Body, he wrote:

If we realize that we are each bound to the other members of the human race in the Mystical Body of Christ, that we must love the human race as a whole, and love all the groups which constitute it, then we can scarcely fail to realize the evil as well as the stupidity of hating any part of the Mystical Body of Christ.... There are persons who feel quite acutely the duty of individual kindness to persons of other races, and yet who seem to be totally unconscious of the injustice of race relations as a whole...who are violently antagonistic to any effort to reform the political, economic, social, and even religious oppression of the colored race. Would this be possible to any one who really believed in the doctrine of the Mystical Body?[3]

Would it be Harlem or Gethsemani? Merton resolved the choice by entering the monastery in December 1941, but he did not forget Harlem, or the racial injustice that its poverty revealed, or Fr. Furfey's notion of the interdependence of the races.

Twenty years later, Merton, whose post-*Seven Storey Mountain* books on contemplation and monasticism, had continued to attract a wide readership, suddenly began to speak out forcefully on social issues -- on war and nonviolence in 1961, and on civil rights and race in 1963. What, many of his readers wondered, did this new "turn toward the world" have to do with spirituality? Quite a lot as one of his most perceptive interpreters argues:

What had happened to him was that his solitude had issued into what all true solitude must eventually become: compassion. Finding God in his solitude, he found God's people, who are inseparable form God and who, at the deepest level of their being...are at one with one another in God, the Hidden Ground of Love of all that is. This sense of compassion bred in solitude... moved him to look once again at the world he thought he had left irrevocably twenty years earlier...when he had entered the monastery. He now felt a duty, <u>precisely because he was a contemplative</u>, to speak out...[4]

Merton asserted that it was the particular task of the contemplative monk, as a man on the margins, to speak out of his silence and solitude with an independent voice in order to clarify for those who were "completely immersed in other cares" the true value of the human person amid the illusions with which mass society surrounds modern people at every turn.

During the summer of 1963 Merton wrote a series of three "Letters to a White Liberal." Revised and published in several journals, they formed a major part of *Seeds of Destruction*, published in 1964. The book attracted critical attention, especially a negative review in the "Book World" Sunday Supplement to the *New York Herald Tribune* by the University of Chicago historian of Christianity Martin Marty. Taking issue with Merton's criticism of white liberals and his assessment of the limitations of the Civil Rights movement, Marty accused Merton of posing as the white James Baldwin from behind the safety of his monastery's walls.

Marty was upset especially by Merton's accusation that white liberals were unprepared for the radical social change required to effectively solve America's race problem. White Americans were primarily interested in profits not persons. A truly radical reordering of priorities was needed. Once they realized the cost of such change, white liberals would end up supporting the status quo. Addressing white liberals directly, Merton claimed that their participation in the March on Washington was not because the Negro needed them, but because they needed the Negro. Actually their participation blunted the revolutionary impact of the March. Mincing no words, Merton lambasted the liberal's hypocrisy:

> "North or South, integration is always going to be not on our street but 'somewhere else.' That perhaps accounts for the extraordinary zeal with which the North insists upon integration in the South, while treating the Northern Negro as if he were invisible, and flatly refusing to let him take shape in full view, lest he demand the treatment due to a human person and a free citizen of this nation."[5]

Merton had indeed read James Baldwin's *Nobody Knows My Name* (1961) and *The Fire Next Time* (1963) and agreed with Baldwin's "statements about the futility and helplessness of white liberals, who sympathize but never do anything." Merton, locating himself alongside the liberal as a "guilty bystander," observed that their and his "impotency is in our love of abstraction, our inability to connect with a valid image of reality. In a word, total alienation is the real tragedy, the real root of our helplessness. And our lotus-eating economy is responsible for that."[6] The roots of white racism he argued were tangled up with the materialism, alienation, fear, and violence spawned by a society bent on mindless, mass consumption. Consumerism commodified human relationships and trivialized freedom of choice, so that individuals became alienated not only from others, but also from themselves. "Our trouble," he stated in *Seeds of Destruction*, is that we are alienated from our own personal reality, our true self. We do not believe in anything but money and the power of the enjoyment which comes from the possession of money."[7] The ironic tragedy of this condition is that the white man who thinks himself to be free "is actually the victim of the same servitudes which he has imposed on the Negro: passive subjection to the...commercial society that he has tried to create for himself, and which is shot through with falsity and unfreedom from top to bottom. He makes a great deal of fuss about 'individual freedom' but one may ask if such freedom really exists. Is there really a genuine freedom for the person or only the irresponsibility of the atomized individual members of mass society?"[8] The alienation of the person from the true self, Merton insisted, led to violence: "The problem of racial conflict is part and parcel of the whole problem of human violence... all the way up from the suppressed inarticulate hate feelings of interpersonal family and job conflicts to the question of the H-bomb and mass extermination. The problem is in ourselves. It is only one symptom."[9] Merton's pessimistic assessment, then, of the Civil Rights movement was due to his analysis of the need for profound social change, if the deep and tangled sources of the racial problem were ever to be addressed.

He agreed with white liberals that passing Civil Rights legislation was good and necessary, but, he also concluded it was insufficient. How effectively and quickly would the laws be enacted on the local level? The resistance of southern whites to desegregation, backed by outright violence, seemed intransigent. In the North, "where such rights are still guaranteed in theory more than practice" Civil Rights legislation aroused "pressures and animosities" between whites and blacks. He noted perceptively that even if the law "were perfectly enforced it would still not be able to meet critical problems that were more strictly economic and sociological (jobs, housing, delinquency, irresponsible violence)." In short he concluded, "Civil Rights legislation is not the end of the battle but only the beginning of a new and more critical phase in the conflict."[10] Our problem is that too many of us have concluded that the battle already is won.

The paternalistic attitudes of white liberals would have to give way to a new modesty and respect for the independent leadership of blacks in the movement. White benevolence still served as a mask for white leadership, and, blacks readily saw it for what it was: an attempt to hold onto some control over the "Negro's fight for rights, in order to be able to apply the brakes when necessary." For the African-American knows, Merton caustically observed, "that your material comforts, your security, and your congenial relations with the establishment are much more important to you than your rather volatile idealism, and that when the game gets rough you will be quick to see your own interests menaced by his demands. And you will sell him down the river for the five hundredth time in order to protect yourself."[11]

Merton had no doubt that the Civil Rights movement was a *kairos* for African Americans, a providentially appointed moment in history: "It is the Lord of History who demands of the Negro a complete break with his past servitudes. And the break must be made by the Negro himself without any need of the white man's paternalistic approval. It is absolutely necessary for the Negro to dissolve all bonds that hold him, like a navel cord, in passive dependence on the good pleasure of the white man's society."[12]

According to Merton, "one of the most striking and mysterious characteristics of the Negro freedom movement ... is this sense, which awakening everywhere in the Negro masses of the South, especially in the youth, has brought them by the hundreds and thousands out of the ghettos" and "has moved them to action." Earlier, than most, he understood the African-American movement to be part of a larger worldwide movement by which "the entire Negro race, and all the vast majority of 'Colored races' all over the world, have suddenly and spontaneously become conscious of their real power and... of a destiny that is all their own."[13]

But this destiny was not solely theirs alone. Black writers, such as James Baldwin and William Melvin Kelley, insisted that "there is one *kairos* for everybody. The time that has providentially come for the black man is also providential for the white man." Acknowledging both authors' distrust and alienation from Christianity, Merton insisted that

[Their] view is still deeply Christian and implies a substantially Christian faith in the spiritual dynamism with which man freely creates his own history, not as an autonomous and titanic self-affirmation, but in obedience to the mystery of love and freedom at work under the surface of human events. In the light of this, then, the hour of freedom is seen also as an hour of salvation. But it is not an hour of salvation for the Negro only. The white man, if he can possibly open the ears of his heart and listen intently enough to hear what the Negro is now hearing, can recognize that he is himself called to freedom and to salvation in the same *kairos* of events which he is now, in so many different ways, opposing or resisting.[14]

Why should the white man listen? Merton's answer to this question harkens back to his youthful intuition of Harlem as a site of holiness and of judgment. In a passage that rivals Baldwin for eloquence, Merton interpreted the profoundly religious meaning of the nonviolent Civil Rights movement to his white readers, many of whom had initially viewed it as a merely political conflict between extremists:

The Negro children of Birmingham, who walked calmly up to the police dogs that lunged at them with a fury capable of tearing their small bodies to pieces, were not only confronting the truth in an exalted moment of faith, a providential *kairos*. They were also in their simplicity, bearing heroic Christian witness to the truth, for they were exposing their bodies to death in order to show God and man that they believed in the just rights of their people, knew that those rights had been unjustly, shamefully and systematically violated, and realized that the violation called for expiation and redemptive protest, because it was an offense against God and His truth. They were stating clearly that the time had come where such violations could no longer be tolerated. These Negro followers of Dr. King are convinced that there is more at stake than civil rights. They believe that the survival of America is itself in question.... [They] are not simply judging the white man and rejecting him. On the contrary, they are seeking by Christian love and sacrifice to redeem him, to enlighten him, so as...to awaken his mind and his conscience, and stir him to initiate the reform and renewal which may still be capable of saving our society.[15]

Why should the white man listen?—because of the authenticity of
the black voice, an authenticity born of suffering:

> The voice of the American Negro began to be heard long ago,
> even in the days of his enslavement. He sang of the great
> mysteries of the Old Testament, the *magnalia dei* which are at
> the heart of the Christian liturgy. In a perfect...spontaneous
> spirit of prayer and prophecy, the Negro spirituals of the last
> century remain as classic examples of what a living liturgical
> hymnody ought to be, and how it comes into being...where
> men suffer oppression, where they are deprived of identity,
> where their lives are robbed of meaning, and where the desire
> of freedom and the imperative demand of truth forces them
> to give it meaning: a religious meaning. Such religion is...a
> prophetic fire of love and courage, fanned by the breathing of
> the Spirit of God who speaks to the heart of His children in
> order to lead them out of bondage. Hence the numinous force
> of the...'Freedom Songs' which he now sings, in the Baptist
> Churches of the South where he prepares to march out and face
> the police of states...which arm themselves against him with
> clubs, fire hoses, police dogs and electric cattle prods, throw-
> ing their jails wide-open to receive him. His song continues to
> resound in prison like the songs of Paul and his companions
> in the Acts of the Apostles.[16]

If whites chose not to listen to the message that blacks were trying to give America, Merton warned at the end of his "Letters to a
White Liberal," "the merciful *kairos* of truth will turn into the dark
hour of destruction and hate."[17]

On August 30, 1967, an open letter from Martin Marty to
Thomas Merton appeared in the *National Catholic Reporter*. Near
the end of the "long hot Summer of Sixty Seven" Marty took occasion to apologize for his negative 1963 review of Merton's *Seeds
of Destruction*. Merton had, after all, he acknowledged, "told it like
it is, and like it probably will be." Responding in the same Journal
a few weeks later, Merton expressed his pleasure at the renewal of
their friendship but remained somber about the outbreak of racial
riots around the country. "The injustice and cruelty which are by
now endemic beneath the surface of our bland and seemingly
benign society are too deep and too serious to be cured by legislation...[The]un-Christianity of American Christianity is going to
be inexorably exposed and judged: mine perhaps, included." He

tentatively held out "some hope that out of this hot summer we may at last get the serious beginning of a really effective radical coalition where, in spite of all the black separatism...there may in fact be collaboration between white and black on the left toward peace, new horizons constructive change..."[18]

In the two and a half years between Marty's review and his recantation, the rhetoric of the "black liberation struggle" seemed to have shifted from integration to black power, and from King's non-violence to Malcolm X's "by any means necessary."

Responding to the appeals for black power, Merton took the militancy of H. Rap Brown and Stokely Carmichael seriously, refused to demonize them, and carefully explained the sources of their anger in the violence suffered by black people and their impatience at the slow pace of change. He wrote an appreciative review of Malcolm X's posthumous *Autobiography*, concluding that Malcolm was "a person whose struggles are understandable, whose errors we can condone. He was a fighter whose sincerity and courage we cannot help admiring, and who might have become a genuine revolutionary leader—with portentous effect in American society!"[19]

All the while he extended his discussion of racism beyond the situation of African-Americans to include Indians in North and South America and the cargo cults of Melanesia, noting their common experience of western imperialism. "In one word, the ultimate violence which the American white man, like the European white man, has exerted in all unconscious 'good faith' upon the colored races of the earth (and above all on the Negro) has been to impose on them invented identities, to place them in positions of subservience and helplessness in which they themselves came to believe only in the identities which have been conferred upon them."[20]

In his last published statement on race, "From Nonviolence to Black Power," published in 1968 in *Faith and Violence*, Merton described his own role in the Civil Rights struggle: "The job of the white Christian is then partly a job of diagnosis and criticism, a prophetic task of finding and identifying the injustice which is the cause of all violence, both white and black, which is also the root of war..."[21] Aware that the *kairos* moment of Christian non-violence seemed to have passed, he did not despair, but continued to hope for the realization of an earlier vision, a Catholic approach to the issue of race which bore a family resemblance to the doctrine of the Mystical Body as propounded by Fr. Furfey's retreat so many years before:

> A genuinely Catholic approach to the Negro would assume not only that the white and the Negro are essentially equal in dignity (and this, I think we do generally assume) but also that they are brothers in the fullest sense of the word. This means to say a genuinely Catholic attitude in matters of race is one which concretely accepts and fully recognizes the fact that different races and cultures are <u>correlative. They mutually complete one another</u>. The white man needs the Negro, and needs to know that he needs him. White calls for black just as black calls for white. Our significance as white men is to be seen <u>entirely</u> in the fact that all men are not white. Until this fact is grasped, we will never realize our true place in the world, and we will never achieve what we are meant to achieve in it.[22]

In this passage, I believe, Merton echoes the closing sentences of Baldwin's *The Fire Next Time*: "If we—and now I mean the relatively conscious whites and the relatively conscious blacks, who must, like lovers, insist on, or create, the consciousness of the others—do not falter in our duty now, we may be able, handful that we are, to end the racial nightmare, and achieve our country, and change the history of the world."[23]

With extraordinary sensitivity and sympathy Merton listened to the voices of black Americans and tried with honesty and candor to convey what they were saying during a time of social crisis to white Americans. Seeking to communicate across a racial divide that many whites did not even perceive, he pressed on toward the ultimate end of communication: compassion and community, based upon his own contemplative experience of the hidden wholeness of us all. The path to racial reconciliation remains, as he predicted, difficult and steep.

1. It requires the radical realization that alienation from our true selves, fed and disguised by mass consumerism, leads to violence and to the reduction of persons into things. As Martin Luther King put it "we must move rapidly from a thing oriented society to a person oriented society."

2. Contemplation and action need to be joined lest our activism become merely another form of violence and our contemplation another form of self gratification. Contemplative silence, solitude, and simplicity are necessary in order to come into contact with the

true self, what the Orthodox Christian tradition calls "hesychia"— the stillness at the heart, the center of each of us. But action is also required in identification with, solidarity with, presence among the poor, in the tradition of Dorothy Day, Catherine DeHueck, and St. Maria of Paris, lest we remain "guilty bystanders," obsessed by our desire to enjoy "spiritual" experiences.

3. Kairos time may be accurate, but misleading, if we use it as an excuse for inaction. "The time has passed; the movement is over." It is not over, unless it is over in our lives. The struggle goes on in local communities across the nation, just as it did before "the movement" began. We can get stuck within the past as a recollection of dead heroes to be memorialized in Civil Rights museums. Our memory of the struggle for racial and economic justice needs to be enlivened by a sense of liturgical memory or *anamnesis*. *Anamnesis* is our response to Jesus' words at the Last Supper: "Do this in remembrance of me." It is our Eucharistic remembrance and repetition of his transformation of bread and wine into his body and blood, which is then extended out into the world in the "liturgy after the liturgy," where we see the body of Christ, as Mother Teresa and St. John Chrysostom remind us, in the distressing disguise of our poor and oppressed brothers and sisters.

4. Moreover, this re/membering involves telling and listening to our stories, sharing them with each other truthfully and receiving them openly so that our hard hearts may be softened to *penthos* – a sorrowful mourning for our nation's history of racism. This mourning, as Merton (and King) well knew, is a difficult but necessary step before we can be comforted and truly reconciled.

Endnotes

1. Thomas Merton, *Run to the Mountain: The Story of a Vocation*, ed. by Patrick Hart, O.C.S.O. (New York: Harper Collins, 1995), p. 464.

2. Letter of Thomas Merton to Catherine DeHueck Doherty, December 6, 1941, *The Hidden Ground of Love*, ed. by William H. Shannon (New York: Farrar, Straus, Giroux, 1985), p. 10.

3. Paul Hanley Furfey, *Fire on the Earth* (New York: Macmillan, 1943) pp. 51-52.

4. Thomas Merton, *Passion for Peace: The Social Essays*, ed. by William H. Shannon (New York: Crossroad, 1997) pp. 2-3. The quotation is from Shannon's Introduction. *Passion for Peace* includes the essays in "Part One: Black Revolution" from *Seeds of Destruction* (1964) as well as several later essays of Merton on race.

5. Merton, *Passion for Peace*, p. 163.

6. Merton's journal entry of February 13, 1963, published in *Turning Toward the World: The Pivotal Years*, ed. by Victor A. Kramer (New York: Harper Collins, 1996), p. 297.

7. *Seeds of Destruction* (New York: Farrar, Straus, and Giroux, 1964) p. 25.

8. *Passion for Peace*, p. 196.

9. *Passion for Peace*, p. 289.

10. *Passion for Peace*, p. 155.

11. *Passion for Peace*, p. 169.

12. *Passion for Peace*, p. 196.

13. *Passion for Peace*, p. 191-192.

14. *Passion for Peace*, pp. 197-198.

15. *Passion for Peace*, pp. 174-175

16. *Passion for Peace*, pp. 189-190.

17. *Passion for Peace*, p. 187.

18. *Hidden Ground of Love*, pp. 456-457.

19. *Passion for Peace*, p. 275

20. Thomas Merton, *Ishi Means Man* (Greensboro, NC: Unicorn Press, 1976), p. 11.

21. Reprinted in *Passion for Peace*, p. 216

22. *Passion for Peace*, p. 183.

23. James Baldwin, *The Fire Next Time* (1963, reprinted New York: Modern Library, 1995), pp. 104-105.

Terrible Days:
Merton/Yungblut Letters and MLK Jr.'s Death

William Apel

> These have been terrible days for everyone [Dr. King's murder]
> and God alone knows what is to come.
> Letter from Thomas Merton to June Yungblut[1]

Thomas Merton was devastated. In his letter of April 9, 1968 to his Quaker friend June J. Yungblut, he wrote of the "terrible days" which surrounded the murder of Martin Luther King Jr. Like so many others, Merton had placed tremendous hope in the witness and work of Dr. King. He also knew, however, that one individual could only accomplish so much. And now Dr. King had sacrificed his very life for God's cause of love and justice in a racist and war-torn world.[2]

Merton's most immediate concern was to get a note of condolence to Coretta Scott King. He did not have the King family's home address in Atlanta, but he was confident that June Yungblut could pass his message along to Dr. King's widow. Merton knew June and John Yungblut to be reliable and dedicated friends in the struggle for peace and social justice. As longtime members of the Society of Friends (Quakers) and the American Friends Service Committee, the Yungbluts had worked closely with Dr. King in his nonviolent protest against racism, poverty and war. Merton could rest assured that through June Yungblut his words of condolence would be delivered to Coretta King.

Thanks to June Yungblut's correspondence with Merton, we gain an eye-witness account of events surrounding the death of Martin Luther King, Jr.—especially those that occurred inside the King family home after the assassination. As an interfaith friend, June Yungblut shared information with Merton, which he otherwise would not have had. Because of the June Yungblut letters, Merton was brought close to the pain and suffering of the King family.

Many familiar with Merton's life are aware of the train of events related to his discovering of the news of Martin Luther King, Jr.'s murder. This terrible news came to Merton over the car radio as he was returning from Lexington after having visited Shakertown with his friend and English guest Donald Allchin. Rather than return to Gethsemani, Merton headed to Bardstown instead. He wanted to spend the evening with Colonel Hawks – a close African American friend.[3]

Merton had predicted several years before Dr. King's death that the civil rights movement would soon fall upon harder times. In fact, Merton wrote in print about a coming crisis of leadership. Several of his essays in *Seeds of Destruction* (1964) anticipated this coming crisis. Merton envisioned a future in which many in the white community who had supported the civil rights movement would lose courage and drop away. This prophecy was to come true. After Dr. King's assassination, black leaders insisted on more control and leadership of the movement. This caused many white liberals, some in leadership positions to back off.

These terrible times that Merton forecast were indeed visible during the long, hot summer following Dr. King's death. The old coalition between white liberals and black leadership did, in fact, begin to dissolve. The rise of a new generation of black militants, the popularity of Malcolm X's brand of black nationalism, and Dr. King's own decision to broaden his social agenda to include poverty at home and the Vietnam War abroad, created great unease among white liberals and their leadership.

Merton's criticism of his white liberal friends for their withdrawal of support from the movement was frank and direct. In his essay from *Seeds of Destruction* entitled "Letters to a White Liberal," Merton accused many white liberals of growing soft in their commitments to the cause. He wrote:

> It is one of the characteristics of liberals that they prefer their future to be vaguely predictable (just as the conservative prefers only a future that reproduces the past in all it's details), when you see that the future is entirely out of your hands and that you are totally unprepared for it, you are going to fall back on the past, and you are going to end up in the arms of the conservatives.[4]

The future Merton predicted had arrived. Much faith and renewed courage for the tasks ahead would be needed. But for the immediate present, Merton wanted to get a message of condolence to Coretta Scott King. The rest would have to wait for now. First things first: Thomas Merton turned to June J. Yungblut for help. She was well suited to be his emissary to Mrs. King.

June J. Yungblut

June Yungblut was born in the American South. She came from a very distinguished Quaker family whose roots could be traced back to William Penn. Yungblut graduated from Keuka College in upstate New York and then earned a Master's degree from Yale and a Doctorate in Philosophy from Emory University. June and her husband John (a Quaker theologian) were serving as directors of the Quaker House in Atlanta when correspondence between June Yungblut and Merton began in 1967.

During this time in Atlanta, the Yungbluts became friends with Martin Luther King, Jr. and his family. In fact, John and June Yungblut were prime movers in an attempt to arrange a meeting at Gethsemani between Dr. King and Thomas Merton. The idea was to provide a time of retreat and relaxation for Dr. King along with a low-key meeting with a few members of the Catholic peace movement.[5] During this same period of time, June Yungblut had developed a close friendship with Coretta Scott King.

In his biography of Thomas Merton, Michael Mott marks the year 1967 as a time when three important women entered Merton's life. According to Mott, each woman brought a "wholly different perspective" to Merton. June Yungblut was one of these aforementioned women; the other two were Rosemary Radford Ruether and the teenager Suzanne Butorovich.[6]

A natural bond of friendship arose immediately between Yungblut and Merton. From the start of their correspondence, they shared common literary interests. In addition, Yungblut's Quaker activism connected with Merton's ongoing concerns for peace and justice. And beyond all this, they were poets! In fact, June's best-known poem entitled "This is the Child," written after Merton's death, illustrates for us what kindred spirits they must have truly been.

Yungblut's poem portrays the brutality of war—especially the suffering and slaughter of innocent civilians—something that deeply troubled Merton as well. Yungblut's poem memorialized an image, which haunts those who lived through the Vietnam War: The unforgettable scene of a Vietnamese child whose napalmed body, and cries of pain, are affixed forever on the cover of *Life* magazine.

> This is the child
> who danced naked down the road in Vietnam

her clothes torn from her body
by frenzied fingers
the dance of death, dürer woodcut
etched in napalm
come forward on the stage
leaping, running, mouth aflame
we are your audience
we watch you play
where will it all end? [7]

As a dedicated Quaker, June Yungblut did all she could to oppose war. And like her interfaith friend Thomas Merton, she knew that to oppose war was to confront the violence inside herself—beginning with the violence within her own heart.

What also drew Merton and Yungblut together was their love of the arts—most especially dance. Professionally trained by Martha Graham, Yungblut's work with the Barbara Mettler studio of Creative Dance rounded out a fascinating fusion of Quaker commitment to peace and human rights with a love of literature, poetry, and dance. Without question, June Yungblut's creative and compassionate life fueled both her faith and her commitment to peace and justice. Her friendship with Merton and the King family was surely an extension of that commitment.

The Death of Martin Luther King, Jr.

Both Thomas Merton and June Yungblut feared that Dr. King's life might come to an early end. In Merton's April 9 letter to Yungblut immediately after King's murder, he noted, "What a terrible thing and yet I felt that he was expecting it."[8] On her part, Yungblut also feared for Dr. King's life. She wrote Merton about her reservations concerning Dr. King's last visit to Memphis. Although the letter itself is lost to history, Merton copied part of its content in his journal entry of April 6, 1968. Yungblut wrote:

Martin is going to Memphis today…He won't be back until the weekend…I hope both he and Nhat Hanh will soon go to Gethsemani…If Martin had taken a period there he might have had the wisdom in repose to stay out of Memphis in the first place, and it was a mistake to go there.

In her perceptive letter to Merton, Yungblut anticipated Dr. King's "Jerusalem." She wrote about her deep concern regarding King's involvement in the sanitation workers' strike in Memphis.

> He [Dr. King] had done no preparation and came in cold to a hot situation where the young militants had him just where they wanted him...If there is violence today Memphis will be to King what Cuba was to Kennedy...If Memphis is to be Martin's Jerusalem instead of Washington, how ironical that it is primarily a nightclub for Mississippi, which is dry where the crucifixion may take place and that the Sanhedrin will be composed of Negro militants.[9]

The Sanhedrin, rather than being "Negro militants," was a white racist named James Earle Ray. Death for Dr. King was nevertheless the verdict—coolly and calculatingly executed without mercy.

Condolences

As mentioned earlier, Merton's most pressing response to Dr. King's death was to send a message of condolence via June Yungblut to Coretta Scott King. This was first and foremost a matter of the heart. His note to Mrs. King was not intended for public record or future publication. Instead, as a monk and a priest, Merton wrote to Coretta Scott King from the depth of his own grieving spirit. He longed to communicate his love to the King family, and June Yungblut was indeed the channel for this love.

The central paragraph of Merton's message to Mrs. King is quintessential Merton. Here he speaks spirit to spirit, as one broken heart to another. He laments the loss of one of God's greatest servants – a man who lived his life as best he could in the imitation of Christ. Merton's words to Mrs. King revealed both a personal and universal dimension. He knew that Dr. King, in all his particularity, had now become a universal man—one who belonged to the ages. Merton writes to Coretta Scott:

> Let me only say how deeply I share your personal grief as well as the shock, which pervades the whole nation. He [Dr. King] had done the greatest thing anyone can do. In imitation of his master he has laid down his life for friends and enemies. He knew the nation was under judgment and he tried everything to stay the hand of God and man. He will go down in history as one of our greatest citizens.[10]

On April 11, June Yungblut wrote back to Merton of her own personal heartbreak. She reported how she had helped at the King home; how she cared for the smaller King children; how she grieved as Coretta Scott flew to Memphis to bring home her husband's body. June Yungblut told Merton of her sadness as she observed the younger King children trying to grasp the reality of their family's tragedy. She also told Merton about her deep admiration for Coretta Scott's courage. June noted how Coretta Scott grieved in private, while displaying tremendous strength and dignity in public.[11]

An Act of Redemption?

June Yungblut noted to Merton one small sign of hope during those bleak days in the King household. She reported to Merton a conversation she overheard involving the younger King children. It was an exchange between the King and Abernathy children. This exchange was poignant and deeply moving. Perhaps it was redemptive? Yungblut tells Merton:

> The Abernathy children asked Andy Young if they could hate the man that fired the shot [that killed their father]. Martin and Dexter King answered before Andy could and said, "no", they couldn't hate the man because their Daddy told them they were not to hate anyone.[12]

The words of Dr. Howard Thurman, a longtime friend of the King family and mentor to Martin Luther King Jr., may be instructive in this regard. Several years before Dr. King's death he wrote:

> To be to another human being what is needed at the time that the need is most urgent and most acutely felt, this is to participate in the precise act of redemption.[13]

Could it be that "the precise act of redemption" in this situation were the simple words of Dr. King's children? No to hatred, yes to love.

Strength to Love

Looking back on the letters exchanged by Thomas Merton and June J. Yungblut at the time of Dr. King's death, we are reminded of the price that is often paid by those who labor for the realization of God's kingdom. Martin Luther King, Jr. and Coretta Scott King knew the price of divine glory. So did Thomas Merton and June Yungblut. The price has always been high – the Hebrew prophets and Jesus knew it better than anyone. Costly grace must always replace cheap grace if God's work is to be done.[14]

I'm sure Merton and Yungblut both understood that Martin Luther King, Jr. had followed – as best as he could – the way of Jesus his Redeemer in living out the "moral imperative of love." In her forward to the 1982 edition of *Strength to Love*, Coretta Scott King quotes directly from her husband's speech to the anti-war group Clergy and Laity Concerned. These words, perhaps better than any other of Dr. King's statements, express the universal nature of God's redemptive love. They also go to the very core of Thomas Merton's own understanding of love. In the words of Martin Luther King, Jr.:

> When I speak of love I am not speaking of some sentimental and weak response. I am speaking of that force which all of the great religions have seen as the unifying principle of life. Love is somehow the key that unlocks the door which leads to ultimate reality. This Hindu-Moslem-Christian-Jewish-Buddhist belief about ultimate reality is beautifully summed up in the first epistle of Saint John: "Let us love one another; for love is of God and everything that loveth is born of God and knowth God."[15]

Love has no equal. The courage to love has no equal. Martin Luther King, Jr. and Coretta Scott King knew of this love and this courage. So did Thomas Merton and his interfaith friend June Yungblut. They too affirmed love as a "Hindu-Moslem-Christian-Jewish-Buddhist-belief." Indeed, God's love is without boundaries.

Ultimately, Thomas Merton and June J. Yungblut believed in Dr. King's witness to love because it was of God. Nothing, not even our mortal shortcomings, can keep this love from doing its work. Even in the "terrible days," God's love prevails. This is the great truth that Thomas Merton and June Yungblut shared through their correspondence and friendship. This is the legacy of the strength to love found in the life and witness of Coretta Scott King and Martin Luther King, Jr.

Endnotes

1. William H. Shannon, ed., *The Hidden Ground of Love: The Letters of Thomas Merton on Religious Experience and Social Concerns* (New York: Farrar, Straus and Giroux, 185), 645.

2. Parts of this present article are adapted from chapter nine of my

book *Signs of Peace* published by Orbis Books in 2006. The content has been refocused and expanded with an emphasis upon Martin Luther King, Jr.'s death and the additional use of unpublished letters of June J. Yungblut at the time of Dr. King's death.

3. Michael Mott, *The Seven Mountains of Thomas Merton* (Boston: Houghton Mifflin, 1984), 519-520

4. Thomas Merton, *Seeds of Destruction* (New York: Farrar, Strauss and Giroux, 1964), 36.

5. Mott, *The Seven Mountains of Thomas Merton*, 519.

6. Mott, *The Seven Mountains of Thomas Merton*, 487.

7. June J. Yungblut, *This Is the Child* (Tuscan, AZ: Mettler Studios, 1975), page not numbered

8. Shannon, ed., *The Hidden Ground of Love: The Letters of Thomas Merton on Religious Experience and Social Concerns*, 644.

9. Patrick, Hart, ed. *The Other Side of the Mountain* (San Francisco: Harper San Francisco, 1995), 79.

10. Shannon, ed. *The Hidden Ground of Love: The Letters of Thomas Merton on Religious Experience and Social Concerns*, 451.

11. June J. Yungblut to Merton, April 11, 1968, archives of the Thomas Merton Center, Bellarmine University, Louisville, Kentucky

12. Yungblut to Merton, April 11, 1968.

13. Howard Thurman, *Mysticism and the Experience of Love* (Wallingford, PA: Pendle Hill Pamphlet, 1961), 18.

14. My reference to cheap and costly grace recalls Dietrich Bonhoeffer's opening chapter of, *Cost of Discipleship, especially* with which Merton was familiar.

15. Martin Luther King, Jr., *Strength to Love* (Philadelphia: Fortress Press, 1963), 5. Coretta Scott King reported in her 1982 forward to the book that people constantly told her this book "changed their lives."

Merton as Method
for Inter-religious Engagement:
Examples from Buddhism

John D. Dadosky

This paper seeks to highlight the achievement of Thomas Merton's contribution to inter-religious engagement both as a *pioneer* and as a *model* for the Church whose example gives us a clue how to proceed with dialogue in this pluralistic age while maintaining one's religious identity. I will reference two of Merton's successes with Buddhism.

A. The Context

I begin with the context for Merton's contribution relative to how the official church has weighed in on Buddhism within the past few years. John Paul II made important strides in improving relations with other religions, especially with Muslims and Jews; perhaps because they are monotheistic religions. However, with respect to Buddhism, he states clearly that "the doctrines of salvation in Buddhism and Christianity are opposed." He says: "The *Buddhist doctrine of salvation* constitutes the central point, or rather the only point, of this system. Nevertheless, both the Buddhist tradition and the methods deriving from it have almost an exclusively negative soteriology." He continues by suggesting that John of the Cross offers a kind of fulfillment of Buddhism.[1]

Consider Pope Benedict's more recent comments: "I repeat with insistence [that] research and interreligious and intercultural dialogue are not an option but a vital necessity for our time"[2] In keeping with the Pope's insistence let us look at the example of Merton who dialogued successfully with Buddhists and others and who had a deep understanding of those religions. His method of dialogue is on par with the historical successes of Matteo Ricci and Roberto de Nobili.

B. A Shift in Method

Vatican II represented a paradigmatic shift in the Church's self-understanding. In previous work I have argued that this paradigm shift is represented in a movement from *a strictly self-mediating identity* that viewed its relationship with the Other in terms of a *one-way* relationship to a more *two-way* direction or *mutually self-mediating* direction.[3] In turn, the Vatican II documents represent the official recognition that the Church has mutual relations with the Other. For example, consider the title of the final chapter of *Gaudium et Spes* "The Church and the World as Mutually Related." I call this the Church's self-understanding as *mutually self-mediating* as opposed to a *strictly self-mediating* stance, which views the 'world' antagonistically and with suspicion. Vatican II is the official recognition that just as the Church has treasures to share with the Other, likewise it recognizes that the Church is also enriched by the treasures it finds in the Other.

This recognition that the Church has mutual relations with the Other has put the Church in a precarious position. The affirmation of the Other, that is, of other Christian faiths, religions, cultures, and secular culture, runs counter to an ecclesial self-understanding that preceded Vatican II where the distortions of the Church's self-understanding lead to triumphalism, clericalism, and juridicism. While a movement beyond these attitudes is a welcome development, it has put the post-Vatican II church in a kind of 'identity crisis' in the face of a vast pluralism. One example of this is the struggle that the Church has dealing with the question of evangelization and dialogue with respect to other religions. When does the Church evangelize and when does it dialogue with the Other? How does one avoid dialogue as simply a veiled form of evangelization? How does one remain faithful to the evangelical mission of the Church in the dialogue? Indeed there is a tension between proclamation and dialogue and they need not be mutually opposed. Moreover, dialogue is now considered to be a part of the mission of the Church.[4] How does one keep one's Christian identity in this dialogue? Consequently, the question of how to relate to the Other comes to the forefront and this is a question of *method*. I think Thomas Merton's life example gives us a clue as to how dialogue can be successfully carried out. In this way, I think Merton was significant for two reasons. He was a pioneer by successfully carrying on dialogue before it was fashionable (a half a century before the quote above from Pope Benedict christening intercultural and interreligious dialogue). Secondly, Merton was successful at it, perhaps more successful than any other major Christian thinker. In this way, Merton exemplifies the method of mutual self-mediation.

Of course, the latter is technical language; the more descriptive language of his methodology would be *friendship*.

James L. Fredericks argues that friendship is an "invaluable" approach for interreligious dialogue.[5] For example, when the Buddhist and the Christian sit down together for dialogue in a spirit of friendship, this context provides the best context for mutual enrichment, for mutual challenge, and for the 'surprise' of something new emerging through their respectful sharing and camaraderie. The spirit of friendship provides a context for engaging the different types of differences including contradictory ones: "… Christians will do well to develop deep and abiding friendships with the non-Christian neighbors as a useful way to disagree with honesty and depth."[6] Interreligious friendships enrich the Church's self-understanding in two ways. On the one hand, it keeps our self-understanding from falling into complacency: "Making new friends requires us to step out of our security and enter into a less comfortable world where the unpredictable replaces the tried and true."[7] On the other hand, the encounter is enriching in that it offers "new and welcome ways" of understanding oneself.[8]

Mutual self-mediation as a method involves befriending one another in the arena of interreligious encounters, mutually sharing the authentic aspects of each other's cultural and religious treasures, and confronting contradictory differences respectfully. Friendship is the only context where one can challenge dialectical (contradictory) differences. Good friends challenge each other on bad habits in a loving way wherein one is less likely to get defensive and more likely to listen and grow. Good friendships are also complementary, talents and knowledge can be shared among each party in a mutually enriching supportive context. Some friendships can give way to something more than the sum of their members such as Jesus' claim when two or more gathered in his name, he is present.[9] When one considers Merton's success with interreligious dialogue one must consider that his method, like that of Matteo Ricci of the 17th Century, was one of friendship.

A brief survey of his encounter with two significant representatives of Buddhism, the Dalai Lama, and D.T. Suzuki, will demonstrate that Merton's life example, exemplifies the method of mutual self-mediation, or friendship with the Other.

C. The Dalai Lama

Merton's encounter with the Dalai Lama is one that demonstrates mutual sharing, challenge, trust, respect; in short—friendship. It is clear that the Dalai Lama considered him a friend as well as a dialogue partner. "When he died," his Holiness states, "I felt that I had lost personally one of my best friends, and a man who was a contributor for harmony between different religions and for mental peace."[10] Similarly, Merton describes the encounter: "It was a very warm and cordial discussion. And at the end, I felt we had become very good friends. And were somehow very close to each other. And I believe too, that there is a real spiritual bond between us".[11]

Merton met with the Dalai Lama three times during his visit to Dharamsala, India. During their encounter, the Dalai Lama quickly sensed that Merton was a good human being: "Honest. Truthful."[12] His Holiness was impressed by Merton's interest in Eastern philosophy, meditation, his deep understanding and open-mindedness—a pioneer in East-West relations.

In this encounter we see the mutual enrichment occur. Through Merton's understanding, open-mindedness and good heart, the Dalai Lama acquired an appreciation of Christianity stating "through him my understanding and my respect about other religions, particularly the Christian, was very much increased." They found areas of common agreement: the similarity of monastic life, "that spiritual beliefs are one of the major contributions for world peace," and that "Compassion, love, tolerance—these are the same for Christian and Buddhist." [13] They spoke of Western and Eastern monastic practices both philosophically and very practically in terms of monastic vows, basic rules, and meditation postures. Their conversations ranged from the abstract of metaphysics (and even beyond it, in the case of *madhyamika*) to the more concrete social-political situations in discussions of Marxism and monasticism. However, in addition to mutual enrichment, they discovered mutual challenges. As the Dalai Lama states: "It is useful for the Christian to adopt some Buddhist ideas. And similarly for Buddhists to learn from Christian tradition. To help each other. It will help to enrich both traditions."[14] The Dalai Lama admits that Christianity has challenged him to incorporate the social responsible dimension of Christianity that includes social welfare, social action, and education.

Buddhism with its developed tradition of meditation practice can challenge the Christian to deeper meditation practices and contemplation. Merton was impressed by the precision of their discussion of conscious interiority. He was challenged as a Christian contemplative by the encounter with the Buddhists to articulate "the depth of spiritual experience" which he believes the Buddhists have a "deeper attainment and certitude" than Catholic contemplatives.[15] Hence, in the encounter of these two spiritual pioneers one finds a mutual enrichment and mutual challenge.

In the spirit of Merton, a monastic inter-religious dialogue continues today. There have been historic meetings at Merton's former monastery, Gethsemane, Kentucky. The Dalai Lama suggested the dialogue continue there beginning in 1996. The inter-monastic dialogue, and continues as Joseph Raab suggests, it is "largely a continuation of the friendship between Thomas Merton and the Dalai Lama."[16]

D.   D. T. Suzuki

From 1959 to 1966 Merton carried on a rich and substantial dialogue with a prominent authority on Japanese Zen, Daisetz T. Suzuki. The dialogue was unique and pioneering because both scholars were experts in their own traditions and both had an intense interest in each other's tradition.[17] The relationship exemplifies the process of mutual self-mediation in that it is mutually enriching and mutually challenging.

A formal dialogue between the two takes place in print in Merton's *Zen and the Birds of Appetite*. Later, Merton writes an article titled "A Zen Revival" that prompts Suzuki to declare after reading it that Merton has the best grasp of any Westerner he has ever met.[18]

At one point in the dialogue Suzuki ventures an opinion:

> I would like to say that there are two types of mentality that fundamentally differ from one another: (1) affective, personal, dualistic, and (2) nonaffective, nonpersonal and nondualistic. Zen belongs to the latter and Christianity to the former[19]

Suzuki continues to explain the basic difference between the two through an illustration of emptiness. However, as stated, his comments are intriguing in that, invoking the language of Bernard Lonergan, the Christian mentality speaks to the world *mediated by meaning* and the Zen mentality refers to *the world of immediacy*.

The latter, is used by Lonergan to refer to a mystical experience as *a mediated return to immediacy.* In this way, what Merton refers in his later writing on Zen as 'the Zen insight' is really not an insight in the strict sense of acquired knowledge but rather an *experience.* It is quite distinct in the sense that is not mediated by the cognitional operations of understanding and judgment, but rather an immediacy of consciousness that is facilitated by the methods of contemplation.[20]

Indeed, while I have suggested that Merton's method of interreligious engagement is one of friendship, perhaps it is more accurate to say that his method is one of contemplative prayer, where contemplation is fruit of those efforts or the experience, the mediated return to immediacy, if you will. Merton's interreligious friendships afford a context where he can delve deeper into understanding those experiences with those with whom he can identify and those who have traversed the terrain more deeply. Merton's 'passing over' to Suzuki's point of view invites Christians to a re-appreciation of a lineage of mysticism that has been misunderstood and in some cases dismissed, such is the case with Meister Eckhart.[21] We get a clue to Merton's successful attempts with dialogue in his article "Contemplation and Dialogue." A fruit of the contemplative life is contemplation or "the direct intuition of reality" a pure, direct awareness that is a gift.[22] The contemplative life that sets the conditions for such experiences is a 'lost art'—one that is recovered not by escaping or isolation from the 'world' but with openness to it. Hence, there is an indication of the value of the East for Merton because the Zen practioners have traversed the terrain of the experience more deeply.

In a recent article by John Keenan in the book *Merton & Buddhism,* he offers a critique of Merton's grasp of Zen based on the fact that scholars have begun raising serious questions concerning Suzuki's knowledge of Zen. This, in turn, would have affected Merton's understanding of Zen, which Keenan finds to be simplistic and more a product of the context of the time. Keenan is concerned to counter the simplistic understanding of Zen as completely experiential in its goal and as not interested in intellectual reflection, doctrines etc. In contrast, Keenan emphasizes that Zen has a wealth of traditions and doctrines and therefore cannot be reduced to simply trying to have an experience of awakening. "In a word, Zen is not the bare and pure experience of the ultimate that is beyond all words and doctrines. The Zen notion that one must go beyond doctrine itself is a Zen doctrine!"[23]

At the center of this critique is the question concerning pure experience, or unmediated experience as the basic core of not only Zen but all 'religious-mystical' experience. This question has been raised by other scholars as well and deserves greater attention than I have time to address it here. Keenan refers to the work of Bernard Lonergan in this regard. Keenan suggests, and I think rightly so, that unmediated experiences can be commonplace and often occur outside of a religious context. However, he overlooks a subtle point in Lonergan's treatment of the issue that is important. For Lonergan, there is unmediated experience but in the context of religious-mystical experience, the experience itself is *a mediated return to immediacy*. The individual's tradition is the context where one is mediated to the experience of immediacy. For example, one could say that *the doctrine of no doctrine*, would be a key part of the cultural-religious language that prepares the conditions for Zen practitioners to be 'jerked clean out' of themselves in a mediated return to immediacy, if I can invoke a description from Merton's own religious experience. Consequently, the subsequent reflection on the encounter is carried out within the context of the tradition. However, Keenan is aware of this latter point, once one has returned to the mediated consciousness and begins reflecting on that experience.[24]

If Keenan is correct then my interpretation above may be open to the same critique. However, while I believe Keenan, Roger Corless and others have valid arguments which I will take up in a lengthier essay, suffice it to say, I do not think their critique detracts from Merton's understanding of Buddhism or his pioneering contribution to interreligious engagement in the Catholic Church. While Keenan may not dispute the latter, the former he would probably dispute. I think one has to consider that Merton had a spiritual authority that flowed from his commitment to the contemplative life, which the intellectual and spiritual authorities of his day could recognize. It is one thing to critique Merton's understanding of Zen from an intellectual standpoint, however, one cannot dispute the spiritual authority that Merton possessed, who significant Buddhist scholars and practitioners could recognize. For example, during his visit with Merton, the Dalai Lama demonstrated some meditation techniques by actually sitting on the floor with Merton, a gesture that would be considered "unthinkable" in Tibet considering the custom that the Dalai Lama remains in an elevated seated position.[25] If anything, this signifies an atypical respect that his Holiness showed towards Merton. The same can be said of the Tibetan monk Chadral Rinpoche, who after having a stimulating dialogue with Merton, called him a *rangjung*, a naturally arisen Buddha.[26] All this to say Merton had an authority that was not the result of strictly academic knowledge of Buddhism. Again, he had a commitment to the spiritual life, the fruits of which were identifiable by the some of the leading spiritual figures and Buddhist authorities of his day. This can be overlooked by simply focusing on Merton's academic study of Buddhism regardless of how imperfect or historically conditioned it may have been.

Another issue Keenan relays is related to that of pure experience, the method of dialogue with Buddhism and between other religions in general. Keenan suggests that dialogue has often been naively focused on commonalities between human beings and with it, the commonality of religious-mystical experience. It does not take seriously enough the differences between religious traditions. I agree with him that there are fundamental differences between the various religions of the world and we should take pains to understand these differences carefully and realize that some of these differences are irreconcilable. However, in our current age of increasing tension between conflicting religious worldviews fueled by religious extremism, I find it refreshing that Merton and the Dalai Lama were finding commonalities between Buddhism and Christianity, which included the common values of compassion.

In light of Keenan's concern, what we are lacking is an appropriate method for engaging with other religions that accounts for the distinct types of differences and allows one the wisdom to differentiate and distinguish among them, while simultaneously embracing fundamental commonalities between the various religions.

E. The Future of Buddhism and Christianity?

To bring this paper to a conclusion I return to the place where I began. It is interesting that Thomas Merton and Josef Ratzinger both had opinions regarding the future of Christianity and Buddhism. It is clear that Ratzinger saw Buddhism as a challenge to Christianity. In a French interview Ratzinger quotes a source he agrees with that the biggest challenge to Christianity in the twentieth century "would not be Marxism but Buddhism."[27] The comparison to Marxism makes Buddhism appear more of a threat than a challenge to Christians. Ironically, Merton's last lecture was a comparison between Marxism and Monasticism. I asked the former Archbishop Weakland about this several years ago and he told me that one of Merton's greatest gifts was his intuition. Weakland was speaking about how Merton's final lecture was a head of its time—that several years later, the topic had become a centerpiece of concern for the Conference.

Similarly, one must wonder what to make of comments ascribed to Merton near the end of his life that "Christianity and Zen are the future."[28] Is Merton anticipating some kind of syncretism? I would suggest that Merton's comments should not be taken for their religious implications but rather for their philosophical import. That is, in both his dialogues with the Dalai Lama and with Suzuki, they speak of the philosophical issues pertaining to interior consciousness. One could say the Christian comes from a *logos* or theoretical tradition involving speculation, whereas the Zen practitioner sees the limits of such theory as a hindrance to *the mediated return to immediacy* of which *Satori* is a dramatic instance. When Merton was at Polonaruwa, he was "jerked clean out" of himself, that is, he is mediated by way of the giant Buddha images to an immediacy that is presumably Zen-like in character. He cannot describe it in Western vocabulary.[29] Perhaps he views Christianity and Zen as the future because they are the philosophical complementarities of the *world mediated by meaning*, or the logos of Christianity on the one hand, and the world of immediacy that Zen strives to obtain through experiential rather than by way of theory on the other hand. In this way, the differences between Zen and Christianity need not be seen as contradictory but rather as complementary, or mutual in their philosophical emphases. They can also be mutually challenging as well. Zen can challenge the Christian who might be clinging to 'the word' or 'dogma' at the expense of the transformative experience; and the Christian can challenge Zen to reexamine the value of theory and the world of the logos as not a hindrance but an aid to at lease a proximate understanding of the experience—there is an intrinsic value to theoretical knowledge.

Endnotes

1. John Paul II, *Crossing the Threshold of Hope* (New York: Alfred A. Knopf, 1994), 85. In fairness, Dr. John Borelli of Georgetown told me that this does not reflect the full complexity of John Paul's thinking on Bud-

dhism and there were other published statements that would nuance his position—some which were made after the controversy that followed the publication of these original comments. However, most Catholics do not have the ready access to these alternative statements that could nuance John Paul's thinking. Moreover, *Crossing the Threshold of Hope* was a kind of catechetical-inspirational type of work that reached many Catholic readers. Therefore, while his statements may not be explicitly *ex cathedra*, they do have an impact on many Catholics' common perceptions of Buddhism.

2. *Zenit* News Service, February 1, 2007.

3. John Dadosky, "The Church and the Other: Mediation and Friendship in Post-Vatican II Roman Catholic Ecclesiology," *Pacifica* (October, 2005), 302-322; and "Towards a Fundamental Theological RE-Interpretation of Vatican II," *The Heythrop Journal*, Volume 49 Issue 5 (September, 2008): p 742-763.

4. See the joint pontifical statement *Dialogue and Proclamation* (1991), ¶ 38.

5. James L. Fredericks, *Faith Among Faiths: Christian Theology and Non-Christian Religions* (Mahwah, NY: Paulist Press, 1999), 173ff, at 175.

6. Ibid., 177.

7. Ibid., 175.

8. Ibid., 176.

9. John Dadosky, "The Church and the Other, 316, 322.

10. Paul Wilkes, *Merton By Those Who Knew Him Best*. (San Francisco: Harper & Row, 1984), 147.

11. Thomas Merton, *Asian Journal*, (New York: New Directions, 1973), 125.

12. Wilkes, 145.

13. Wilkes, 146.

14. Wilkes, 146.

15. Thomas Merton, *The Other Side of the Mountain: The End of the Journey, The Journals of Thomas Merton, Vol. 7 1967-1968*, ed. Patrick Hart, O.C.S.O (San Francisco, Harper: 1989), 265.

16. Joseph Q. Raab, "Comrades for Peace: Thomas Merton, the Dalai Lama, and the Preferential Option for Nonviolence." *The Merton Annual* 19 (2006): 256-267, at 264.

17. Their relationship can be divided into two periods, 1) from Merton's initial correspondence in 1959 to their face to face meeting in New York City in 1964; 2) from that initial meeting until Suzuki's death in 1966. Joseph Quinn Raab, *Openness and Fidelity: Thomas Merton's Dialogue with D.T. Suzuki, and Self-Transcendence*. (Thesis for the degree of Ph.D. in Theology, University of St. Michael's College, Toronto, 2000), 135, n. 9

18. D.T. Suzuki's comments to Mr. Lunsford Yandell. See Christmas Hum-

phrey's forward to *The Zen Revival* (London, The Buddhist Society, 1971).

19. Thomas Merton, *Zen and the Birds of Appetite,* (New York: New Directions, 1968), 133.

20. It goes without saying that when practitioners speak of what Zen is and is not about, they are now relying on insights and affirmations mediated by consciousness which cannot be avoided. Hence I suppose one could say there is a sense in which there is also "Zen insight"; although it is an insight into the limits of our understanding in the face of mystery.

21. Ibid, 63.

22. Thomas Merton, *Mystics and Zen Masters* (New York: Farrar, Straus, Giroux, 1999), 203.

23. John P. Keenan, "The Limits of Thomas Merton's Understanding of Buddhism," in Bonnie Bowman Thurston (ed.), pp. 118-133, *Merton and Buddhism: Wisdom, Emptiness and Everyday Mind* (Louisville, KY: Fons Vitae, 2007), p. 126.

24. Ibid., 130.

25. Thurston, *Merton & Buddhism*, 71.

26. Ibid., 75.

27. See Leo D. Lefebure, "Cardinal Ratzinger's Comments on Buddhism," *Buddhist Christian Studies* 18 (1998): 221-223. I would agree with Lefebure who believes Ratzinger was just expressing his personal opinion and not speaking officially for the Church, 221.

28. Cited in Raab, *Openness and Fidelity*, 95.

29. See Joseph Q. Raab, "*Madhyamika* and *Dharmakaya*: Some Notes on Merton's Epiphany at Polonoruwa" *The Merton Annual*, (2004): 195-205.

"Those Going Among the Saracens and Other Nonbelievers": Thomas Merton and Franciscan Interreligious Dialogue[1]

Daniel P. Horan, OFM

Introduction

Hidden within Thomas Merton's 1966 text, *Conjectures of a Guilty Bystander,* stands a telling passage only seven paragraphs long that presents perhaps the most succinct expression of his model and inspiration for interreligious dialogue. He begins this section with a quote from Eulogius, an Orthodox Metropolitan, and notes its significance in his life.

'Men like the Seraphic Saint, Saint Francis of Assisi, and many others, accomplished in their life the union of the churches.' This profound and simple statement…gives the key to ecumenism for monks, and indeed for everyone.[2]

In the last two decades much has been published regarding the latent, and at times more explicit, Franciscan influence on the writing and spirituality of Merton.[3] However, exploration of the particular way the Franciscan charism affected, and perhaps directed, Merton's approach to interreligious dialogue has been overlooked. What's more striking is the similarity in methodology and praxis utilized by both Francis of Assisi and Merton. It is clear from the quote above and elsewhere in his writings that Merton held Francis as a paragon of interreligious dialogue in the forefront of his interreligious and ecumenical consciousness.

Having applied, been initially accepted and later rejected by the Order of Friars Minor (Franciscan friars) in 1939,[4] Franciscan spirituality influenced Merton significantly during a formative period in his life. Merton's admiration for, and desire to emulate, Francis is a reoccurring theme in his writing. As we also will see, Merton adopted Francis's approach to interreligious dialogue and made it his own.

This paper will explore the connection between the nearly eight-hundred-year-old Franciscan tradition of peaceful interreligious dialogue and its impact on the twentieth-century monk, while illuminating the present-day implications for hearing "the voice of the stranger." The methodological approach for this study will include a threefold examination of Francis's, Merton's and our experiences as they relate to interreligious dialogue.

First, we will look at Franciscan interreligious dialogue. Since every interreligious experience is rooted in a particular historical setting, I will present a brief historical context. Without an appreciation for the ecclesiastical and socio-political world serving as a backdrop to the interreligious experience of Francis, the full significance of hearing the other is lost. Next, I will present a summary of Francis's interreligious encounter with the Sultan in Egypt. The most famous of Francis's interreligious encounters, this will serve as a case study. From our examination of Francis's encounter with the Sultan, I will suggest three characteristics that arise from our methodological reflection that will allow us to locate the operative hermeneutic in the work of Francis.

Second, I will use the three characteristics of Franciscan interreligious dialogue identified in the first section as a lens through which to examine the interreligious work of Merton. As we will see, Merton's interreligious encounters bear a strong resemblance to Francis's meeting with the Sultan. Through his own words and action, Merton expresses the Franciscan spirit of peaceful and authentic encounter with the "stranger."

In closing, I will suggest considering our present time as not unlike those of Francis and Merton, examine the contemporary relevance of the model for interreligious dialogue that Francis and Merton leave us, and show how an adoption of the method of Francis and Merton might open new pathways for interreligious dialogue today. As twenty-first century citizens, we are inheritors of a rich tradition shaped by these two prophetic voices that continue to speak with great pertinence today. We are better able to hear the voice of the stranger in our own day aided by their wisdom and guided by their example.

Franciscan Interreligious Dialogue

Historical Context

In April of 1213 Pope Innocent III released his encyclical *Quia maior*, which introduced his plan for the fifth crusade (1217-1221). The second crusade to be called by Innocent III – his first was from

1202-1204—was seen as the final step in recapturing the Holy Land and was doubtless the talk of the town. The two hallmarks of *Quia maior* were the general call for everyone in Christendom to support the effort and the encyclical's great detail concerning the manner in which this fifth crusade was to be launched. Whereas the preceding crusades had been launched largely due to the activity of the emperors, the fifth crusade was completely an effort of Innocent III.

In addition to the unique nature of the crusade being called by the pope, its announcement through a papal encyclical presented a new theological dimension to understanding the purpose of the crusade. No longer was a crusade to be interpreted, however superficially, as an act of civil authority or aggression. Innocent III's encyclical placed the papacy and all of Christendom behind the effort.[5] Innocent III set the plan in motion, but it would be ordinary Christians who would pay the bill, staff the army and pray for military success. Further developing a theological purpose for the crusade, he declared that this effort was part of God's divine command.[6] Horrifically, this view was rooted in Innocent III's understanding that the Gospel call to 'love one's neighbor' compelled Christians to liberate their fellow Christians in the Holy Land, "who are being held in the hands of the perfidious Saracens in dire imprisonment and are weighed down by the yoke of most severe slavery."[7] The operative hermeneutic of the time was one of fear, relegating Muslims to otherness. By excluding Muslim men and women from the Christian obligation to 'love one's neighbor,' they were dehumanized.

This attitude of the dehumanized-other had been developing for nearly a century by this time. Innocent III was greatly influenced by the theology and preaching of Bernard of Clairvaux who believed that while God could easily liberate the Holy Land from the Saracens, God had provided an opportunity for all Christians to prove themselves faithful to Christ by becoming involved in the crusade.[8] Not only was the defeat of the Holy Land Muslims a matter of military strategy, it was also viewed as God's will. Evidence of similar disdain for Muslims exists among chroniclers of the time such as in the writing of Bishop Jacques de Vitry, who, in addition to providing a personal account of Francis's encounter with the Sultan, describes the Saracens as "sacrilegious disciples of [the] Antichrist."[9] The general attitude of the time was one of great hostility toward Muslims.

Interreligious Dialogue

Revolutionary in lifestyle and ambitious in scope, Francis of Assisi's first rule of life for the Order of Friars Minor, tentatively approved by Pope Innocent III, included a chapter dedicated solely to the way the friars were to engage non-Christians. Francis's desire, articulated in summary at the onset of his Rule, was simply to live the Gospel of Jesus Christ.[10] It is clear that the experience of Gospel living informed the lens through which Francis viewed his world. Beginning with the famous encounter with the leper, when Francis himself recognized his own need for conversion, and continuing throughout his earthly journey, Francis set an example for Christian engagement with "the stranger." Nowhere in his writings is this example more clear than in the chapter of his way of life that instructs his followers on how to encounter the strangers of his time: the Muslims and other nonbelievers.

Chapter sixteen of the *Regula non bullata*, titled "Those who are going among the Saracens and other nonbelievers,"[11] resulted from the experience of Francis and his companions in their peaceful mission among the Saracens in 1219.[12] At a time when the Christian world was rallying support for and contributing to the efforts of the fifth crusade, Francis – initially motivated by zeal for the gift of martyrdom, and later inspired to promote peaceful resolution to war[13]—traveled to Egypt with a few of his companions to preach to the Muslims and oppose the crusade.[14]

His journey began in 1212, prior to the formal launching of the fifth crusade. Strongly moved to preach the message of the Gospel to the Muslims, Francis set out on a journey to Syria and shortly afterward to Morocco, but his mission was cut short due to travel complications and poor health.[15] Francis would eventually succeed with his plan and reach Damietta. Upon arriving, having traveled to Egypt with Italian crusaders, Francis saw the devastation of battle and the inevitable defeat that lay ahead for the Christian army. While staying in the crusaders' camp, Francis challenged the crusaders to consider whether their engagement in battle with the Saracens was really the will of God. Francis's most famous biographer, Thomas of Celano, suggests that the crusaders were warned by the Saint that their losses in battle were the result of their disregard for the true will of God, that of peacemaking and not war. Francis's espousal of nonviolence and his efforts to dissuade violent action by the crusaders speaks volumes of the countercultural position embraced by this man from Assisi. According to scholar Jan Hoeberichts, "Francis occupied an exceptional position among his contemporaries with regard to the crusades and the attitude they expressed towards the Saracens and Islam. This is all the more striking since virtually the entire church from high to low was committed to the crusade."[16] Francis DeBeer suggests that, "Francis's attitude appears strange, to say the least."[17] Certainly Francis's opposition to the direction the Church and the political world was moving was seen as odd, considering his loyalty to the Church and its leadership. However, his commitment to following the Gospel trumped even his steadfast fidelity to the Church.

Francis, having preached to the crusaders, left the protection of their camp to go among the Saracens. His vision of universal fraternity and connectedness as children of God allowed him to approach the Saracens, viewing them not as "enemy" but as friend, remembering the call of Christ to "love your enemies and do good to those who hate you."[18] Jesus' command to love was for Francis a central truth, and by radically adhering to this truth, he was an example to his followers of what it meant to follow Christ by living as a *frater minor* (lesser brother). Becoming vulnerable to the point of risking his very life, Francis humbly lived as a brother to all.

Along with his companion, Brother Illuminato, Francis crossed the Saracen threshold and requested permission to see the Sultan. They were at first denied but after persistent request, they were siezed and beaten and eventually taken to Sultan Malek-al-Kamil. The Saracens most likely thought Francis and Illuminato were negotiators sent by the crusaders in response to the Sultan's earlier attempt at calling a truce.[19] However, Francis had come on his own with his own agenda: a message of peace.

This message included the preaching of the Gospel to the Sultan in a way that was respectful and inviting. Francis never insulted or denigrated Islam—as his contemporaries were known to do—but his disarming approach created an atmosphere of conversation and dialogue. It is believed that Francis and his companion spent up to three weeks with the Sultan and his advisors discussing religious matters and sharing their experiences.

Malek al-Kamil was known to be a kind and just man in his own right. His attentive listening to Francis, and graciously allowing a Christian to preach in his court, demonstrates the openness to dialogue the Sultan had toward a humble man who posed no threat and sought peace amid violence. Jacques de Vitry chronicles this experience of openness as he notes,

> When the cruel beast [the Sultan] saw Francis, he recognized him as a man of God and changed his attitude into one of gentleness, and for some days he listened very attentively to Francis as he preached the faith of Christ to him and his followers...At the end he said to Francis: 'Pray for me, that God may deign to reveal to me the law and the faith which is more pleasing to Him.'[20]

When the time had come for Francis and his companion to depart from the Sultan's court, Malek al-Kamil showed his admiration and affection for the *poverello* in a personal request for a prayer. As Kathleen Warren notes, the Sultan was sincerely moved by Francis's goodness and sincere desire to promote peace and truth among the Christians and Saracens.[21] The Sultan was surely aware that Francis saw the Muslims as children of God and his brothers and sisters. Francis DeBeer identifies this encounter, signified by the Sultan's prayer request, as a moment when Francis transcended "the cloister of Christianity," and invites the Sultan to likewise transcend his own boundaries.[22] While the Sultan is not yet ready to make that move, it was clear that a seed was planted and, "a dialogue was initiated which transcended all quarrels, discussions, and arguments. And no one could go any further: neither Francis nor the Sultan. One must wait for the hour of the Spirit. And the suspense has lasted for centuries."[23]

Methodological Reflection

A question naturally arises concerning the manner with which Francis was able to engage in such peaceful dialogue: how did Francis do this? To appreciate the significance of Francis's encounter with the Sultan, and his entire interreligious attitude, we must first explore his method and primary hermeneutic. In the interest of brevity, I suggest three factors that operate concurrently throughout Francis's interreligious encounter with the Sultan that form the foundation of what we might today call "Franciscan interreligious dialogue." These factors are:

1. The radical adhering to the evangelical value of solidarity.

2. The preferential option for the discovery of common faith.

3. The position of minority rooted in a commitment to lifelong conversion.

While the person and charism of Francis of Assisi can not be limited to these three attributes, by naming them we might establish a starting point from which an analysis of Franciscan interreligious dialogue can advance.

The Franciscan movement, rooted in Gospel living, has always collectively embodied the notion of fraternity. The quintessential expression of this principle is found in Francis's most famous writing, "The Canticle of the Creatures."[24] Here Francis expresses his radical worldview of the interconnectedness of all creation stemming from the One, Loving God. While this Franciscan expression has often been diluted to a caricature of the *poverello* and a birdbath, its most honest reading suggests an intense appreciation for the gift of life and existence shared by all. Beyond the poetry of "The Canticle of the Creatures," this view is found in the living example of Christian charity of Francis encountering the Sultan. From prayer to praxis, Francis saw himself as another blessed creature of God, in many ways no different from the Sultan and the Saracens. In understanding himself as brother to all, Francis transcended the boundary of "us" versus "them" categories and embraced the marginalized and abused outcasts of his day.

There is a strong temptation to romanticize this encounter and neglect the sacrifice and vulnerability of Francis. His decision to welcome the Sultan and other Muslims into his life as brothers and sisters was in stark contrast to the policies and practice of the Church and the social order of his day. In choosing to stand in solidarity beside the Muslims, he moved outside the comfort of inclusion to the live at the margins and became better able to "hear the voice of the stranger," because he had become a stranger to his own culture.

Our second characteristic, the preferential option for the discovery of common faith, is found explicitly in Francis's Rule of life. The recent work of Franciscan scholar Laurent Gallant has shed a great deal of light on the true meaning of Francis's 16th Chapter of the *Regula non bullata*. The text has always been interpreted to have an ecumenical tone and understood as the product of the experiences of Francis and his brothers' mission among the Saracens.[25] Take for example verse 6 concerning how the friars are to live spiritually among the Saracens, "One way is not to engage in arguments or disputes, but to be subject to every human creature for God's sake and to acknowledge that they are Christians."[26] The significance of Gallant's study is the extent to which Francis's directive expresses a preferential option for the discovery of common faith. While previously acknowledged as explicit instructions for his followers to encounter the stranger, the method of dialogue seems to have been skewed over time.

The traditional translation, influenced by the proliferation of copied manuscripts that include the addition of the word *in* (*ut credant* in *Deum omnipotentem*),[27] has been understood as instructing evangelization efforts to promote Christianity among the Muslims. This verse has been read as,

> The other way is to announce the Word of God, when they see it pleases the Lord, in order that [unbelievers] may believe *in almighty God, the Father, the Son and the Holy Spirit, the Creator of all...*[28]

This reading suggests an exclusively Christian approach toward encountering the other. Gallant believes that this is a copyist error that dates back to at least the seventeenth century and has reoc- curred in every major edition since. Gallant posits that this error was easily overlooked and replicated because of the possible influ- ence of and resemblance to the Christian Creed.[29] The familiarity of the copyists with the Christian Creed (which begins *Credo in Deum omnipotentem*) would naturally lead them to "correct" the written Rule of Francis by inserting the word "in." Subsequently, this copying error has led to the diminishing of the radical example of interreligious dialogue over several centuries.

Serious textual criticism of the manuscript tradition has only been explored since the middle of the twentieth century, beginning with the work of scholars like David Flood and Thadee Matura.[30] Gallant's re-visiting of the *Regula non bullata* text is the most re- cent contribution to this field. His reading of the text suggests a more radical expression of Francis's desire that the friars meet the stranger on common ground. Gallant asserts that Francis's instruc- tion in verse 7 be read as follows:

...in order that they may believe

(1) that almighty God [in which they already believe] *is* Father, Son, and Holy Spirit,

(2) that the Creator of all [in which they also already believe] *is* the Son [i.e., God's creating Word], who is Redeemer and Savior.[31]

This interpretation suggests an effort to unite the Muslim and Christian through doctrinal agreement as a starting point. The establishment of common doctrinal ground is the first step of a two-tiered enterprise. The second step is the explication of the Christian conception of "Almighty God" as Trinity, and that "Creator of All" includes the Son. This second step is only possible built on the foundation of the preferential option for the discovery of common faith. Francis's goal here was not to preach exclusive Christian dogma to the Muslims and other nonbelievers. Rather, by discovering articles of faith shared by both groups, a peaceful conversation can begin rooted in solidarity. Gallant also observes that historians and theologians of the Franciscan movement often emphasize Francis's "acute conscience of the presence of God and of the working of the Spirit in all human beings. This shared Christian-Muslim belief in ['Almighty God'] and 'Creator of all' would certainly be an example of common faith."[32]

In many ways our third category suggests the most original and classically "Franciscan" of the three characteristics found in Francis's encounter and his vision which his brothers were to follow. The position of minority rooted in a commitment to lifelong conversion is also the most organic and dynamic of the three, which further complicates a systematic analysis of his interreligious approach.

Francis held that in order to live a truly authentic form of Gospel life, one was never to place one's self above another. In Chapter 6 of the *Regula non bullata* Francis remarks that this attitude is to be held even among the brothers: "Let no one be called 'prior,' but let everyone in general be called a lesser brother. Let one wash the feet of the other."[33]

Minority is not synonymous with passivity. Rather, Francis viewed a life as minor when one courageously stood against the power differentials that divided the people of his day. A product of his time, Francis was all too familiar with the medieval authoritarian structures that made up his world. Even with the rise of the merchant class in the 13th century, Francis could not escape the social pressure to achieve some sort of noble status. As a young man both he and his father desired that Francis become a successful knight. It was not until the beginning of his conversion in 1206 that Francis began seeking a life of minority. Thomas of Celano describes his outward change in appearance, "He who once enjoyed wearing scarlet robes now traveled about half-clothed."[34]

The humility that naturally accompanies such a state of living helped to create a non-threatening space for dialogue. If one is not interested in winning, being correct or ranking above another, then he or she is not a threat. The Sultan had nothing to fear of Francis. The way Francis lived his life demonstrated his willingness to be subordinate to every other person for God's sake. Francis recognized himself as a sinner and therefore knew of his own need for continued conversion, garnering a great deal of patience for those who he encountered. While considering what was so non-threatening about Francis, Franciscan theologian Kenneth Himes said, "It was the fact that no one ever had to fear Francis. Francis never sought to dominate, manipulate, or coerce anyone. No person ever looked into the eyes of Francis and saw a lust for power or control."[35]

In many ways these characteristics of "Franciscan interreligious dialogue" show but a snapshot of the complex and inspiring charism they aim to convey. It is my hope that by articulating these factors, we might better appreciate the Franciscan spirit that so touched and influenced Thomas Merton.

Thomas Merton's Interreligious Dialogue

Ascertaining the explicit moments of Franciscan influence in Merton is a nebulous task. The truth is, human beings are influenced and informed by many people, principles, ideas, places and events, which blend together to form an eclectic composite. However, even as complex and unique individuals, we can still trace significant factors of our intellectual, emotional and spiritual formation. Such is the case with Thomas Merton and his Franciscan influence. In a letter to a staff writer at the Catholic periodical *Magnificat* dated February 12, 1966, Merton closes with this admission, "[I] will always feel that I am still in some secret way a son of St. Francis. There is no saint in the Church whom I admire more than St. Francis."[36]

The occurrence of Merton's frequent and direct references to Francis of Assisi throughout his written corpus alone testifies to the conscious reflection of this twentieth-century monk on the medieval saint. However, what's more is the strong resemblance of Merton's implicit worldview to that of Francis. While their historic contexts are separated by centuries, their core principles remain powerfully parallel. Simply put, the lifelong significance of Francis and Franciscan spirituality for Merton helped shape the way he viewed those of other faiths. Similarly, we see this in other areas of his life. His prayer and poetry often maintain a style that reflects Franciscan views of Christology, environmental theology, Trinity, human relationship, poverty, and humility, to name a few. It seems appropriate to name Franciscan interreligious dialogue as a major source of Merton's own interreligious approach.

Here we will explore some of the interreligious work of Merton through the lens of Franciscan interreligious dialogue as outlined above. It is my hope that after careful consideration we can affirm the resemblance to and likely influence of Franciscan interreligious dialogue in Merton's life and work.

The Radical Adhering to the Evangelical Value of Solidarity

For Francis, fraternity summarized his radical living in solidarity with all of humanity and creation. Abstracted in the vernacular poetry and prayer of the "Canticle of the Creatures" and exemplified in the encounter with the Sultan, Francis's starting point rested in the faithful recognition of his relationship to the other. Merton shares a similar starting point for his interreligious encounters. Best articulated as openness and eremitical prayerfulness, Merton's radical adherence to solidarity with the 'other' stood as a foundation for his interreligious work.

Authentic Gospel living is not based on building up the toleration of and emphasis on individuality, as was the emerging tendency at the dawn of postmodernity toward the end of Merton's life. Rather, Merton asserted the need for unity and end of division, envisioning a community like the Acts of the Apostles describes, "They devoted themselves to the apostles' teaching and fellowship, to the breaking of bread and the prayers...all who believed were together and had all things in common."[37] It is this ardent faithfulness to the Gospel that we can describe as radical adherence to solidarity.

If we look at Merton's essay, "A Letter to Pablo Antonio Cuadra Concerning Giants,"[38] we see an assertive critique of those unwilling to stand in solidarity with the rest of humanity. He names the affluent antagonist the "tourist." Merton opines,

> He cannot possibly realize that the stranger has something very valuable, something irreplaceable to give him…the tourist lacks nothing except brothers. For him these do not exist. The tourist never meets anyone, never encounters anyone, never finds the brother in the stranger.[39]

While this is an explicit polemic aimed at the United States, it is perhaps an implicit reference to when the young Merton was something of a globetrotter himself and much less open to the 'stranger.' Rooted in his own experience, Merton can empathize with – and in turn criticize – the "tourist," challenging the Western citizen to growth in the evangelical life.

Merton's own spiritual maturation led to his identification with the rest of humanity. Seeking a life of solidarity in which he might live in a way other than the "society of isolated individuals," Merton recognized that Christians are called to build communities of persons and not collections of individuals.[40] Concerning the world of isolated individuals, Merton explains, "[that] they do not know that reality is to be sought not in division but in unity, for we are 'members one of another'…the [one] who lives in division is not a person but only an 'individual.'"[41]

Solidarity appears as a recurring theme throughout Merton's work. For Merton, solidarity is seen as openness to both God and humanity. William Apel describes this feature as one of the greatest lessons we can gather from Merton's life.[42] What's more, placing Merton's response of solidarity within the context of his time we see, as Allan McMillan put so well, "Merton had insights not typical to the times in which they occurred and his learning had an experiential base."[43] McMillan goes on to suggest "seven lessons" learned by Merton during his interreligious encounters. The fourth such lesson is that of solidarity.

> That one cannot understand the depth of feelings and faith experiences of another person unless one has experienced and wrestled with them in his or her own life. This compassion, this willingness to 'suffer with' *the other* opens us to the appreciation of the greatness of how other people respond to the Divine call.[44]

This position of solidarity, while not necessarily present in the behavior and writing of the young Merton, is a recurring characteristic of the later Merton's interreligious *modus operandi*.

Merton's interreligious efforts were made at a time marked by great suspicion of outsiders. Long before the Second Vatican Council's "Declaration on Religious Freedom" (*Dignitatis Humanæ*) and the "Constitution on the Church in the Modern World" (*Gaudium et Spes*), Merton chose to stand with the "stranger" and to engage the "other," setting himself outside the popular limit of any interreligious encounter endorsed by his peers, culture and Church. His decision to embrace a position of solidarity risked the rejection of some, to be open to all. Merton knew his own identity was inescapably intertwined with the rest of humanity. He says in *New Seeds of Contemplation*, "I must look for my identity, somehow, not only in God but in other men [and women]. I will never be able to find myself if I isolate myself from the rest of [hu]mankind as if I were a different kind of being."[45]

The Preferential Option for the Discovery of Common Faith

With a worldview shaped by the desire to form a community of persons as opposed to a collection of individuals, Merton moves from a foundation of solidarity with the "other" or "stranger" to engage in interreligious encounters. At this point the preferential option for the discovery of common faith emerges with force. Returning to *Conjectures of a Guilty Bystander*, we observe Merton's explicit expression of this characteristic.

> The more I am able to affirm others, to say 'yes' to them in myself, by discovering them in myself and myself in them, the more real I am. I am fully real if my own heart says *yes* to *everyone*. I will be a better Catholic, not if I can *refute* every shade of Protestantism [or other faiths], but if I can affirm the truth in it and still go further.[46]

Merton, like Francis, recognized that true dialogue could never be based on proselytizing or evangelization in the narrow sense. Both Francis and Merton reflect the truth that God dwells in each person, and each saw the need to affirm that truth in the "stranger" as paramount to fruitful dialogue.

Merton's relationship with D.T. Suzuki illustrates this well. In a journal entry dated April 11, 1959, Merton reflects on the experience of a spiritual encounter with Suzuki.

Thus if I tried badly and bluntly to 'convert' Suzuki, that is, make him 'accept' formulas regarding the faith that are accepted by the average American Catholic, I would, in fact, not 'convert' him at all, but simply confuse and (in a cultural sense) degrade him. Not that he does not need the Sacraments, etc. but that is an entirely different question. On the contrary – if I can meet him on a common ground of spiritual Truth, where we share a real and deep experience of God, and where we know in humility our own deepest selves…then I certainly think Christ would be present and glorified in both of us and this would lead to a *conversion of us both.*[47]

Those who knew Merton, such as Amuya Chakravarty, Glenn Hinson, D.T. Suzuki and John Wu, have commented on his ability to engage with members of other faiths through his openness to their experience. Merton expresses in *Mystics and Zen Masters* that the true meaning of "catholic" includes "a readiness to enter into dialogue with all that is pure, wise, profound and humane in every kind of culture."[48] He spends much of this volume drawing connections between Christianity and Zen Buddhism, which remains one of his most explicit examples of the preferential option for the discovery of common faith.

Mystics and Zen Masters chronicles Merton's step-by-step exploration of eastern spirituality through the lens of common faith. His discovery of existential similarities among Christians and "the stranger" has led me to lightheartedly rename this volume "A Treatise on Interreligious Parallels." Merton cannot help but identify the ways that Zen Buddhism corresponds to Christianity. He compares the tea ceremony with Franciscan simplicity;[49] "Buddhahood" with passages in 1 Corinthians;[50] the Zen notion that "zero equals infinity" with John of the Cross's "*todo y nada*" (all and nothing);[51] the tradition of Kung Tzu with the tradition of St. Benedict;[52] the wisdom of the *Tao Te Ching* as resembling the Sermon on the Mount;[53] the philosophical insights of *Hsiao Ching* reflecting Christian Neoplatonic thought like that of Pseudo-Dionysius;[54] and so on. Following Francis, Merton's *modus operandi* is that of a preference for the discovery of that which unites humanity in God, or as Merton often described it, "The Hidden Ground of love."

This ongoing quest to identify with those of other beliefs through the discovery of common faith led Merton to return to the polemical metaphor of "the Tourist." Like Merton's own growth from naïve Catholic convert to interreligious ambassador *par excellence*, he calls the "tourists" of the world to find themselves in the "other" and "strangers" who are most unlike them. In doing so, they will have made a successful pilgrimage. Merton says, "It was in this spirit that St. Francis went on pilgrimage—on his own original kind of 'crusade'—to meet the [Sultan]; as a messenger not of violence, not of arrogant power, but of humility, simplicity and love."[55] Merton refers us to his pilgrimage guide and model with the hope that we too emulate St. Francis.

The Position of Minority Rooted in a Commitment to Lifelong Conversion

Finally, we examine how Merton emulated Francis's position of minority rooted in a commitment to lifelong conversion. Lawrence Cunningham suggests that Merton's most radical conversion, or "series of conversions," occurred through the 1950s and reached a climax with the 1966 publication of *Conjectures of a Guilty Bystander.*[56] Any reader of his life work will notice the gradual shift in emphasis from internal reflection to include external action. One struggle that remained constant for Merton was discerning the relationship between his vocation to the eremitical life and the call to engage the world. Eventually, and most explicitly, the nexus of monk and prophet became manifest in his strong interreligious interest and peace activism of the 1960s.

Like Francis, who was something of a "playboy" in his youth, Merton lived a rather pleasure-seeking life during his early years. Outlined in *The Seven Storey Mountain*, Merton's initial conversion to Catholic Christianity took shape in a manner much like Francis's own. A clear liminal experience marked the beginning of the conversions of Francis and Merton. I say beginning because both men saw this process as an ongoing experience of reorientation upward toward God and outward toward the rest of humanity after the pattern of the Gospel. As Cunningham noted, this experience of conversion will continue to shape Merton's life and lead him toward the "stranger" through interreligious dialogue.

Those familiar with Merton's life and work know of his struggles with ego. In a strikingly honest passage in *New Seeds of Contemplation*, Merton prays, "Give me humility in which alone is rest, and deliver me from pride which is the heaviest of burdens. And possess my whole heart and soul with the simplicity of love."[57] The almost instant fame resulting from the best-selling success of his autobiography early in his religious life, and his subsequent battle with egotism, is an example of his struggle to find balance, humility and vocational clarity. Merton discovered the answer to his dilemma in the full embrace of his vocation to solitude.

Contemplation is many things for Merton. Much of his writing expresses his struggle to specifically identify its meaning. Merton describes contemplation as that which is beyond all other forms of experience, as that which reaches out to the inexpressible God, as an awareness of the gift of our contingent existence and finally as a response to God.[58] Contemplation is understood in varied ways, but every perspective views contemplation as an ongoing process. To experience contemplation, Merton tells us that continual divesting of our ego, self-centeredness and sinfulness is necessary to recognize that in our true poverty we are free to more perfectly follow Christ. This experience of humility beckons an awareness of the poverty and need of those around us. In turn, such a process of ongoing conversion, or contemplation, leads one upward to God and outward toward the rest of humanity.

Francis's mendicant life of minority is reflected in Merton's monastic life of contemplation. Minority encompasses those aspects of the *vita evangelica*, poverty, chastity and obedience, common to religious life. It is also a conscious renunciation of power and status. It requires voluntary subordination of one's self for the sake of solidarity and communion with the "other." Reaching the state of minority is a process of ongoing conversion. Another way to appreciate Francis's minority and Merton's contemplation is to consider these terms as describing two sides of the same coin. Francis's minority most accurately describes the manifestation of the process of ongoing conversion whereas Merton's contemplation reflexively embodies the action (or lack thereof) of the process.

The dynamic result of this ongoing process of conversion is the discovery of one's true identity. In order to hear the "voice of the stranger" and authentically encounter the "other," I must know who I am. An oft-cited fruit of Merton's life of contemplation is the emergence of his conceptualization of "the true self." Merton finds the "true self" in God's image of him rather than his own skewed perception. To find who he is, Merton must find who God is.

In order to know and love God as He is, we must have God dwelling in us in a new way, not only in His creative power but in His mercy, not only in his greatness but in His littleness, by which He empties Himself and comes down to us to be empty in our emptiness, and so fill us in His fullness.[59]

The act of God's kenosis that Merton describes serves as a model for his own life. It is the Incarnation that articulates God's choice to live out a position of minority among us. Discovering and following this example, we live as our true selves. Through contemplation and openness to ongoing conversion from the false self, we discover who we really are in who God really is. To live the life of the Gospel is to live a life of self-emptying service, finding God in our emptiness and poverty. From that position of minority, we, like Merton and Francis, are able to authentically encounter "the stranger" to hear his or her voice.

Hearing the Voice of the Stranger Today

We live in a world of strangers. While technology, science, travel and other forms of discovery have shaped our contemporary culture to appear unlike Francis's 13th century Italy and even Merton's early 20th century United States, some aspects of life transcend the boundaries of geography and time. Unfortunately, we, like Francis and Merton, find ourselves in a world of broken humanity. The ongoing struggles of the human condition call us to help advance reconciliation and dialogue.

We are challenged daily by threats of violence, war, unrest, discrimination, inequality, racism and other forms of injustice. In an age marked by the overt presence religious pluralism and secular governments, openness to other people, cultures and religious expressions is surprisingly sparse. It is even difficult to recognize the faux form of acceptance Merton decries as a "society of isolated individuals," when violence erupts in the form of genocide in Sudan, authoritarian oppression and coercion in China, political unrest in Kenya, terrorist attacks in Britain and Spain, school shootings in the United States, utter chaos in Iraq, turbulence in Afghanistan and in manifold manifestations in every corner of the globe. As citizens of a postmodern, globalized, twenty-first-century world, we have much to learn about seeing, hearing and loving the "stranger."

I believe we can benefit greatly from Franciscan interreligious dialogue and Merton's model of and contribution to that tradition. Following the lead of Francis and Merton, and learning from their examples, we might move from living in a society of isolated individuals and strangers to living an expression of God's Kingdom with our sisters and brothers.

Models for Interreligious Dialogue

Both Francis and Merton speak a prophetic word to us today. Francis maps the path to hear the voice of the stranger, while Merton demonstrates that the path can still be traveled today. Both exemplars of interreligious dialogue embody the three characteristics outlined above, and our desire to emulate their model of interreligious dialogue must lead us to similar embodiment of these characteristics. If we hope to effect change in our world, we must first be willing to change ourselves.

The change required of us is essential to implementing Franciscan interreligious dialogue. This change is not a matter of exterior practice, political affiliation, social networking, branding or the use of fashionable and politically correct buzzwords. The change demanded of us is internal, foundational and spiritual. It is the adoption of a new way to live our lives; it is the willingness to rethink our worldview; and it is re-visioning the way we see God in our world and in one another.

The new way to live our lives is found in the embodiment of the position of minority rooted in a commitment to lifelong conversion. When capital gain and power over others are the measures of success, voluntarily embracing minority is indeed a novel way to live. Francis demonstrates that authentic Christian living is rooted in becoming subject to our brothers and sisters, and by doing so, avoid the pitfalls of power and unjust authority. Merton teaches us that it is God who models the greatest example of humility through the Incarnation, and it is through contemplation that we come to see this more clearly. The lives of Francis and Merton show us that this is not an overnight process. Rather, we must remain committed to the process of lifelong conversion that draws us nearer to God and each other.

The willingness to rethink our worldview is located in the embodiment of the preferential option for the discovery of common faith. When winning and advancing at the expense of another is broadly accepted and preferred in our society, seeking to form connections and identifying similarities with others is a radical paradigm shift. Francis started at the level of the other, wherever that might be. Instead of condemning the differences of the stranger, Francis embraced the shared faith and experiences of those he encountered. Likewise, Merton saw a reflection of God in the faith and life of those different from him.

Re-visioning the way we see God in our world and in one another is manifest in the radical adherence to the evangelical value of solidarity. When our society defines our personal identities by what makes us different, we must uncover the truth of God's presence on earth – that all citizens of this world share our humanity. Francis saw his life as interdependent and connected to every other aspect of God's creation. This fraternal view of the universe marks a path for us toward a global community. Merton saw the intrinsic value of each person as an interrelated participant in God's creation. He walked Francis's path away from understanding society as a collection of individuals to the Christian experience of a community of persons.

The opportunity for the internal, foundational and spiritual transformation placed before us today is an invitation to radically change the way we encounter all we meet. Embodying the characteristics of Francis and Merton's method of interreligious dialogue will allow us to become the new prophetic voices our world so desperately needs. We can become the voices that announce the possibility of a world that welcomes, no longer strangers, but brothers and sisters all.

Conclusion

Scott Thomas makes the argument that Franciscan interreligious dialogue speaks a message to today's world that confirms tolerance and appreciation for the religious sensibilities and traditions of others is not based on, nor leads to, skepticism, relativism and syncretism. Rather, authentically hearing the voice of the stranger is the fruit of remaining firmly rooted in one's own religious tradition with a genuine openness to encountering another.[60]

Thomas Merton's work in the middle part of the 20th Century demonstrates the life-giving nature of a tradition that speaks to our contemporary world as much as it did some 800 years ago. Merton saw the great need for valid religious renewal in order to maintain any semblance of relevance in our modern world.[61] Franciscan interreligious dialogue provides a schema for ecumenical relevance in a broken and divided world. I believe that this powerful model of authentic encounter with "the other" informed the action of Merton over time and possesses the possibility to steer our interreligious efforts in a positive direction today.

Some will dismiss the work of Francis and Merton as irrelevant to their lives because of the extraordinary nature of the work of these two exceptional men. Some will suggest that both Francis and Merton lived and acted in another time, in another place and in another manner foreign to the time, locations and issues of to-day. Some will suggest that the challenge of engaging in authentic dialogue is too difficult.

The last objection is the most honest and accurate, if only a flaccid excuse. It is difficult to engage in authentic dialogue, to change our image of 'other' to 'brother or sister.' This experience demands a comprehensive change in lifestyle, worldview and communication. It is, as our third characteristic of Franciscan inter-religious dialogue suggests, truly a process of life-long conversion that requires our commitment to relationship.

Like Francis and Merton, we must answer the call to enter into this relationship wholeheartedly, risking much for the sake of an-other. We are shown a way of solidarity, seeking common faith and lifelong humility. We are asked to change and be God's instrument of change in the world. Only then will our ears be open to hear the voices of the strangers, and our hearts be open to love them.

Endnotes

1. This paper was first presented 5 April 2008 at the Seventh General Meeting and Conference of the Thomas Merton Society of Great Britain and Ireland in Oakham, Rutland (U.K.).

2. Thomas Merton, *Conjectures of a Guilty Bystander* (New York: Image-Doubleday, 1966; 2000) p. 143. The translation of the quotation from Eulogius is mine from the original French, *"Des hommes comme Saint Seraphim, Saint François d'Assise et bien d'autres, ont accompli dans leur vie l'union des Eglises."*

3. See Timothy J. Shaffer, "Thomas Merton's Franciscan Spirituality," *The Cord* 57 (January/February 2007) pp. 63-81; Kathleen Deignan, "Road to Rapture: Thomas Merton's *Itinerarium Mentis in Deum*," *Franciscan Studies* 55 (1998) pp. 281-297; Michael Downey, "Merton's Franciscan Heart," *Franciscan Studies* 55 (1998) pp. 299-309; and Sean Edward Kin-sella, "'Where the Grey Light Meets the Green Air': The Hermit as Pilgrim in the Franciscan Spirituality of Thomas Merton," *Franciscan Studies* 55 (1998) pp. 311-322.

4. Thomas Merton, *The Seven Storey Mountain* (New York: Harcourt Brace & Company, 1998) pp. 289-298. Merton was later received into the Third Order of St. Francis (Secular Franciscans) on February 19, 1941. See Thomas Merton, *Run To The Mountains: The Journals of Thomas Merton*

Volume One 1939-1941, ed. Patrick Hart (New York: HarperCollins, 1995) p. 309.

5. Kathleen Warren, *Daring to Cross the Threshold: Francis of Assisi Encounters Sultan Malek al-Kamil* (Rochester, MN: Sisters of St. Francis, 2003) pp. 22-23.

6. J. Hoeberichts, *Francis and Islam* (Quincy, IL: Franciscan Press, 1997) p. 10.

7. Hoeberichts, *Francis and Islam*, p. 10.

8. Hoeberichts, *Francis and Islam*, p. 11.

9. Francis DeBeer, "St. Francis and Islam," in *Francis of Assisi Today*, eds. Christian Duquoc and Casiano Floristán, *Concilium* 149 (November 1981) pp. 11-12.

10. Chapter I of the *Regula non bullata* begins as follows: "The rule and life of these brothers is this, namely: 'to live in obedience, in chastity, and without anything of their own,' and to follow the teaching and footprints of our Lord Jesus Christ." Francis of Assisi, "The Earlier Rule," in *Francis of Assisi: The Early Documents*, Vol. 1, eds. R. Armstrong, W. Hellmann and W. Short (Hyde Park, NY: New City Press, 1999) pp. 63-64. [Hereafter *FAED* 1]

11. *FAED* 1, p. 74.

12. There is some debate concerning the dating of Francis's encounter with Malek al-Kamil. Manselli places the entire trip within the time between May 9, 1218 and August 29, 1219; see Raoul Manselli, *St. Francis of Assisi*, trans. Paul Duggan (Chicago: Franciscan Herald Press, 1988) pp. 222-223. Walbert Bühlmann, developing his theory based on the creation of Chapter 16th of the *Rugula non bullata*, suggests that Francis and his companions stayed in Egypt between July 1219 and spring 1220. See Walbert Bühlmann as quoted in Hoeberichts, *Francis and Islam*, p. 45. Warren supports the dating between 1 and 16 September of 1219. See Warren, *Daring to Cross the Threshold*, p. 46.

13. DeBeer, "St. Francis and Islam," pp. 16-17.

14. While there is still some debate over whether Francis's mission to Egypt was in fact a peaceful opposition to the crusade, I concur with those scholars who believe this to be Francis's primary motive. For a list of those writers who agree with this theory, see Warren, *Daring to Cross the Threshold*, n.18, pp. 36-37.

15. Warren, *Daring to Cross the Threshold*, p. 33.

16. Hoeberichts, *Francis and Islam*, p. 5.

17. DeBeer, "St. Francis and Islam," p. 15.

18. Warren, *Daring to Cross the Threshold*, p. 42.

19. Warren, *Daring to Cross the Threshold*, pp. 44-45.

20. Jacques de Vitry, *Historia Occidentalis*, in *FAED* 1, p. 584.

21. Warren, *Daring to Cross the Threshold*, p. 49.

22. Warren, *Daring to Cross the Threshold*, p. 49.

23. Francis DeBeer, *We Saw Brother Francis*, trans. Despot and LaChance (Chicago: Franciscan Herald Press, 1983) p. 88.

24. See Francis of Assisi, "The Canticle of the Creatures," in *FAED* 1, pp. 113-114.

25. Hoeberichts, *Francis and Islam*, p. 61.

26. Francis of Assisi, "The Earlier Rule" (*Regula non bullata*), ch. XVI, v. 6, in *FAED* 1, p. 74.

27. Laurent Gallant, "Francis of Assisi Forerunner of Interreligious Dialogue: Chapter 16 of the Earlier Rule Revisited," *Franciscan Studies* 64 (2006) pp. 58-59.

28. Francis of Assisi, "The Earlier Rule" (*Regula non bullata*), ch. XVI, v. 7, in *FAED* 1, p. 74. See also Gallant, "Francis of Assisi Forerunner of Interreligious Dialogue," p. 63 n.15. Emphasis added.

29. Gallant, "Francis of Assisi Forerunner of Interreligious Dialogue," pp. 59-60.

30. See David Flood and Thadee Matura, *The Birth of a Movement*, trans. Paul LaChance and Paul Schwartz (Chicago: Franciscan Herald Press, 1975), originally published David Flood and Thadee Matura, *La Naissance d'un Charisme* (Paris: Editions Franciscaines, 1973).

31. Diagram as presented by the author in Gallant, "Francis of Assisi Forerunner of Interreligious Dialogue," p. 61.

32. Gallant, "Francis of Assisi Forerunner of Interreligious Dialogue," p. 73.

33. Francis of Assisi, "The Earlier Rule" (*Regula non bullata*), ch. VI, vv. 3-4, in *FAED* 1, p. 68.

34. Thomas of Celano, *The Life of Saint Francis*, Ch. VII, v. 16, in *FAED* 1, p. 194.

35. Kenneth Himes, "The Inaugural Keynote Address on the Occasion of Inauguration of Fr. Kevin Mullen, O.F.M., Tenth President of Siena College," (1 October 2007), unpublished text, pp. 7-8.

36. Thomas Merton, *The Road To Joy: Letters to New and Old Friends*, ed. Robert Daggy (New York: Harcourt Brace, 1989) p. 298.

37. *NRSV* Acts 2:42,44.

38. Thomas Merton, "A Letter to Pablo Antonio Cuadra Concerning Giants," in *The Collected Poems of Thomas Merton* (New York: New Directions Publishing, 1977) pp. 372-391.

39. Merton, "A Letter to Pablo Antonio Cuadra," p. 387.

40. William H. Shannon, *Thomas Merton: An Introduction* (Cincinnati: St. Anthony Messenger Press, 2005) p. 95.

41. Thomas Merton, *New Seeds of Contemplation* (New York: New Directions Publishing, 1962) pp. 47-48.

42. William Apel, *Signs of Peace: The Interfaith Letters of Thomas Merton*

(Maryknoll, NY: Orbis Books, 2006) p. 105.

43. Allan McMillan, "Seven Lessons for Inter-faith Dialogue and Thomas Merton," *The Merton Annual* 15 (2002) p. 194.

44. McMillan, "Seven Lessons," p. 198. Emphasis added.

45. Merton, *New Seeds of Contemplation*, p. 51.

46. Merton, *Conjectures of a Guilty Bystander*, p. 144. Emphasis is Merton's.

47. Thomas Merton, *A Search for Solitude: The Journals of Thomas Merton, Volume Three 1952-1960*, ed. Lawrence Cunningham (New York: HarperCollins, 1996) p. 273.

48. Thomas Merton, *Mystics and Zen Masters* (New York: Farrar, Straus and Giroux, 1967) as quoted in Apel, *Signs of Peace*, pp. xiv-xv.

49. Merton, *Mystics and Zen Masters*, p. 10.

50. Merton, *Mystics and Zen Masters*, p. 17.

51. Merton, *Mystics and Zen Masters*, p. 39.

52. Merton, *Mystics and Zen Masters*, p. 65.

53. Merton, *Mystics and Zen Masters*, p. 70.

54. Merton, *Mystics and Zen Masters*, p. 79.

55. Merton, *Mystics and Zen Masters*, p. 112.

56. Lawrence Cunningham, *Thomas Merton & The Monastic Vision* (Grand Rapids: William B. Eerdmans Publishing, 1999) pp. 51-52.

57. Merton, *New Seeds of Contemplation*, p. 45.

58. Merton, *New Seeds of Contemplation*, p. 2-3.

59. Merton, *New Seeds of Contemplation*, p. 40.

60. Scott Thomas, "Franciscan Guide to Dialogue," *The Tablet* 260 (7 October 2006) pp. 8-9.

61. Thomas Merton, *Contemplation in a World of Action* (Notre Dame: University of Notre Dame Press, 1999) pp. 182-183.

A (Not So) Secret Son of Francis: Thomas Merton's Franciscan Lens for Seeing Heaven and Earth[1]

Timothy J. Shaffer

Wide Open to Heaven and Earth

In the midst of a turbulent world both internal and external to himself, Thomas Merton continually opened himself to the sacredness of the world of which he was a part. "Heaven" is not a reality beyond the pain and violence of existence. The reign of God is not necessarily (or most likely to be) ushered in with the breaking-open of the sky through divine intervention. Rather, through the participation of the people of God as a "pilgrim people" in this in-breaking, an image of a collective journey is more fitting and highly applicable for a world crying for healing and understanding. God is not separate from humanity. Humanity is empowered by the spirit to be change in a broken world. No longer can heaven be the finish line for a person of faith who has maintained individual piety and adherence to religious practices. Heaven must be what drives people to change to world today…and to change the world tomorrow because it will not be accomplished today. Merton was one with great acuity to this understanding and challenged himself as an individual seeking holiness while not forgetting that either we all make our way or heaven or no one does. This pilgrimage together is one of the central themes in Merton's writing, though it would be easy to only read a monk's thoughts on one's personal life while there is this deeper level operating throughout his writing.

Much like the image of the "great city" in one of Merton's dreams, he knew the human journey was long, but the knowledge of being within the safety of the "two arms of the harbor" allowed him to continue on his spiritual journey.[2] The movement toward eremiticism was dramatically shaping his vocation as a monk in addition to his continually developing and maturing understanding of what it meant to be more than simply a guilty bystander watching the world dismantle itself without realizing it. Merton was greatly influenced by many thinkers and prophets, of earlier times as well as his contemporaries. Yet, as Lawrence S. Cunningham has noted, it is quite interesting to note how few commentators on Merton have "noticed the influence of Bonaventure, whose writings Merton read when teaching with the Franciscans in upstate New York before he entered the monastery."[3] This note by Cunningham can be expanded to encompass the entire Franciscan tradition and Merton's relationship with the lesser brothers from Assisi. This is not to exclude other influences in Merton's thinking but rather to emphasis a tradition which has been, by and large, excluded from works about the paradoxical modern monk of Gethsemani.

The subtitle of the Tenth General Meeting of International Thomas Merton Society, "contemplation, community, and culture," captures quite beautifully Merton's multiple influences because being open to both heaven and earth is not limited to a select few prescribing to one particular religious tradition. The beauty of this gathering was the ability to come together as a community shaped by the insight and companionship of a person who sought to enter more deeply into the questions pertaining to these three dimensions rather than simply trying to answer them as many others are apt to do.

In *Conjectures of a Guilty Bystander*, Merton wrote about one of the "Berlin Crises" and how this quasi-ritual game of the Russians and Americans was both fun and profitable to not only the governments but also the businesses which saw profits rise because of this environment. He noted how these two warring nations politely continued the political and media-sensationalized dance with one another in Berlin which was "Good not only for the newspaper business, but for *all* business. Everything, they say, is booming."[4] How Merton continued this thought is not only telling of the events and pseudo-events of this period, but it connects with the subtitle of the most recent meeting of ITMS and this particular essay exploring the impact the Franciscan worldview had upon Merton. To quote Merton directly:

> Meanwhile a man in Chicago has built himself a fallout shelter in his cellar, and declares that he and his family will occupy it, keeping out all intruders with a machine gun. This is the final exaltation of our culture: individualism, comfort, security, and to hell with everybody else. (As if other people might be interested in getting in there, being baked slowly to death by the fire storm, in warm togetherness.)[5]

How this shows Merton's relationship with Franciscan thought and practice through the hermit life is quite clear. The Franciscan influence on Merton was one that cultivated a space to align a desire for solitude with a strong sense of engagement and participation to challenge a dominant culture that would prefer to build fallout shelters and defend them with machine guns.

In this essay, I will demonstrate why Merton's brief article entitled "Franciscan Eremiticism" must be seen as more than simply a short writing project along side many others. Rather, I will argue that writing "Franciscan Eremiticism" allowed Merton to articulate a worldview that defied popular convention of how to meaningfully participate in the numerous issues of the day while also moving beyond a purely Trappist understanding of the monk in the modern world. Merton's monastic and eremitical life was authentically "Cistercian" yet it may more appropriately be understood as bearing marks of Franciscanism in its articulation and expression. And it was this Franciscan lens that allowed Merton to see and engage the world much like Francis did in a world not all that different. Before exploring "Franciscan Eremiticism" from the late 1960s, I will first show the early connections Merton had with the Franciscan tradition before entering the monastery.

The title of this essay comes from one of Merton's own letters written on February 12, 1966, to Anthony L. Bannon. Here he wrote about connections he had with St. Bonaventure's College (now University). Concluding his letter to Bannon, Merton wrote, "[I] will always feel that I am still in some secret way a son of St. Francis. There is no saint in the Church whom I admire more than St. Francis."[6] These are not words to be taken lightly. They demonstrate the way in which Merton's early roots planted in Franciscan soil brought forth a flowering bud that included many other strains of influence, yet can be understood to come from ground fertilized ironically by the saint so often associated to the ecological world and the canticle of creatures. And in the end, it seems that by looking more deeply at the latter years of his life with this influence in mind, one is able to see how Merton was not such a secret son after all.

Franciscan Formation: Lasting Roots

The Franciscan connection and influence for Thomas Merton started early in his life shortly after his baptism in the Roman Catholic Church. While the focus of this essay is on an article published in 1966, it is important to recognize the foundation from which Merton developed spiritually and one of the sources of continued influence throughout his life. While this earlier period demonstrates Merton's interest in the more theological aspects of the Franciscan tradition, it connects with the eremitical experience because it is all part of the Franciscan tradition of which Merton was a student. I have addressed these periods more fully elsewhere and would encourage one to consider looking at that material in order to more appropriately frame the content of this article within the Franciscan setting.[7]

Merton's Magnetic North

Sadly, an often overlooked period of Merton's life is when he was considering a religious vocation to the Franciscans and his subsequent teaching at St. Bonaventure's College in Olean, New York. He spoke with the Franciscans and was to enter the novitiate in August of 1940. After spending time at Robert Lax's cottage in Olean, New York, and on the campus of St. Bonaventure, Merton was anxious to join the Franciscans. After a period of life as a quasi-Franciscan at St. Bonaventure, Merton realized that those close to him, such as Walsh and Father Edmund, the Franciscan who had helped him discern his vocation, did not know about his life before entering the Church. This was of great concern for Merton, and after telling Father Edmund, it was suggested he write to the Provincial and tell him he had reconsidered his application.[8] Merton was lost spiritually because he was told he did not have a vocation to the Franciscans.

After accepting that he would not be a Franciscan, Merton recognized he needed to find a job, preferably one where he would still able to live a holy life, a monk of sorts in the secular world. Seeking employment, Merton returned to St. Bonaventure College and spoke with Thomas Plassmann, O.F.M. who was the president, and he gave him a job teaching English. He lived in Devereux Hall with friars, lay professors, and some students. [9]

During his time teaching, Merton considered making a retreat during Holy Week and Easter in 1941. He recalled the monastery Daniel Walsh spoke of, the Abbey of Our Lady of Gethsemani. Merton traveled from St. Bonaventure to Kentucky to make a retreat and was greeted at the gate by a monk who had once been a Franciscan.[10] Immediately Merton was drawn to the life of the Trappists (Order of Cistercians of the Strict Observance) at Gethsemani, though he stated clearly during that initial retreat that he was not intending on staying beyond the predetermined length of his retreat.

Merton would indeed leave Gethsemani and return to St. Bonaventure, yet he would desire to return to Gethsemani and eventually did, permanently. Merton had a discussion with Boehner at St. Bonaventure which served as the impetus for his return to the monastery in Kentucky. Merton again journeyed to Gethsemani and finally felt he had understood his vocation, rather than embracing a false one. Merton left St. Bonaventure's in the middle of the academic year, leaving his courses, students, and many belongings behind. He had found his vocation, as long as the Trappists agreed with his self-assessment.

Tom Merton and Medieval Theologians

The overarching Bonaventurean influence in Merton's life must be central to understanding the Franciscan-Merton relationship not only in identifying those aspects of the Franciscan tradition which he refers to, but more broadly the way in which he used Bonaventure's *Itinerarium Mentis in Deum* as a model for his own contemplative ascent.[11] Kathleen Deignan notes that while Merton did not fully employ Bonaventure's map, it "nevertheless inspired and encouraged him to set out on the mystical quest and find his own road to rapture."[12]

The impact of Bonaventure upon the life of Merton is as profound as it is subtle.[13] Similarly, the overall Franciscan influence on Merton is crucial to understanding the development of Merton as a (spiritual) person during the formative years leading up to his entrance into the monastery. Merton's Franciscanism *is not* to be understood as the dominant influence in his writings. The monastic school is the richest source for him. Nevertheless, the Franciscan school, especially Bonaventure and Dun Scotus, gave Merton material to consider as he began his own spiritual journey and also provided a language and understanding that would help him to articulate his life as a monk and a hermit.[14]

Merton's journals reveal a man seeking an understanding of himself as a writer and as one who was unsure of which direction he was heading in life. Unfortunately, the journals which remain from Merton's early life date only from 1939-1941, leaving out the earliest parts of his life because he did not keep a journal or because of the destruction of journals. The latter is known to have occurred because Merton noted that he had occasionally kept a journal in his youth.[15] The years from 1939 to 1941 provide Merton's thoughts on many topics ranging from war to his spiritual journey as he sought a deeper commitment to his new faith.

Run to the Mountain and *The Secular Journal* include virtually all of Merton's journals from this period. Yet, there are gaps in the published material. Mott notes that the "St. Bonaventure Journal" (which would be published, for the most part, as *Run to the Mountain*) is the truest representation of Merton's feelings during this time. *The Secular Journal* is something of a distortion of Merton's true feelings, according to Michael Mott. He notes that Merton was at times a "very odd editor of Thomas Merton the writer."[16]

The journals that comprise *Run to the Mountain* include entries which were not printed in the edited journals of this period. During his time at Cambridge, Merton had been drawn to Dante and his understanding of the movement towards God through various stages and states of existence. His interest in Dante continued throughout his time at Columbia and remained with him during the years he was teaching English at St. Bonaventure. The theme Merton took from Dante was that of *ascent*, the theme Merton would then explore through the writings of Augustine and Bonaventure.

The importance of Dante in Merton's life, during this time, is essential to understanding the role of the *Itinerarium* for him. Dante's relationship with the Franciscan tradition is well noted as one reads the notes from Merton's classes. It becomes clear Dante helped Merton enter more deeply into the journey as presented by Bonaventure.[17] While there is great doubt about the authenticity of the claim that Dante was himself a Franciscan who left the Order before making profession, the claim demonstrates the connection Dante had with the Franciscans, especially Peter John Olivi and the "Spirituals."[18] Dante's *Commedia* presented a medieval map which not only speaks symbolically of the movement towards God, but reflects Dante's own journey.[19] Dante, along side Bonaventure, gave Merton an understanding of the Christian life as a journey into God that involved various stages and levels.

The "Fitzgerald File" found in the Thomas Merton Collection at St. Bonaventure University contains a broad spectrum of Merton's writings during the period prior to Gethsemani.[20] The "Fitzgerald File" or "Fitzgerald Notebook," includes Merton's journals, drawings, novels, essays, and notes on Dante's works.[21]

Within this collection are his notes on Dante and the description of movement through the different levels in the ascent to God. In reference to writing about canto 11 of the *Inferno*,[22] Merton noted with an asterisk, "compare S. Bonaventura."[23] Later, in reference to the "Action of the Divine Comedy," he noted that "the voyage is an *ascent*—even in Hell: Dante keeps right on going in same direction."[24] Merton depicted this ascent in the pages of his notebook. Following this statement is an image showing the ascent towards God, depicted by a cross coming from a circle, seemingly symbolizing earth. The "Inferno" is a triangle at the base of the circle with a line leading to a triangle just outside the circle which is "Purgatory," then from there the line, which to that point has been "wavy," becomes straight and leads into a cross identified as "Paradise."[25] There is an arrow showing the direction one is to take in this ascent towards "Paradise." This drawing demonstrates Merton's understanding of *ascent* and how one moves from hell to a state beyond this reality but not fully removed from sin, and then finally reaching the divine.

Later in the "Fitzgerald Notebook," Merton devoted an entire page to "Dante and St. Bonaventura" and in the pages following wrote about "Dante and St. Bonaventure on Mariology," "Dante and Franciscans," and "St. Francis in the Divine Comedy."[26] Here Merton noted that where Dante and Bonaventure parallel one another, there usually is a common source in Augustine. Merton went on to write about the "Doctrine of Spiritual Gravitation," "Rewards and Punishment," "Exemplarism," and finally, "Itinerarium—The Ascent of St. B and that of Dante." Though these pages are in a collection that consists of Merton's writings on numerous topics, it is important to note the way in which Merton returned often to the theme of ascent in regards to the Christian life oriented towards God found throughout Christian writing, but specifically in Augustine, Dante, and Bonaventure. Merton used the concept of ascent, or more appropriately *journey* as understood by Bonaventure, to express the move towards intimacy with God through the world and then eventually beyond it into the divine, transcending human limitations, language, and understanding.

During his time at St. Bonaventure, Merton learned about Bonaventure's *Itinerarium* and Scotus' *De primo principio* from Boehner,[27] but his introduction to these two Franciscan theologians originated with his studies under the direction of Daniel Walsh while at Columbia. In his correspondence with Naomi Burton

Stone regarding editing of *The Seven Storey Mountain*, Merton noted he would, "like to keep as much as I can of the references to Duns Scotus as possible because even Catholics don't know him as they should."[28] When *The Seven Storey Mountain* was being edited in 1947, Merton's recollection of reading Duns Scotus helps to reinforce the contention that Merton's time at St. Bonaventure, though transitional in many ways, nourished his spiritual journey as he sought a deeper commitment to living as a Christian and even more so as a monk.[29] Though Merton did not expand on his reading of Duns Scotus as he did in regards to Bonaventure in *The Seven Storey Mountain*, the influence of Scotistic thought runs through the text.

As noted above, Merton had been reading Scotus' *De primo principio*. The theme of *De primo principio* is the notion that God is the first cause of all things and that God is the "ultimate goal of activity."[30] But as much as Scotus was a philosopher, he was first a Franciscan theologian who employed philosophical language to articulate reasons for belief in a God not requiring the proofs he argued for in his works. The opening lines from *De primo principio* express this faith:

> May the First Principle of things grant me to believe, to understand and to reveal what may please his majesty and may raise our minds to contemplate him.
>
> O Lord our God, true teacher that you are, when Moses your servant asked you for your name that he might proclaim it to the children of Israel, you, knowing what the mind of mortal could grasp of you, replied: "I am who am," thus disclosing your blessed name. You are truly what it means to be, you are the whole of what it means to exist. This, if it be possible for me, I should like to know by way of demonstration. Help me then, O Lord, as I investigate how much our natural reason can learn about that true being which you are in we begin with the being which you have predicated of yourself.[31]

Though Duns Scotus thought in a sophisticated, philosophical manner, he was a brother of Francis and remained committed to his life as a lesser brother while engaging theological issues of the medieval world. God, the First Principle and goal of human activity, is understood through human experience and language. The account of God speaking to Moses (Exodus 3:14) exemplifies the desire of humanity to know and be able to name God while being unable to fully grasp the ineffable mystery of God. Importantly, Merton understood Scotus to be a scholar with faith. While this combination was not foreign to Duns Scotus or his contemporaries, Merton's experience of the twentieth century was much different. As Merton explored Christian theology, under the tutelage of Walsh and others, he recovered the deep commitment of theologians such as Duns Scotus and Bonaventure (in addition to many other theologians) and worked to integrate this type of thinking into his own beliefs about Christianity and Christian theology. Duns Scotus, much like Bonaventure, became a model for Merton as he sought a deeper understanding of his journey into God through the deepening of his faith.

The entire journal entry dated January 21, 1941, concerns Bonaventure's *Itinerarium*.[32] The second chapter, which Merton is writing about, is about seeing God in creation, but more specifically it is when the "enlightened mind turns its imagination, that is, its power of representing things, to sense data and beholds in these psychological facts vestiges, that is, faint analogies of the mystery of the Blessed Trinity and especially of the Incarnation."[33] The outside world enters into the soul through the five senses, but more broadly, experience. Merton was not simply reading Bonaventure leisurely; he was reading the *Itinerarium* as a means to articulate technical theological points that had an influence upon everyday life. Merton employed Bonaventure's steps in his own journey in recognizing the presence of God in all of God's vestiges as experienced through the senses as he engaged the physical world around him while also seeking God through the mind.

Merton picked up again with the second chapter of the *Itinerarium* and quoted Bonaventure verbatim where he wrote about God the "Father" as fountain-source and object of the impression which is on all of creation as experienced in the world.[34] This is important because Merton's identifies in Bonaventure's writing the central theme of God's outpouring love into the created world.

In the final pages of *The Seven Storey Mountain*, Merton wrote as one who had found his place in the world, within the enclosure of the monastery. Giving the title "The Sweet Savor of Liberty" to a chapter at the end of *The Seven Storey Mountain* demonstrates Merton's happiness living as a Cistercian. Yet, in the midst of Merton's praise for life as a monk, hidden away in his "four walls of…new freedom,"[35] he turned again to Bonaventure as a guide in his spiritual life. The importance of this reference to the *Itinerarium* cannot be overlooked. To quote at length:

> Look in Saint Bonaventure's *Itinerarium* and you will find one of the best descriptions ever written of this highest of vocations. It is a description which the Seraphic Doctor himself learned on retreat in and solitude on Mount Alvernia. Praying in the same lonely spot where the great founder of his Order, Saint Francis of Assisi, had had the wounds of Christ burned into his hands and feel and side, Saint Bonaventure saw, by the light of a supernatural intuition, the full meaning of this tremendous event in the history of the Church. "There," he says, "Saint Francis 'passed over into God' (*in Deum transiit*) in the ecstasy (*excessus*) of contemplation and thus he was set up as an example of perfect contemplation just as he had previously been an example of perfection in the active life in order that God, through him, might draw, all truly spiritual men to this kind of 'passing over' (*transitus*) and ecstasy, *less by word than by example.*"

Here is the clear and true meaning of *contemplata tradere*, expressed without equivocation by one who had lived that life to the full. It is the vocation of transforming union, to the height of the mystical life and of mystical experience, to the very transformation into Christ that Christ living in us is directing all our actions might Himself draw men to desire and seek that same exalted union because of the joy and the sanctity and the supernatural vitality radiated by our example—or rather because of the secret influence of Christ living within us in complete possession of our souls.

And notice the tremendously significant fact that St. Bonaventure makes no divisions and distinctions: Christ imprinted His own image upon Saint Francis in order to draw not some men, not a few privileged monks, but *all* truly spiritual men to the perfection of contemplation which is nothing else but the perfection of love. Once they have reached these heights they will draw others to them in their turn. So any man may be called at least *de jure*, if not *de facto*, to become fused into one spirit with Christ in the furnace of contemplation and then go forth and cast upon the earth upon the earth that same fire which Christ wills to see enkindled.[36]

The *Itinerarium* is a roadmap, not only for monks or friars, but for all people seeking God through a deep interior life, and allows one to pass along the fruits of such a life on to others.[37] Francis is the model for Bonaventure when he wrote the *Itinerarium,* and it was through Bonaventure's writing that Merton was able to enter into the Franciscan journey blending deep contemplation with a desire to be an instrument of God's peace and love in the world.

In short, his early exposure and attraction to the Franciscans was more than just a transitory experience but rather planted roots which would bloom later in the last few years of Merton's life. Nevertheless, the focus of this article is a brief article and its context in Merton's later life, long after the Allegany Hills had been a backdrop for his meditative walks considering religious life.

A New Lens Through Franciscan Eremiticism

In 1966, Thomas Merton published a brief article in *The Cord* entitled, "Franciscan Eremiticism." In this brief essay (little more than eight typed pages as it would appear in *Contemplation in a World of Action*) Merton focused on a very important but often overlooked theme in the life of Francis and, more broadly, within the Franciscan tradition: the eremitical life.

The importance of this essay for Merton is imperative to note. As Merton sought to articulate his life as a hermit and recognize his place within the broader context of humanity and creation, it is easy to see how Francis' continued presence in his life manifested itself in this article. The implications of this essay in Merton's life are dramatic if one looks at the content of the brief pages, explaining how the eremitical aspect of the Franciscan life was for Francis "intimately related to his conception of a poor and wandering life."[38] Sean Edward Kinsella writes, "There is both a tension and a complimentarity between Thomas Merton's yearning for the solitary life and his simultaneous desire to be immersed in the world."[39] Kinsella notes that Merton shared many of the same concerns as Francis (e.g., the desire for solitude while remaining actively involved with the life of the Church outside of the institutional framework of religious life), and this suggests a Franciscan influence.[40] Kinsella recognizes the Franciscan component of Merton's eremitical spirituality was a retrieval of a period of early monastic life that saw the expression of that life leading monks out into the world to preach. Merton desired to more adequately understand both his life as a hermit and as a member of the human race and drew heavily from Francis and his expression of life to achieve this in his own "Umbrian valley."

The content of Merton's essay demonstrates not only his interest in the Franciscan expression of the eremitical life, but more importantly the ways in which it was applicable to his vocation as a Cistercian monk. What distinguishes Franciscan eremiticism from monastic expressions of the hermit life is the reality that for a Franciscan, the solitary experience of being a (temporary) hermit living in the "midst of nature and close to God" is related to the concepts of "poverty, prayer and the apostolate."[41] As eremiticism within the monastic setting was experiencing a revival, Merton considered the historical context in which Franciscan hermits lived. Merton rightly connected the itinerancy of the mendicant Franciscans with the "pre-Franciscan movement of itinerant and preaching hermits in the tenth to twelfth centuries."[42] These earlier mendicant monks and the later mendicant orders were not that different in their disposition and understanding of the role of the religious in the world.

The eremitical experience prior to the Franciscans was based on the notion that such a life was "considered higher because [it was] more perfectly and unequivocally 'monastic' and world-denying."[43] During this period, in addition to monks seeking more reclusive lives, many laypersons and secular clerics also embraced such a lifestyle though they did not first move through the prescribed monastic formation. This movement of both the laity and secular clerics into hermitages caused a dramatic shift in the role of the hermitage. These new hermits engaged the world in a "new and special way" because parish churches lacked the presence of preaching while the monks remained a self-contained community and did not reach out beyond their own cloisters.[44] The new hermits became the ones who embraced itinerant lives preaching to the poor in a language understandable to them. Peter the Hermit, an itinerant preacher during the time of the First Crusade, is an example of such an individual.[45] While there was great energy around this movement, by the thirteenth century the movement was reabsorbed back into cenobitic monasticism.[46]

The glorification of the monastic life, the "angelic perspective," was shattered by the mendicant orders in the thirteenth century.[47] For Francis, the world was not evil and the world was not unlike and distant from God, "because the world had been created by a God who was loving and good and, therefore, his presence was to be felt and experienced in the world and was not excluded from it."[48]

While Merton saw how the eremitical movement was diminished within the monastic orders, Francis was "in the direct line of the earlier hermit tradition."[49] Early on for the Franciscans, the hermitage was a place in which they sought solitude in order to go out and preach the Gospel. Francis followed the earlier itinerant hermit tradition which was "completely open to the world of the poor and the outcast."[50] The hermit was not to place himself above thieves and was called to see the fraternal relationship between two persons made in the image of God.

Francis' "Rule for the Hermitage" was more of a framework or guideline for those seeking to have a "practical guide" for life in a hermitage in contrast to a "Rule" in a strict or legal sense for the friars.[51] Merton recognized in the "Rule" given by Francis the spirit of simplicity and charity which "pervades even the life of solitary contemplation."[52] Francis was able to reconcile the two seemingly contradictory expressions of the eremitical life: solitary prayer and fraternal love.[53] The Franciscan hermitage was one of "solitude... surrounded by fraternal care and is therefore solidly established in the life of the Order and of the Church."[54] The brothers were dependant upon one another in very practical ways in order to enter into a contemplative state of existence.

While Merton outlined this component of the Franciscan eremitical tradition as found in the "Rule for Hermitages," this aspect of the Franciscan understanding of solitude is what was attractive to him. Merton wrote that Franciscan eremiticism had another aspect: "it was open to the world and oriented to the apostolic life."[55] Merton mentioned the role of Mount Alverna [sic] in Francis' own life and his founding of "at least twenty mountain hermitages."[56] The presence and impact of the eremitical and contemplative aspects of the Franciscan charism are vital to understanding how Francis and his followers engaged the world outside the hermitage. The purpose of the eremitical experience was always to renew oneself in order to return to ministering to the people of God as itinerant preachers.

Merton concluded the short essay with two suggestions, stating that the Franciscan life had always included the eremitical spirit which was *not* necessarily the spirit of monasticism or of "total, definitive separation from the world."[57] Second, the eremitism of Francis and his followers was initially and continues to be "deeply evangelical and remains open to the world, while recognizing the need to maintain a certain distance and perspective, a freedom that keeps one from being submerged in active cares and devoured by the claims of exhausting work."[58] These two points made by Merton are more than his assessment of the Franciscan eremitical tradition which, for the most part, had been absent from the evangelical life of the friars. Rather, this article published in December 1966 expressed his own eremitic life as he more fully embraced his place within the world as a marginal person who spoke out about issues of grave importance from his hermitage. Just as the Franciscan vocation is an evangelical life, a life of prayer and contemplation as well as action, Merton's later life reflected this eremitical expression more authentically than his own Trappist identity. From the very beginning, the Franciscans had the challenge of achieving not just a balance, but rather an integration or synthesis of these two elements, contemplation and action.[59] Fittingly, the title of the work in which Merton's "Franciscan Eremiticism" later appeared bears these words. If one is convinced that Merton was indeed influenced by Francis and those who followed in his footsteps, then this essay on early Franciscan life speaks not only about medieval friars, but also about himself. He was a monk seeking to more fully articulate how he understood his life within the broader context of the world, a part of it rather than apart from it. Concluding "Franciscan Eremiticism," Merton wrote:

> Today more than ever we need to recognize that the gift of solitude is not ordered to the acquisition of strange contemplative powers, but first of all to the recovery of one's deep self, and to the renewal of authenticity which is twisted out of shape by the pretentious routines of a disordered togetherness. What the world asks of the priest today is that he should be first of all a *person* who can give himself because he has a self to give. And indeed, we cannot give Christ if we have not found him, and we cannot find him if we cannot find ourselves.
>
> These considerations might be useful to those whose imaginations and hopes are still able to be stirred by the thought of solitude, and of its important place in every form of the religious and apostolic life, in every age, especially our own.[60]

The importance of this essay cannot be overstated because it allowed Merton to articulate his eremitical life in a way that resonated within the Christian tradition, albeit Franciscan rather than Trappist. Merton looked at his life as a Christian through a Franciscan lens.

In the final part of *Contemplation in a World of Action*, Merton was speaking about the role of the contemplative life in the modern world. In a section entitled "What is Monastic?" Merton took as his starting point a quote from a Franciscan sister who wrote, "I think that what I am objecting most to is the monasticism that has been imposed upon us and has become part of our structure."[61] Responding to this statement from a "Franciscan milieu," Merton noted that this imposition of monastic structure is seen by those within active orders and the laity to be something restraining. Here, Merton tried to clarify what he meant when speaking about monasticism and, by implication, the contemplative life. After speaking for a period about what monasticism was, Merton mentioned the Franciscans. To quote Merton directly:

> The Franciscan way came into the Middle Ages as a salutary revolt against the highly institutionalized monastic system. St. Francis made possible once again an open-ended kind of existence in which there wasn't very much predetermined for you. You were pretty free to do this or that or anything. You could be a pilgrim, you could be a hermit, and you could be a pilgrim for a while and a hermit for a while and then a scholar for a while. Then you could go to the Muslims in North Africa and get yourself martyred if you had the grace! And so forth.
>
> The Franciscan ideal could really be regarded as a return to the authentic freedom of early monasticism. I would venture as a kind of personal guess at this point that actually the ideal of St. Francis was more purely *monastic* in the true original primitive sense than the life lived by the big Benedictine and Cistercian communities of the thirteenth century where everything was so highly organized behind walls.[62]

Merton saw the return to the more primitive expressions of monasticism through this Franciscan lens. In a journal entry from July 27, 1966, writing in reference to Francis the "world-lover," Merton stated, "There is no question I too am really a world-lover after all: but what kind?"[63] Asking this question, the month after submitting "Franciscan Eremiticism" to *The Cord*, shows his struggle with articulating his place in the world, recognizing that indeed there is an important space for a hermit to engage others while questioning and uncertainty remained. The hermit is "hidden in

Jesus Christ [and] he is therefore most intimately present to all the rest of the Church."[64] The actively engaged life, the evangelical life, had a strong influence on Merton exemplified not only through his "quasi-apostolate" of writing in the general sense but specifically in his writing about Francis and the early Franciscans.[65]

A Broader Influence: Franciscan Familial Relationships

In what Kinsella calls "profoundly Franciscan," Merton's writing during this period shows how the solitary is not alone because of the presence of God's grace, and by depending on God's grace and becoming abandoned to God's love, one realizes his or her inner poverty, "a poverty which is emptiness, nakedness, and minority."[66] Merton saw the place of the hermit as being beyond the monastic life and in the world, as exemplified by an individual such as Francis. The role of the hermit is not to hide from the world, but instead is called to be a bridge between the quiet solitude of the hermitage with the dynamic apostolate in the midst of the world.[67] The life of the hermit is directed toward other people through compassionate social awareness while also becoming more aware of one's own life, and has accepted the rootlessness of such a life.[68] Solitude is "the very ground of ordinary life."[69] While this ground of life is in all persons, the hermit is open to learning how to accept this solitude as his or her ground of being. To most people, the notion of solitude as the ground of one's being "is unthinkable and unknown."[70] In a letter dated April 14, 1968, Merton wrote:

> The principle behind my answer is this: it is misleading to talk so much of the *contemplative* life in a way that obscures the fact that what we need to renew is not so much the "contemplative" and enclosed and abstract dimension of our life, as the *prophetic and eschatological* witness out of silence, poverty, etc. Merely to put up walls and gates and to live in formal poverty behind them does not give such witness. The reality of silence and solitude are of course essential. But it should be in a kind of dialectic which charity and help to your neighbors is there. In other words, the help you give should clearly proceed from a love that is nourished by silence and prayer; it should manifest a compassion that is rooted in an intimate awareness of the sufferings of Christ. The fact that you will see Him suffering concretely in the poor there ought to help your contemplative prayer to be deeper and more real. I don't know what else

St. Clare or St. Francis could tell you! The original spirit of Franciscan eremiticism was certainly in a context of occasional going out among the poor, being definitely *of* the poor, and not just a symbol of established religion and a life of devotion supported by the rich.[71]

For Merton, the Franciscan expression of solitude provided a language in which he could articulate his increasing desire to speak out on behalf of and about the members of humanity who had been or were being marginalized by war, racism, and many other injustices which he saw as deeply spiritual issues. While others were more actively engaged, Merton remained within the monastic enclosure, and more specifically, removed even from the monastery in the hermitage. Yet, while he maintained a distance from the forefront of action where there was always encouragement for him to leave the monastery in order to more fully participate in the social spectrum as Christians emerged from an individualistic sense of faith, Merton was fully engaged as a member of humanity because he sought to embrace the ground of his own being in order to relate to others, especially those unaware of the inner self which was the ground of their being. Shaped by such an understanding of the eremitical tradition, Merton's writings on justice and peace, among other topics, came out of this experience of what it meant to be an authentic hermit. Additionally, it is through this understanding of solitude as the ground of one's being that allowed Merton to embrace other religious traditions in a way that saw the sources common to them, while recognizing the distinctions that separate religious expressions have from one another.

Merton's relationship with Thich Nhat Hanh, an exiled Vietnamese Buddhist monk, for whom he wrote "Nhat Hanh Is My Brother," is an example of how Merton sought to understand more fully the ground of being in every person. Merton and Nhat Hanh were like brothers, even more so than those closer because of race or nationality, because, as Merton wrote, "he and I see things exactly the same way."[72] Merton went on to write that both he and Nhat Hanh were monks who had lived similar lives and that it was "vitally important that such bonds be admitted."[73] That which connected these two with one another was their mutual understanding and respect of religious traditions that sought to express the deep inner truths of contemplation, but recognized the ways in which that impacted how one lived in the world. In his work on Merton and Nhat Hanh as examples of "engaged spirituality," Robert H. King writes, "In noting the almost mythic status that Merton and Nhat Hanh have achieved in the eyes of many throughout the world, we should not fail to recognize their ordinary humanity."[74] Their meeting at Gethsemani on May 28, 1966, occurred roughly at the same time Merton would have been writing his essay "Franciscan Eremiticism." Lawrence Cunningham notes that, "Nhat Hanh's worldview had something almost Franciscan about it. It was for that reason, among others, that Merton gave a series of Sunday afternoon talks to the monks on the poetry of this gentle Buddhist monk."[75] It would not be unreasonable to think that a Buddhist monk helped Merton clarify even more so the role of the Franciscan charism in his own life as he sought to more fully be human and more fully enter into the discourse about the world at the time.

Concluding his essay on Merton, Kinsella writes that "the themes of hiddenness and compassion—of homelessness, of solitude, poverty, nakedness, and minority—these are themes to which Merton returned repeatedly throughout his writings."[76] His delight in the writings and examples of the Desert Fathers to Zen masters "is a fundamentally profound appreciation of Francis' own appreciation of the foundational meaning of the monastic experience: the true solitary existing in prophetic dialogue with the entire world."[77]

A Third Way

In *Thomas Merton's American Prophesy*, Robert Inchausti titled a chapter "The Mystic as Public Intellectual" which connects strongly with Merton's societal position challenging the cultural status quo through his becoming "the very epitome of the community-based intellectual who practiced what he preached."[78] If Inchausti is correct in his evaluation of Merton's understanding of how to engage in social reform in the United States, then "we had better begin at the community level with the reformation of our own lives— fighting the fascist within as well as the fascist from without."[79] Here, again, the openness to both the sacred and the profane, heaven and earth, is essential. Later Inchausti quotes an important line from *Contemplation in a World of Action* where Merton notes that what a priest (and I would argue anyone) has to offer to humanity is their own *person*, their *self*.[80] These words, which Merton identified as being useful considerations for those whose imaginations and hopes were able to be stirred by solitude, are for "every age, especially our own" and demonstrate the wide application of his writing on Franciscan eremiticism.[81]

Including these lines from "Franciscan Eremiticism" is important for a chapter on the role of the mystic in the public sphere because it demonstrates Merton's challenge for each person to give of themselves to others. Merton's correspondence with Rosemary Radford Ruether, which is also included in this chapter, demonstrates a cleavage between the academic theologian and the monastic social critic. Nevertheless, both were seeking a new way of being in the world and the ushering in of the reign of God, although the approaches were considerably different from one another. Additionally, Inchausti mentions the advice Merton gave to Jim Forest to seek a "long view of things" rather than choosing to simply engage in the destructive dismantling of American culture through either of the polemical means supported by secular politics. Merton sought a third way of integrity rather than choosing to embrace "the conflicts tearing the country in two."[82] He sought to distance himself from the political thinkers of both the left and the right because "they truly believe they know what needs to be done and so set about doing it."[83] Monasticism allowed Merton to distance himself from such claims because the enclosure was designed to undermine individual intellectual pride and the false notion that one has a full grasp of how to address such monumental issues. The Franciscan influence was a contributing factor in Merton's desire to seek solitude while entering more deeply into the entire process of moving beyond the destructive reality which seemed unavoidable to most persons in a highly volatile world.

The World as a Cloister

Merton saw his own vocation as one that opened up to the world, a posture that allowed the prophetic voice to speak from inner silence. He followed "the dark path of contemplation, which even most monks would tend to eschew, and it opened up for him a depth of love he did not know existed, which he came to call 'the hidden ground of love.'"[84] It was this understanding of a foundational ground of love for Merton that connected all peoples and things together. Echoing Francis' commitment to seeing the world in a familial way, Merton challenged himself and his diverse readership to consider the radical call of living in such a way, searching for the true self and in that journey within one's own life recognizing the ways all peoples are connected and truly are one.

Francis saw the world as his cloister, and in many ways, Merton shared a similar view from his hermitage in the hills of Kentucky. The evangelical life lived by the Franciscans is one that identified the Gospel as being central to mission and disposition in regards to how one is to live in the world. Living as a prophetic hermit, Merton engaged his world in a unique fashion similar to Francis in his own medieval context where he shattered the categorical restrains of his world to embrace a new way of being *in* and *of* the world. As Merton continued to grow as a hermit open to all traditions and schools of though that would help him more fully understand his own tradition, he found a home in the Franciscan tradition because of its explicit desire to walk with the marginalized of our world while "retreating to the hills" to find silence in the contemplative spaces removed from the busy intersections of life. For him, there was no "essential contradiction between contemplation and action" and the two "in his view supported each other in a balanced Christian life."[85]

Merton was not a Franciscan, yet he did look through a lens shaped by Francis and his followers to be an engaged member of the human family seeking a new way of being in a broken world. His writing "Franciscan Eremiticism" was an opportunity to articulate his own journey in the latter years of his life as one who identified and lived out a commitment to seeking inner peace in order to engage others in meaningful dialogue with the aid of his prophetic typewriter.

Endnotes

1. This is an expanded version of "A (Not So) Secret Son of Francis: Thomas Merton's Franciscan Lens" presented at the Tenth General Meeting of the International Thomas Merton Society at Christian Brothers University in Memphis, Tennessee, June 7-10, 2007.

2. Thomas Merton, *Conjectures of a Guilty Bystander* (New York: Doubleday, Image Books, 1989), 188-189.

3. Lawrence S. Cunningham, *Thomas Merton and the Monastic Vision*, Library of Religious Biography (Grand Rapids, Mich.: William B. Eerdmans Publishing Company, 1999), 206.

4. Merton, *Conjectures*, 194.

5. Ibid.

6. Thomas Merton, *The Road to Joy: The Letters of Thomas Merton to*

New and Old Friends, selected and edited by Robert E. Daggy (New York: Farrar, Straus, Giroux, 1989), 298.

7. I have written more extensively about this Franciscan influence on Merton elsewhere, framing the content of this article within the broader context of this relationship between Merton and the Franciscan tradition. See, Timothy J. Shaffer, "A Secret Son of Francis: The Franciscan Influence in the Thought and Writings of Thomas Merton" (Master's thesis, University of Dayton, 2006). For a more succinct essay on this topic see, Timothy J. Shaffer, "Thomas Merton's Franciscan Spirituality," *The Cord* 57, no. 1 (2007): 63-81.

8. Thomas Merton, *The Seven Storey Mountain* (New York: Harcourt, Brace and Company, 1948), 297.

9. Ibid., 303ff.

10. Ibid., 321.

11. Kathleen Deignan, C.N.D., "Road to Rapture: Thomas Merton's *Itinerarium Mentis in Deum*," *Franciscan Studies* 55 (1998): 281.

12. Ibid.

13. Ibid.

14. Referring to Bonaventure and Dun Scotus as the primary Franciscan influences on Merton prior to his entrance into monastic life at Gethsemani is not to exclude the tremendous impact Francis had upon his life, but rather Francis is differentiated from both Bonaventure and Scotus because he is not identified as belonging to the "Franciscan school" of thought as the others are. Francis was the source from which the Franciscan school drew its theological distinction, but this does not warrant classifying Francis with Franciscans who would engage in theological discourse in the medieval world.

15. Patrick Hart, O.C.S.O., preface to *Run to the Mountain: The Story of a Vocation*, vol. 1, ed. Patrick Hart, O.C.S.O. (San Francisco: HarperSanFrancisco, 1995), xi.

16. Michael Mott, *The Seven Mountains of Thomas Merton* (Boston: Houghton Mifflin Company, 1984),161.

17. This is an important point because the connections between Dante and the Franciscans are found in Merton's teaching notes which are not published, thus inhibiting many from identifying this connection which shapes much of Merton's thought during this period and later.

18. Alexandre Masseron, *Dante Alighieri: The Poet Who Loved Saint Francis So Much*, trans. Br. Richard Arnandez, F.S.C. (Chicago: Franciscan Herald Press, 1978), 87-89. Regarding the relationship between Dante and the "Spirituals," see Nick Havely, *Dante and the Franciscans: Poverty and the Papacy in the 'Commedia'* (Cambridge: Cambridge University Press, 2004), and David Burr, *The Spiritual Franciscans: From Protest to Persecution in the Century after Saint Francis* (University Park, Penn.: Pennsylvania

State University Press, 2001).

19. For a detailed study of Dante's autobiographical journey see Mary Alexandra Watt, *The Cross That Dante Bears: Pilgrimage, Crusade, and the Cruciform Church in the* Divine Comedy (Gainesville, Fla.: University Press of Florida, 2005), especially 164-181.

20. See Patrick Hart, O.C.S.O., introduction to *Run to the Mountain*, xv-xvii.

21. Thomas Merton, "Fitzgerald Notebook, 1939 (?)," AD, AMs, and TMs (photocopy), The Thomas Merton Collection, Friedsam Memorial Library, St. Bonaventure University, St. Bonaventure, N.Y.

22. For a modern verse translation of the *Inferno*, see Robert Pinsky, *The Inferno of Dante: A New Verse Translation*, with a foreword by John Freccero and notes by Nicole Pinsky (New York: Farrar, Straus and Giroux, 1994).

23. Merton, "Fitzgerald Notebook," 236.

24. Ibid., 306.

25. Ibid.

26. Ibid., 350-353.

27. Merton, *The Seven Storey Mountain*, 337. Merton later mentions that he had been reading Scotus with a friend in the Seminary. See, Merton, *The Seven Storey Mountain*, 368.

28. Mott, *Seven Mountains*, 232. See also Thomas Merton, *Witness to Freedom: The Letters of Thomas Merton in Times of Crisis*, selected and edited by William H. Shannon (New York: Farrar, Straus, Giroux, 1994), 123-124. In *Witness to Freedom*, pages 123-153 is a section including a small portion of the written correspondence between Merton and Burton Stone which gives the reader a better sense of the relationship the two had with one another.

29. William H. Shannon, *Silent Lamp: The Thomas Merton Story* (New York: Crossroad, 1992), 115. Here Shannon notes that St. Bonaventure College was, for Merton, a place to "mark time, while waiting to be shown what he was to do with his life."

30. Richard Cross, *Dun Scotus on God*, Ashgate Studies in the History of Philosophical Theology (Burlington, Vt.: Ashgate, 2005), 39.

31. John Duns Scotus, *A Treatise on God as First Principle*, trans. and edited by Allan B. Wolter, O.F.M. (Chicago: Franciscan Herald Press, 1966), 1.1–1.2.

32. Merton, *Run to the Mountain*, 297-298.

33. Philotheus Boehner, O.F.M., introduction to *Itinerarium Mentis in Deum*, by Saint Bonaventure, Works of Saint Bonaventure, introduction, translation, and commentary by Philotheus Boehner, O.F.M., vol. 2 (St. Bonaventure, N.Y.: Franciscan Institute, 1956), 26.

34. Merton, *Run to the Mountain*, 307. See Bonaventure, *The Soul's*

Journey into God, trans. and introduction by Ewert Cousins, preface by Ignatius Brady, O.F.M. (Mahwah, N.J.: Paulist Press, 1978), 72-73.

35. Merton, *The Seven Storey Mountain*, 372.

36. Ibid., 418.

37. Ibid., 419.

38. Thomas Merton, *Contemplation in a World of Action*, introduction by Jean Leclercq (Garden City, N.Y.: Doubleday, 1971), 260.

39. Sean Edward Kinsella, "'Where the Grey Meets the Green Air': The Hermit as Pilgrim in the Franciscan Spirituality of Thomas Merton," *Franciscan Studies* 55 (1998): 311.

40. Ibid.

41. Merton, *Contemplation in a World of Action*, 260.

42. Ibid.

43. Ibid., 261.

44. Ibid.

45. Ibid., 262.

46. Ibid.

47. Kinsella, "'Where the Grey Meets the Green Air': The Hermit as Pilgrim in the Franciscan Spirituality of Thomas Merton," 312.

48. Ibid.

49. Merton, *Contemplation in a World of Action*, 262.

50. Ibid., 263.

51. Ignatius Brady, O.F.M., "A 'Rule for Hermitages,'" in *Franciscan Solitude*, ed. André Cirino, O.F.M and Josef Raischl (St. Bonaventure, N.Y.: Franciscan Institute, 1995), 195.

52. Merton, *Contemplation in a World of Action*, 263.

53. Ibid.

54. Ibid.

55. Ibid., 264.

56. Ibid.

57. Ibid., 267.

58. Ibid.

59. Brady, "A 'Rule for Hermitages,'" in *Franciscan Solitude*, 205.

60. Merton, *Contemplation in a World of Action*, 267-268.

61. Ibid., 355.

62. Ibid., 358.

63. Thomas Merton, *Learning to Love: Exploring Solitude and Freedom*, vol. 6, ed. Christine M. Bochen (San Francisco: HarperSanFrancisco, 1997), 103.

64. Merton, *Contemplation in a World of Action*, 258.

65. Chalmers MacCormick, "A Critical View of Solitude in Merton's Life and Thought," in *The Message of Thomas Merton*, ed. Brother Patrick Hart (Kalamazoo, Mich.: Cistercian Publications, 1981), 123.

66. Kinsella, "'Where the Grey Meets the Green Air': The Hermit as Pilgrim in the Franciscan Spirituality of Thomas Merton," 314.

67. Ibid., 316.

68. Ibid., 318.

69. Thomas Merton, "preface to the Japanese Edition of *Thoughts in Solitude*," in *Introductions East and West: The Foreign Prefaces of Thomas Merton*, ed. Robert E. Daggy, with a foreword by Harry James Cargas (Greensboro, N.C.: Unicorn Press, 1981), 97.

70. Ibid.

71. Thomas Merton, *The School of Charity: The Letters of Thomas Merton on Religious Renewal and Spiritual Direction*, ed. Brother Patrick Hart (New York: Farrar, Straus, Giroux, 1990), 377.

72. Thomas Merton, *Faith and Violence: Christian Teaching and Christian Practice* (Notre Dame: University of Notre Dame Press, 1968), 106.

73. Ibid., 108.

74. Robert H. King, *Thomas Merton and Thich Nhat Hanh: Engaged Spirituality in an Age of Globalization* (New York: Continuum, 2001), 182.

75. Cunningham, *Thomas Merton and the Monastic Vision*, 150.

76. Kinsella, "'Where the Grey Meets the Green Air': The Hermit as Pilgrim in the Franciscan Spirituality of Thomas Merton," 322.

77. Ibid.

78. Robert Inchausti, *Thomas Merton's American Prophecy* (Albany: State University of New York Press, 1998), 102.

79. Ibid., 103.

80. Ibid., 104.

81. Merton, *Contemplation in a World of Action*, 268.

82. Ibid., 108.

83. Ibid., 110.

84. King, *Thomas Merton and Thich Nhat Hanh*, 185.

85. Ross Labrie, "Contemplation and Action in Thomas Merton" *Christianity and Literature* 55, no. 4 (Summer 2006): 479. Here Labrie notes that Merton identified three types of contemplation: natural, active, and infused.

In the Zen Garden of the Lord: Thomas Merton's Stone Garden

Roger Lipsey

"You'll find that if that thing is raked properly," he said, "and you sit there looking at it, it gives a tremendous impression of peace, just looking at those lines. Each one in raking it puts his meditation into the sand. It better be a good meditation—you don't want somebody there whose mind is in turmoil, raking; that would have bad effects on the entire novitiate. Still, it's a very peaceful thing."[1] Thomas Merton was speaking to the novices at the Abbey of Gethsemani on October 16th, 1963, speaking of a gravel-and-stone Zen garden just then taking shape outside their separate quarters, the novitiate. The garden, and the novices who found both work and peace in it, enjoyed a perfectly grand view: situated past the east end of the abbey church on a terrace of land below the monks' cemetery, the garden looked out over fields and knobs into the middle distance (fig. 1—an undated late photo, the garden no longer fully intact).

Figure 1

What was this garden, and why was this garden? What did it mean to Merton? What place did it have in his passionate interrogation of Zen Buddhism in the late 1950s and 1960s? What place does this work of the gardener's craft and the monk's dream occupy in the creative life of Thomas Merton? What did it mean to the novices and others who passed that way? How closely did it reflect the traditions of Zen garden design? How much could Merton know of those traditions? Strange to say, these questions haven't been asked. Although Merton's own photographs of the garden have survived, and they are eloquent, the garden itself is long gone. To answer these questions, we will have to look at surviving photographs, search Merton's journals and correspondence, listen to conference tapes from that period, visit the Abbey library, speak with eye witnesses, explore the actual terrain with a geologist, open a dialogue with an expert Zen gardener, and remember Merton's life-changing engagement with Zen Buddhism. The questions are not easily answered, but they can be answered. The Zen garden at Gethsemani slipped into and out of history but held its shape long enough to be noticed and leave a story behind.

The first task, surely, is to become acquainted with the garden through Merton's photographs (figs. 2–5). While there is a short stack of other photographs, also revealing, Merton's own photographs record the garden when it was complete and well cared-for. When was all this coming to pass? His remarks to the novices give us a reliable date mid-stream in the creative campaign. "Of course it isn't anywhere near [finished]," he went on to say at that Sunday conference in mid-October 1963. "Looking at it now," he continued, "you can see absolutely that it lacks something, namely, lacks the big rock to come. Right now it's a wishy-washy thing, but when that big rock gets in there it's going to be striking, I assure you. And we're going to have another medium-size rock in there, and then I think we'll have everything...." Judging by these remarks, by brief journal entries, and by the leafed-out tree and bushes in the photograph, we can surmise that this photograph and all but one other in the series were made in spring or summer 1964, one year before he moved to the hermitage and relinquished most of his responsibilities in the monastic community (fig. 3). But Merton hadn't skipped winter: a striking image, he captured a whorl of raked gravel made more vivid by snow.

It's evident from these photographs and his comments to the novices that Merton cared more for raking than for stones. The

Figure 2

Figure 3

stones were essentially immutable; once placed, they remained what and where they were, while the raked pattern reflected the touch and concern of the novices and needed maintenance. The patterns softened under wind and rain, snagged debris, vanished under autumn leaves. They had to be renewed, and often. The abbey lived under the injunction "ora et labora"—pray and work— and raking the garden was work fully in Cistercian tradition.

This, too, he discussed with the novices on that October day: "We've got our Zen garden going out there," he said, "and it's going to take some raking. We're going to need a few professional rakers, people who can understand the art of raking…. Those who wish to be Zen-garden rakers have to read that little book on Japanese gardens and look at the pictures of raked gardens. We have to keep the leaves off of it. The raking isn't for the leaves, the raking is to get those lines." And so we learn that there was "a little book"— but which little book?

Fig. 2 allows us to inventory the cast of characters or contents of the garden. We are on a slightly raised platform framed by natural paving stones that offered something of an outdoor cloister to the novices, a strolling path to circumambulate the garden. The largest feature of the garden is a long, somewhat sprawling composition in stone suggesting the image of a vast swimming turtle. The other large feature is an "island" in this sea of sand, with a small tree and other foliage, flanked by a feature difficult to characterize—it appears to be a ground-hugging, narrow stone that connects the island, as if by a bridge, to the strolling path. Between the turtle and the island is a smaller stone that juts out from the strolling path; surrounded by ripples of raked gravel, it contributes to the impression of miniature land forms lapped by a sea. On the other side of the island is a small standing stone given great importance by the long belt of raked gravel flowing down from it. Just outside the strolling path at upper right is a massive stone, serving as a marker at what was apparently the entrance to the garden and strolling path. Like all the other stones in this ensemble, it is strikingly eroded, rough-surfaced.

Other photographs by Merton give us closer looks at many of these elements (figs. 4, 5). We can see how the raked patterns ripple out from objects, swirl and yet cling, to convey a pervasive sense of motion; how turtle-like the turtle could be from certain vantage points; and Merton's interest as a garden designer in concentric circles. The abstract quality of the raked pattern is evident. We

Figure 4

know that Merton in these years was exploring abstract imagery with brush and paper, creating Zen-like calligraphy as one phase of his broader exploration of Zen Buddhism, inspired by his mentor and friend, D.T. Suzuki. Some brushed images with dynamic swirls may well date to the period when the Zen garden was being elaborated, late 1963-early 1964—for example, this magnificent bird (fig. 6). Merton had also explored with brush and ink forms that recall the Zen garden turtle—most notably what he called a "swimming dragon" in the collection of the Thomas Merton Center.[2] There are, as well, a few images from this period that are surprisingly monumental. The striking image in fig. 7 is small in

Figure 5

size but large in conception, as if he were designing sculpture for a public space. And so while we cannot recognize an identity between Merton's quickly evolving art of calligraphy and the forms of the Zen garden, the affinity is clear; one sensibility is at work.

Merton's photographs allow a further question: what sort of stone is this? Todd Hendricks, a geologist with the Commonwealth of Kentucky's Department for Environmental Protection, was kind enough to roam the abbey grounds in the company of Mark Meade, archivist at the Thomas Merton Center, and provide an expert report. The stone is local, of course: the abbey rides on bedrock known as Laurel dolomite, a sedimentary formation laid

Figure 6

down more than 400 million years ago in what Mr. Hendricks describes as "warm, tropical, shallow seas." "At that time," he adds,
"Kentucky was between 20 and 30 degrees south of the equator.
The sea and climate were probably similar to today's Persian Gulf—
warm, arid, and tropical."[3] The upper half of the deposit makes
fine construction material; you can see it to this day in many older
buildings in Bardstown, Kentucky, not far from the abbey, including the Old Talbott Tavern. The lower half of the ancient deposit,
exposed through erosion over long periods of time, "weathers to
a light yellowish-gray color with a network of fist-sized holes," as
Mr. Hendricks puts it. And this is the stone Merton found on his
rambles in the woods a half-mile east of the abbey, where Br. Paul

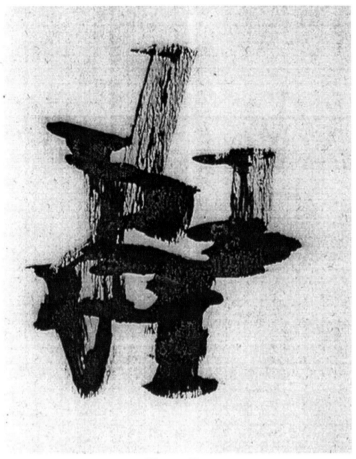

Figure 7

Quenon—one of today's ramblers—could show us plenty of stone Merton left behind.

It is not classic Zen gardening stone. The classic gardens tend to display dense stones, always with interesting surfaces and shapes but rarely so eroded. In my experience of the gardens of Japan, there are few fist-sized holes. That aesthetic does, however, show up in the related East Asian art of so-called scholar's rocks. Scholar's rocks are found objects, never worked like sculpture, although generations of handling can give them a special patina. Great examples are highly prized. The taste for scholar's rocks, as objects of contemplation and wonderment, was shared between China and Japan. To the best of my knowledge, Merton never mentions scholar's rocks and may have been unaware of this tradition, but here as elsewhere Merton tends to fall on his feet: the local stone, useable and at hand, wasn't a classic ingredient of Zen gardens, but its eccentricity recalls the kindred tradition of scholar's rocks.

What did Merton know, what could he know of classic Japanese dry gardens? We have heard him speak of a little book; whatever it was, it doesn't seem to have been retained in the abbey library or among his own books, nor is there anything specifically on Zen gardens. In 1963, when the design of the novitiate garden must have been gestating in Merton's mind and heart, the available illustrated literature was not at all as extensive as it is today. Loraine E. Kuck, who introduced the term "Zen garden" in English, had published *The Art of Japanese Gardens* in 1940. After the war, in 1956, Jiro Harada published *Japanese Gardens*, a much more richly illustrated work. From Gluck and Harada he could have learned a good deal about selecting and grouping rocks, laying out pavement stones, and designing raked patterns to represent the ocean, rivers, or the endless motion in which we are all immersed. He could have learned about the "turtle island," symbol of longevity and depth, which is a recurrent feature in such gardens, and about the "crane island," another recurrent feature. He could have encountered, as well, the Zen gardener's potent approach to the spirituality he revered in the writings of Dr. Suzuki and in the ancient source literature of Zen Buddhism. From an early sixteenth-century text, cited in Harada, he could have heard—and would deeply have agreed—that "the ultimate aim of the landscape garden is to reveal the mysteries of nature and creation. This may be achieved by a simple flat garden with only a few rocks.... When one is about to make a garden, one should not be absorbed merely by the pattern, or carelessly plant even one tree or place one rock without careful discrimination."[4] Did Merton factually encounter this text? Perhaps not. Did he encounter something like it? Almost certainly yes—he knew his Zen sources by 1963.

How skilled a Zen gardener was Thomas Merton? Does this garden meet the test of a knowledgeable eye? Unhappily, but not surprisingly, it does not. Stephen Morrell, curator of a public Zen garden in the New York area and teacher of Zen gardening, had little good to say after generously taking time to look at Merton's photographs. "Crude and simplistic," he felt constrained to say, "reflecting no design technique; the rocks have no relationships with each other."[5] And yet he did express interest in learning how the garden was used at the monastery: use must be for him a significant indicator. The novitiate garden is clearly not at the level of the great Japanese temple gardens, such as the late 15th-century dry garden at Ryoanji, in Kyoto. And the novices did not have the long-cultivated skills of the Buddhist monks who maintain those gardens. Such things duly noted, this Zen garden of the Lord had its good use at the time and remains now an ecumenical sign, a sign of willingness. In 1959, Merton had written as follows to his mentor in Zen, Dr. Suzuki: "I only wish there were some way I could come in contact with some very elementary Zen discipline, even if it were only something like archery or flower-arrangement."[6] What he found was brush-and-ink calligraphy, a quiet way of being in Nature, a quiet way of meditation—and stone gardening.

Historians often make the lordly mistake of saying, for example, that Charlemagne built the chapel at Aachen. Charlemagne did have the idea and provided funds, but an unnoticed workforce actually laid hand to stone and built. Fortunately, the abbey workforce in this instance—the novices—can be recognized. Merton wrote with extraordinary warmth in his journal about the novices who helped to build the garden. On January 4th, 1963, he recorded his satisfaction with an innovation—the merging of the brother novices and choir novices (those who wished to remain brothers only, and those who had the priesthood in mind) into a single body. He had been responsible for the monastic education of the choir novices since 1955. "The merger of the two novitiates is proceeding well," he wrote,

> because all the novices are so good. I am happy with the Brother novices, one loves them immediately. They really have something, a special grace of simplicity and honesty and goodness. It is a great grace to have them here…. I think the grace the brothers have comes from their work, which keeps them perhaps (when properly done) from getting too obsessed with themselves and with their spirituality. It is wonderful how they will go into anything and get it done, not standing around scratching their heads with the dubiousness of the choir, or wanting to be told each next move.[7]

A half-year later, in June, when the thought of the Zen garden may already have come to mind, he recorded distress about his own life but also confidence in the novices. "My projects and relationships, including correspondence and much of my work, are sheer waste," he wrote, not for the first time. But "relationships with the novices," he continued, "...are meaningful and healthy."[8] When he returned from hospitalization and surgery in late September, his sense of return was to the novices and the peaceful novitiate:

> Came home to the monastery Wednesday, shoulder hurting but glad to be back, especially to the novices. This is surely a much more rational life than anything to be found outside. Here at least there is a kind of order and tranquility, and though there is plenty of noise, still in the novitiate everything is quiet and serene. And there is a real joy in the novices, a real peace....[9]

This was Merton's workforce, or part of it. The other part was massive earth-moving equipment, providentially on site at the abbey because James had set in motion a much-needed new water management system. Merton was famously offended, for years and years, by the loud sounds of machinery in the contemplative monastic community: "Today (and all week)," he wrote in his journal soon after returning from hospital, "the frightful racket of the earth-moving machinery around the new waterworks...."[10] But Br. Patrick Hart recalls that the community teased Merton when he returned from hospital because he had arranged, during his absence, for one of those earth-moving machines to carry stone from the woods to the Zen garden and set it in place.[11]

What did the novices think about this enterprise into which they were drawn as stone movers, pavement layers, gardeners, rakers? Dr. James Finley, now a psychotherapist in southern California, then a novice at Gethsemani in the years 1961 through 1967, remembers well. In a recent interview generously offered, he said: "Merton found this huge rock out in the woods. He wanted to make a Zen garden, put the gravel down, and have it raked. We went out to get that rock. The brothers didn't know what to make of all this—it was Uncle Louie's latest idea. I remember raking the Zen garden. I liked it, it was tranquil and fit in well." Asked whether Dom James favored creation of the Zen garden or simply tolerated it, Dr. Finley replied that Dom James almost certainly didn't think of the garden in religious terms. He would have thought of it "in aesthetic terms, not necessarily with any theological content." And Dr. Finley went on to evoke something of the atmosphere of the abbey in those years, and perhaps now also. "Though Gethsemani was conservative," he said, "because of the silence it was also extremely liberal. You found your own way in the silence. There was no pro forma inner way to follow. In this sense, the tradition of monasticism is liberal." Young Finley at the time considered the garden to be Buddhist—he was reading a classic collection of stories, *Zen Flesh Zen Bones*—but in his view many of the novices "probably didn't give it a thought."[12]

Surprisingly, the Zen garden at Gethsemani was not the first to be designed and built under monastic auspices in the United States. Dom Aelred Graham, British-born, somewhat older than Merton, Benedictine, and prior of both the monastery and a well-known prep school in Portsmouth, Rhode Island, completed a lovely Zen garden at the priory in 1962. Its designer was Dom Hilary Martin, a monastic colleague of Dom Aelred's who had two degrees from MIT, one in architecture. He obviously shared with Dom Aelred a keen appreciation for the principles of Japanese garden design. Dom Aelred published in 1963 a pioneering book, *Zen Catholicism*, and he would return to that topic in later years; he had much in common with Merton. The priory garden was more traditionally Japanese in design than the garden at Gethsemani, and rather more luxurious.[13]

Merton was aware of Dom Aelred's garden; it may well have ignited his own thoughts. In April 1963, he had written to Dom Aelred: "...everything I ever hear about Portsmouth always sounds fine. I am particularly glad about the Zen garden...."[14] In the course of things, Dom Aelred visited Gethsemani in March 1964 and was persuaded to offer a Sunday conference to the novices and other listeners. Toward the beginning of the conference, Merton drew him into conversation about the Zen garden:

> **Merton:** Father, you've seen our Zen garden out there.
>
> **Dom Aelred:** Very taken with it, it's very different, but seems to be right in the spirit of it.... Zen monks, when they saw ours, were quite excited about it. But it seems to me that yours is right in the spirit of it, and rather simpler and better in a way, because there shouldn't be too much vegetation or too much ornamentation.... I'm no gardener, somebody else used my book as an excuse.... Wouldn't it be a good idea [he said] if we brought a whole lot of rocks and stone—which cost a little money, incidentally, to do—and I was rather corked about that, but we did it anyhow.
>
> **Merton:** We should have had our fish flag flying. Do you have a fish flag?

Dom Aelred: No, we don't. We don't have that. [The garden] is now a kind of showpiece, and people come to look at *that*—they've forgotten to look at the church![15]

As it was being completed and through seasons to come, what was the life of this garden? Merton's journal entries show that initially he followed and "read" its changes. October 28, 1963: "The falling leaves," he wrote, "crowds of them, flying across the narrow novitiate lawn and the Zen garden…."[16] November 5th, 1963: "This morning, still night, warmer, cloudy, wind, pale night over the Zen garden, cold in the chapel…."[17] New Year's Eve, 1963: "We all went out into the fierce zero cold and stood in the darkness of the garden while a last flake of light resisted for a long time the swallowing globe of dark…. We have a Japanese fish-kite and Brother Dunstan stuck up some bamboo poles in the Zen garden, so I hope we will fly fish and streamers to celebrate the New Year."[18]

But soon the Zen garden fades from his journal. Perhaps it was fully maintained only while he remained master of novices, a position he relinquished in the summer of 1965 when he began living full-time at the hermitage. Photographs in later years show the garden still in use but little cared for—unraked, the tree transplanted or expired, who knows what else changed and diminished. When I saw the garden in 1982, it was a relic of time past, abandoned. Br. Paul Quenon was kind enough to ask Father Timothy Kelly, abbot of Gethsemani in the years 1975 through 2000, what he could recall of the garden. Fr. Timothy reported that it had been replaced by a more standard garden while he was abbot. "No one was caring for it," he said, "weeds were even growing in it…."[19] The stones were returned to the land; just one now remains recognizable.

Was that a defeat? I don't think so. People change, circumstances change, gardens change. The Christian-Buddhist lesson of impermanence is written into this garden as into all things here below. And then, Merton's photographs confer long life on the garden, although in another form—the photographic form he so loved. Through photographs the garden continues speaking to us, just as Merton would have wished.

Merton in the novitiate was the plant at the center of the garden; his vision summoned and sustained it. Merton at the hermitage was elsewhere, planting and nurturing other visions altogether. However, even in the last days of his life the memory of the garden recurred. Standing before the great Buddhist sculptural ensemble at Polonnaruwa in Sri Lanka—one of the wonders of religious art in any tradition—he found himself perceiving the larger setting in terms that he had learned at home: "The whole thing is very much a Zen garden," he wrote, "a span of bareness and openness and evidence, and the great figures, motionless, yet with the lines in full movement, waves of vesture and bodily form, a beautiful and holy vision...."[20] The raked lines of gravel at Gethsemani reappeared for him on the dying Buddha's monastic robe.

Endnotes

1. Published with warm thanks to Dr. Paul Pearson and Mark Meade of the Thomas Merton Center, Bellarmine University; Dr. James Finley; Stephen Morrell; R. Todd Hendricks of the Commonwealth of Kentucky Department for Environmental Protection; Dom Damian Kearney of Portsmouth Abbey; and Brs. Patrick Hart and Paul Quenon of the Abbey of Gethsemani. Recording in the collection of the Thomas Merton Center, Bellarmine University (hereafter, TMC)

2. Catalogue no. 344, TMC

3. R. Todd Hendricks, letter to the author

4. Jiro Harada, *Japanese Gardens*, London: The Studio Limited, 1956, p. 19

5. Stephen Morrell, conversation with the author

6. Merton letter to Suzuki, April 11, 1959, in *Encounter: Thomas Merton and D. T. Suzuki*, Robert E. Daggy, ed., Monterey (KY): Larkspur Press, 1988, p. 18

7. Entry for January 4, 1963, in *Turning Toward the World: The Journals of Thomas Merton, Volume Four, 1960-1963*, Victor A. Kramer, ed., San Francisco: HarperSanFrancisco, 1996, p. 285

8. Idem, June 3, 1963, p. 326

9. Idem, September 28, 1963, p. 20

10. Idem, October 2, 1963, p. 21

11. Michael Mott, *The Seven Mountains of Thomas Merton*, New York: Houghton Mifflin, 1984, p. 395

12. Dr. James Finley, conversation with the author

13. For the Zen garden at Portsmouth Priory, consult archives preserved at the Priory.

14. Merton letter to Aelred Graham, April 24, 1963, TMC

15. Recording dated March 8, 1964, TMC

16. Entry for October 28, 1963, *Dancing in the Water of Life: The Journals of Thomas Merton, Volume Five, 1963-1965*, Robert E. Daggy, ed., San Francisco: HarperSanFrancisco, 1997, p. 28

17. Idem, November 5, 1963, p. 31

18. Idem, December 31, 1963, pp. 51-52

19. Letter to the author

20. Entry for December 4, 1968, *The Asian Journal of Thomas Merton,* Naomi Burton, Patrick Hart and James Laughlin, eds., New York: New Directions, 1973, p. 324

Merton's Reflections on the Christian Artist:
Art as Doorway into Eternity

Pamela Proietti

Merton was greatly influenced by the Thomistic Christian philosophy of Jacques Maritain, whom he considered to be the greatest
living philosopher of the twentieth century. This reasoned and
aesthetic judgment on Merton's part, which I believe is essentially correct, already sets Merton apart from his contemporaries,
who overwhelmingly regarded Martin Heidegger as the greatest
mid-twentieth century philosopher and thinker. Merton's earliest
scholarly work, his Master's thesis on the poetry of William Blake,
already bears the marks of his penetrating artistic and moral intuition. Merton used the guidance he found in Jacques Maritain's
Thomistic understanding of art as the starting point for a profound
understanding of the origin and the transcendent nature of art.
Maritain's Thomistic and Christian understanding of art and the
artist remained with Merton for the remainder of his life as both
artist-mystic and an appreciative observer of genuine art.

While an octogenarian, Maritain remained a prominent French
cultural figure when in the 1960s, he wrote his final book, entitled
The Peasant of the Garonne. At the point in his life when Maritain
wrote this final book, much of the optimism with which he had
faced the post-World War II era had faded. He seemed to despair
of what he saw in the European Christian churches. And Maritain wrote a forceful critique of European culture's drift toward
nihilism, a trend that Maritain believed was prominent and influential among European intellectuals and artists, and also among
European Christian clergy. Maritain wrote this final book at the
same time that Merton was engaging in ecumenical dialogue with
Eastern religious leaders and getting more involved in political and
social movements within the Christian churches of North and South
America. As one looks at the surface of the lives of both men, the
aging Maritain appears to be losing some of his former optimism
and energy for progressive reform in this world. Merton appears
to be, by contrast, moving toward greater engagement with the
world and seeing greater hope for moral and political progress.

In reality, underneath these surface differences, both Maritain
and Merton shared a religious and mystical hope in the Kingdom

of God and in the role of Uncreated Reason within our human world. Maritain regarded Western Christendom as a privileged culture, because the essentially ancient Greek and Biblical pre-philosophic culture of the West was in remarkable harmony with deeper truths about human nature. Yet Maritain saw, as the German philosopher Friedrich Nietzsche had predicted, that this ancient pre-philosophic culture of Western Christendom was being displaced by the revolutionary new culture of modern scientific rationalism. As an old layman looking out at vast cultural changes in Europe in the 1960s, Maritain was fearing that the great culture of Western Christendom "is disappearing before our eyes."[1] The new culture of scientific materialism was triumphing over its much older cultural rivals, the ancient Greek rationalism of Plato and Aristotle, which was transmitted to Western culture through the great Medieval philosophers of both Islam and Christianity, and faith in revealed religion.

Maritain describes with sadness a late twentieth century European culture wherein we see the majority of Christians "kneeling before the world," having lost all awareness of the transcendent: "instead of realizing that our devotion to the temporal task must be that much firmer and more ardent since we know that the human race will never succeed on this earth in delivering itself completely from evil—because of the wounds of Adam and because our ultimate end is supernatural—these intellectuals make of these earthly goals the truly supreme end for humanity."[2]

Yet, at this same moment in time, Merton looks with renewed hope at some promising signs of cultural renewal in both the South American Roman Catholic Christian churches and in Asian religious movements. Both the pessimism of Maritain about old Europe and the optimism of Merton grew out of their shared vision of humanity and human history.

As Maritain understood history, there can be no certainty of the final outcome of our latest cultural movement into a modern scientific cultural horizon: "Things are not predetermined in human history; they depend on our unforeseeable choices…The history of the world progresses at the same time in the line of evil and the line of good. In certain periods—our own for example—one sees the effects of this simultaneous double progress erupting in a kind of explosion."[3] There are immense spiritual and religious aspirations at work within our Western world. Both Maritain and Merton saw hopeful spiritual forces set forth in our world by the genuine artist's love of beauty and commitment to truth. After Merton became a monk, he continued to visit the "secular book-houses" available to him and to read and comment upon the work of religious artists as varied as William Faulkner, Flannery O'Connor, the French existentialist Albert Camus, and the great Christian poets of Russia, of South and Central America, and the Eastern European nations. One can see from reading Merton's commentaries on the great poets of his own time that Merton continued to understand the ground of genuine artistic vision in much the same way that he had understood Blake's poetry two decades earlier.

Merton had a brief dalliance with the false idols of Marxism and Communism during his student days at Columbia. It is difficult to say with certainty why Merton did not join the American Communist Party in the late 1930s, when Party membership was so trendy and fellow travelers so common on university campuses. In his autobiography, *Seven-Story Mountain*, Merton claims that his teacher Mark Van Doren had saved him from a docile and reverent acceptance of the ideology of Marxism and communism,[4] but one can see in his early thesis on Blake and on the nature of Christian art that Merton was a truly independent thinker, and that even as a young man he would not be easily led into embracing the latest fads in art, politics, religion, or culture. Merton's independent and thoughtful spirit would get him into some trouble in his later days at the monastery.

The youthful Thomas Merton first delved deeply into the truths uncovered in Christian philosophy with the aid of Maritain's beautiful early work on Christian art entitled *Art and Scholasticism*, which Merton carefully studied while working on his Master's thesis about the poetry of Blake. It is likely that Merton's earliest experiences of growing up with two artist parents and his early childhood experiences with his father Owen had encouraged him to develop at an early age deep intuitions about the nature of art. Upon reading Jacques Maritain's beautiful and famous essay on the nature of Christian art, Merton must have immediately understood that the author was elaborating fundamental truths about art and the virtue of the artist. Merton writes in his autobiography: "I had always understood that art was contemplation and that it involved the action of the highest faculties of man."[5] Maritain's 1923 essay on religious art remained for Merton a master text on Christian art. In the summer of 1964, Merton organized his talks on art for the novices around the text he called in his notes "A

& S"—Jacques Maritain's *Art and Scholasticism*. Maritain helped
Merton to see that William Blake, like all great artists, experienced
a spontaneous awareness of Truth and Beauty as a kind of second
nature, what Maritain had called "connaturality." The artist does
not create beauty and meaning solely from the force of his will, as
Camus had claimed in his beautiful prose poem *The Plague*. The
artist is able to see what lies hidden within and beyond the merely
sensual beauties of nature, by means of his connatural participation with the Divine Intellect; human intellect participates in the
created world as image of God. All genuine artists participate in an
eternal Reality which transcends the merely natural beauty of our
created world. Art is, before all, intellectual and its activity consists
in impressing an idea upon matter.[6] Both artistic knowledge and
moral knowledge are more than merely intellectual conformity
with the truths involved. The artist, like the moral man, possesses
a mysterious form of knowledge that transcends the scientific
forms of knowledge.

> In this knowledge through union or inclination, connaturality
> or congeniality, the intellect is at play not alone, but together
> with affective inclinations and dispositions of the will, and
> as guided and shaped by them. It is not rational knowledge,
> knowledge through the conceptual, logical, and discursive
> exercise of reason. But it is really and genuinely knowledge,
> though obscure and perhaps incapable of giving account of
> itself. St. Thomas explains in this way the difference between
> the knowledge of divine reality acquired by theology and the
> knowledge of divine reality provided by mystical experience…
> Knowledge through connaturality plays an immense part in
> human life. Modern philosophers have thrown it into oblivion,
> but the ancient Doctors paid careful attention to it and estab-
> lished upon it all their theory of God-given contemplation. I
> think we have to restore it, and to recognize its basic role and
> importance in such domains as moral practical knowledge
> and natural or supernatural mystical experience—and in the
> domain of art and poetry.[7]

Without this connatural awareness of the sacred, a skeptic like
Camus could not have created the moving celebration of human
courage and human goodness that we find in his story *The Plague*.
Maritain describes the connection between beauty and joy in the
fifth chapter of his famous essay on art:

St. Thomas defined the beautiful as what gives pleasure on sight. Man's pleasure in seeing the beautiful is based in an intuitive knowledge...Beauty is essentially the object of *intelligence*, for what *knows* in the full meaning of the word is the mind, which alone is open to the infinity of being. The natural site of beauty is the intelligible world: [from] thence it descends...The beautiful is what gives joy, not all joy, but joy in knowledge; not the joy peculiar to an act of knowing, but a joy superabounding and overflowing from such an act because of the object known... The beautiful exalts and delights the soul by the bare fact of its being given to the intuition of the soul.... The peculiar beauty of our art is to work upon a sensible matter for the joy of the spirit. [Art] has the savor of the terrestrial paradise, because it restores for a brief moment the simultaneous peace and delight of the mind and the senses.[8]

The young Thomas Merton demonstrates an early intuitive awareness of this Platonic and Thomistic philosophy of art which is described so compellingly by Maritain. Merton begins his early Master's thesis on Blake with a defense of the essentially religious ideas of Blake against a modern secular scholar of the 1930s who would remake Blake in his own secular and atheistic image. Nearly three decades later, Merton will again rush to the defense of his beloved poet in a review Merton writes of a scholarly book published in the mid-1960s by a neo-Hegelian theologian. In this later critical commentary, Merton is a bit more charitable than he had been in 1939; the mature Merton graciously acknowledges that the scholar who distorts Blake's poetry "does not get Blake's ideas entirely wrong"! The neo-Hegelian new theologian who comments on Blake's poetry is able to understand Blake's dissatisfaction with much of the orthodox, traditional Church Christianity of his time. But this new theologian wants to substitute his own version of the Hegelian dialectic for the old worn orthodoxies of the established Christian Church. Merton writes: The fact that Hegel ends up with the deification of the State shows the danger of comparing him and Blake too glibly, and [the author's] final embrace of Satan and the Antichrist has a carefree facility about it that makes one wonder if he has lost Blake and ended up with Hegel only."[9]

Merton's early understanding of Blake's artistic vision was remarkable for someone so young. The young Merton, while still a graduate student, understood why Blake opposed both the neo-

Platonists and the Romantics of his time. The Platonists he viewed as too abstract in their mathematical idealism. Their philosophy was too cold and inhuman. Yet Blake believed that the poems of Wordsworth and Coleridge, the Romantic poets of the eighteenth century, were idolatrous in their worship of natural beauty for its own sake. In Blake's poetry, Ulro is the equivalent of Hell. Ulro is a state of almost complete materialism, matter without spirit. For Blake, matter and evil are bound together. Only form is intelligible; matter is the principle of change and change denies intelligibility. For Blake, like the Gnostics, matter is tied up with the Fall and expulsion from Eden. In Eden, man was eternal. He fell from Edenic eternity into matter, into illusion, into chaos and death. Urizen, one of the eternals, fell into matter and dragged the others with him. Urizen appears to be modern Enlightenment man, who is a moral and philosophic skeptic, a materialist, an empiricist, and an atheist. For Blake, the man of imagination, the artist, sees more than his eyes present to him. He does not rely entirely on the evidence of his senses. Urizen, the skeptical materialist and empiricist, "is blind and in chains, and is trying to impose that blindness on the whole world."

By contrast, Los and Enitharmon, who are male and female, are Blake's images for artistic vision. In his poetry, Los and Enitharmon

> Walked forth on the dewy earth
> Contracting and expanding their all flexible senses
> At will to murmur in the flowers small as the honey bee
> At will to stretch across the heavens and step
>   from star to star.[10]

In describing art and the virtue of the artist, Merton loved to quote a favorite passage from Maritain: "The beauty of art is found in integrity, proportion, and clarity. Integrity, because the mind likes being; proportion because the mind likes order and likes unity; lastly and above all brightness or clarity, because the mind likes light and intelligibility."[11]

For Blake and for Merton, as for all religious artists, the brightness of *claritas* is the glory of form shining through matter. To see the splendor of form in matter is to look through matter into eternity. The young Thomas Merton wrote about the shared intuition of the artist and the mystic. Merton compares Meister Eckhart with William Blake in this early thesis. Although the later Merton will become a famous spiritual guide on the apophatic path toward the Divine Reality, he continued to be a lover of religious poetry and religious fiction. Merton's deep understanding of the nature of and the beauty of religious art made him perhaps the finest commentator on the great artists of his age. His essays on the essentially religious ideas that inspired both the Russian Christian poet Pasternak and the French agnostic existentialist artist Camus are astonishing in both insight and beauty. And Merton's own Christian reinterpretation of the Prometheus myth of ancient Greece is a work of genuine Christian art in its own right. For Merton, a new reading of the myth of Prometheus is required after Christ enters human history. The struggle of Prometheus against the Divine is the result of a tragic misunderstanding. Merton's new version of the Prometheus myth is a fitting rebuttal of Camus's tragic *Myth of Sisyphus.*

Merton's beautiful and compelling vision of art and the artist was made possible within his essentially Christian religious vision of the human person. He shared William Blake's and Jacques Maritain's Christian vision of the origin of art:

> Whatever be the nature and the ends in usefulness of the art under consideration, by its object it participates in something superhuman: for its object is the creation of beauty.... In that respect, the artist imitates God, Who created the world by communicating to it a likeness of His beauty. And as the artist also stamps the mystery of form on the material of his art, a form which he discovers in his own soul and mind, the artist realizes in action one of the fundamental aspects of the ontological resemblance of our soul to God.... For this reason the mind, despite the manifold defects peculiar to our species, strives to engender in us...a work at once material and spiritual, like ourselves, with something of our soul over and above.... This requirement of mind explains the presence of artists in our midst.[12]

The young Merton also praises a traditional Hindu scholar's description of the artist. The traditional Hindu scholar, taking a religious view of the Source and nature of art, describes the artistic process and inspiration much the same as Maritain does in his Christian philosophy of art. There is no significant difference to be found in Eastern and Western religions concerning the understanding of art and the virtue of the artist:

The artist imposes upon the natural model the form which his mind, his intellect is prepared to see in it…Just as the soul is the form of the body, so the art in the artist is the form of the work of art…The logic of the pure naturalist in art finally breaks down…A man's portrait is his essential image, his image as he is in God; that is, expresses his own character, whatever it is that makes him who and what he is.[13]

This is how all religious men understand art in both the East and the West. The divide in our contemporary world is between those who understand the Source and purpose of art from a religious perspective and those secular thinkers who would seek to use art to promote profane political and social purposes having no connection with either Beauty or Truth. The noble spiritual vision of the role of art in human life has been lost for men in the modern world.

The [thinkers] of the Middle Ages did not make town dwellers, bookworms, and graduates the sole object of their studies; they were concerned with the mass of mankind [The artist] did not work for society people and the dealers, but for the faithful commons; it was his mission to house their prayers, to instruct their minds, to rejoice their souls and their eyes…More beautiful things were then created, and there was less self-worship. The blessed humility in which the artist was situated exalted his strength and his freedom.[14]

The medieval world was filled with spiritual light, because the men of that age had not lost sight of the Divine ground of being. For Maritain, the period of time in human history beginning with Socratic and Platonic philosophy, in the ancient Greek city-state of Athens, and continuing through the Middle Ages was a Golden Age in Western civilization. Maritain's understanding of the arc of recorded human history differs fundamentally from what the contemporary university students will learn about history.

Maritain does not view man's entry into the modern scientific age as a passage from barbarism into a brave new world of endless progress toward a better future for humanity. Maritain fears that moral and political progress for future generations of modern scientific men is not inevitable. The past century has not been encouraging; the great 19th century German philosopher Nietzsche was justified in his fears about the underlying nihilism in Western man's modern scientific culture. Maritain writes:

> But now the modern world, which had promised the artist all things, will soon scarcely leave him even the bare means of subsistence. Founded upon the two *unnatural* principles of the *fecundity of money* and the *finality of the useful*, multiplying its needs and servitudes without any possibility of there ever being a limit, ruining the leisure of the soul…imposing on man its puffing machinery and its speeding up of matter, the modern world is shaping human activity in a properly inhuman way, in a properly devilish direction, for the ultimate end of all this frenzy is to prevent man from remembering God.[15]
>
> The pitiable state of the modern world, a mere corpse of the Christian world, creates a specially ardent desire for the reinvention of a true civilization. If such a desire were to remain unfulfilled and the universal dissolution to take its course, we should still find consolation, because as the world breaks up we see the things of the spirit gather together in places in the world but not of the world. Art and poetry are among them, and metaphysics and true wisdom; the charity of the saints will lead the choir. None of them has any permanent dwelling here below; each lives in casual shelters, waiting for the storm to pass. If the Spirit which floated over the waters must now hover above the ruins, what does it matter? It is sufficient if it comes. What is certain, at all events, is that we are approaching a time in which any hope set below the heart of Christ is doomed to disappointment.[16]
>
> Persecuted like the wise man and almost like the Saint, the artist will perhaps recognize his brethren at last and find his vocation once again: for in a way he is not of this world, being, from the moment he begins working for beauty, on the road which leads upright souls to God and makes invisible things clear to them by visible {images]. However few they may then be who will disdain to gratify the Beast and turn with the wind, in them, for the simple reason that they will be exercising a *disinterested* activity, the human race will live.[17]

Will there be a revival of genuine art and a larger revival of the best and truest elements of Western Judeo-Christian culture? Perhaps. Perhaps not. Perhaps the cultural renewal that mankind presently requires will take place in the East, with the religious inspiration of Eastern religious insight, rather than here in the West. Both Thomas Merton and Jacques Maritain believed that the Divine flame of Beauty and Truth would continue to remain alive and well within the souls and the minds of the genuine artists in both the East and the West.

February 21, 2007 marked the 100th birthday celebration of arguably the greatest Christian poet of the past century, W H Auden. Auden shared with both Maritain and Merton an intuitive and connatural understanding of the meaning and purpose of Christian art. I will close with the famous final stanza of the poem that he wrote at the beginning of the Second World War, *September 1, 1939*:

> Defenceless under the night
> Our world in stupor lies;
> Yet dotted everywhere,
> Ironic points of light
> Flash out wherever the Just
> Exchange their messages:
> May I, composed like them,
> Of Eros and of dust,
> Beleaguered by the same
> Negation and despair,
> Show an affirming flame.

Endnotes

1. Maritain, Jacques. *The Peasant of the Garonne: An Old Layman Questions Himself about the Present Time*; translated by Michael Cuddihy and Elizabeth Hughes, (NY: Macmillan, 1968), pp. 27-30.

2. Maritain, *The Peasant of the Garonne*, pp. 27-30.

3. Maritain, *The Peasant of the Garonne*, p. 13.

4. Merton, Thomas. *The Seven-Storey Mountain* (NY: Garden City Books, 1951), p. 141.

5. Merton. *The Seven-Storey Mountain*, p. 203.

6. Maritain, Jacques, *Art and Scholasticism*; (Ditchling, England: St. Dominic's Press, 1923), p. 8.

7. Maritain, Jacques. *Creative Intuition in Art and Poetry*, (Princeton, NJ: Princeton University Press, 1953), p.117.

8. Maritain, *Art and Scholasticism*, p. 19.

9. Merton, Thomas. *The Literary Essays of Thomas Merton*; edited by Brother Patrick Hart,(NY: New Directions Publishing Corp., 1981), p. 6.

10. Merton, Thomas. *The Literary Essays of Thomas Merton*, p. 6

11. Maritain, *Art and Scholasticism*, p.16

12. Maritain. *Art and Scholasticism*, p. 8.
13. Maritain. *Art and Scholasticism*, p. 8.
14. Maritain. *Art and Scholasticism*, pp. 16-18.
15. Maritain. *Art and Scholasticism*, pp. 29-30.
16. Maritain. *Art and Scholasticism,* pp. 29-30.
17. Maritain. *Art and Scholasticism,* pp. 30.

Nurture by Nature:
Emblems of Stillness in a Season of Fury

Patrick F. O'Connell

Emblems of a Season of Fury,[1] Thomas Merton's sixth book of verse, published in 1963, is the last volume of shorter poems to appear before his death five years later. As the title suggests, many of the poems deal with the crucial social issues of war, racial injustice and political oppression that drew Merton's attention and motivated much of his prose writing during the final decade of his life. But the poetry of social protest is complemented by poems that express Merton's continued commitment to the Christian contemplative tradition as well as his deepening exploration of the wisdom of other religious paths, particularly Zen. In a season of fury, a time of upheaval, shot through with illusion and deceit, there is a heightened need, Merton seems to suggest, to be grounded in and nurtured by stillness, silence, solitude and love for God and God's creation. Among these poems of contemplative awareness are four which focus on the natural world as a privileged locus of divine encounter. Considering these poems as a group provides an opportunity to reflect on Merton's continued recognition that "To the true Christian poet, the whole world and all the incidents of life tend to be sacraments—signs of God, signs of His love working in the world,"[2] and to discover how that recognition is articulated in distinct but related ways in poems that are generally regarded as among the most well crafted and fully realized of his later lyrics.

* * * * * * *

Probably the earliest of this group of poems,[3] "Love Winter When the Plant Says Nothing"[4] presents a series of natural "emblems" that are called upon to function as meaningful signs in a season, if not of fury, at least of emptiness and apparent deadness. The barren natural landscape with its hidden vitality serves as an analogue for the inevitable and necessary winter periods of the human heart and spirit, which are summoned to undergo the detachment and purification of naked faith, "the evidence of things not seen" (Heb. 11:1).

117

The opening stanza is composed of two pairs of parallel lines, each an apostrophe, a pattern that will predominate throughout the poem:

> O little forests, meekly
> Touch the snow with low branches!
> O covered stones
> Hide the house of growth! (ll. 1-4)

Here the visible, animate and organic is juxtaposed with the unseen, inanimate and inorganic in complementary constructions. While trees are traditionally associated with reaching upward toward the heavens, here the image of the branches of (presumably) fir trees weighted down with snow to touch the ground is presented as a sign of humility (perhaps a reminiscence of the beatitudes, in which the meek inherit the earth [Mt. 5:5]), reinforced by the diminishment represented by the phrase "little forests."[5] The second image, linked to the first by the assonance of "snow" and "low" with "stones" and "growth," moves beneath the snow-covered ground to suggest an invisible vitality below, but the admonition to the stones, themselves unseen,[6] to conceal this growth implies that exposing what is taking place to the harsh surface conditions would be inopportune and even dangerous at this particular time; humility must be matched by patience. The most disconcerting aspect of these opening lines is the speaker's repeated use of the imperative. It is unclear at this point why trees and stones should be commanded to perform certain actions that presumably they are already doing without any human instruction. Any satisfactory explanation for this rhetorical strategy will have to wait for the poem's further development.

The lines immediately following are the only section of the poem that is not part of an imperative construction—simply comprising a catalogue of loosely connected elements:

> Secret
> Vegetal words,
> Unlettered water,
> Daily zero. (ll. 5-8)

The epithet "Secret," given a line to itself, suggests that at least the first item on this list describes what is hidden in the "house of growth," while the identification of plants as "words" implies a potential, as yet unrealized revelatory quality of this growth. But the second element seems to contradict, or at least contrast with, these "Vegetal words": as "Unlettered," the water is not formed into words itself, nor, interpreting "Unlettered" as "illiterate," is it able to "read" the language of the plants—since water in winter would be frozen as ice and snow, at this point it is unable to penetrate the surface of the earth and therefore unable to penetrate the meaning of the hidden, secret words that lie below. Consequently, at present everything adds up to "Daily zero," presumably on one level a reference to the temperature, but on another to the emptiness and lack of life perceptible if one remains on the surface. The unnumbered "zero" corresponds to the "Unlettered" snow and ice—an apparent void—which forms a stark contrast with the "house of growth" of the opening stanza. It is unclear at this point in the poem how, or even whether, the two can be reconciled.

The third stanza returns once again to the imperative, with the first element of a second pair taking up the entire four-line segment:

> Pray undistracted
> Curled Tree
> Carved in steel—
> Buried zenith! (ll. 9-12)

Once again the initial focus is on the visible and organic, this time a single tree also bent over from the weight of the snow, in a posture reminiscent of reverence and humility (perhaps suggestive of a Cistercian profound bow) that calls forth the speaker's directive to "Pray undistracted"—an explicitly religious dimension is introduced for the first time as the natural world is imagined as participating in an act of divine worship, more readily done in the absence of external distractions. The description of the tree as "curled" might seem to indicate difficulty in withstanding the harsh weather,[7] but such an impression is immediately countered by the phrase "Carved in steel"—linked to the previous line both by the consonance of "Curled" and "Carved" and the assonance of "tree" and "steel"; it is suggestive at once of being frozen into stillness and immobility but also of having the toughness to withstand the buffeting of the elements. The final line[8] once again points below the observable surface of the scene, implicitly suggesting the source of this resilience. The true "zenith" is found in the depths where the tree's roots hold it firmly anchored.

Paired with the address to the "Curled tree" is one to fire—not an actual flame in this case but a metaphor of vital heat; while the personifications and apostrophes of the previous descriptions have of course suggested a spiritual application for the winter land-scape, by turning his attention to an element that, unlike the trees and stones, is presented only on the figurative plane, the speaker is gently redirecting the audience to pay greater attention to the human application of his images:

> Fire, turn inward
> To your weak fort,
> To a burly infant spot,
> A house of nothing. (ll. 13-16)

Here the paradox of the "weak fort" (from *"fortis"*—"strong") combining protection with vulnerability, both contrasts with the "steel" tree of the previous stanza and suggests St. Paul's statement, "When I am weak, then I am strong" (2 Cor. 12:10). It is identified with a contrasting paradox, in which the "infant spot" is character-ized as "burly," a site of new beginnings, a life-generating womb, that has unexpected strength and substance. This "fort" and "spot" is finally identified as "A house of nothing"—apparently the op-posite of "the house of growth" hidden in the opening stanza, but properly to be identified with it. Recognition that "the house of growth" must also be "A house of nothing" is the essential insight of the poem, the point at which the lessons of winter are revealed as a paradigm for authentic spiritual development: only by be-ing reduced to nothing, by dying to autonomous, self-generated aspiration, can genuine growth take place. The concluding lines of the poem provide the context in which such a recognition can take place.

The third and final set of paired imperatives is addressed not to material objects but to personified abstractions, a final stage in bringing into focus the spiritual significance of the natural scene:

> O peace, bless this mad place:
> Silence, love this growth. (ll. 17-18)

The word "mad,"[9] contrasting in sound with the sibilent endings of "peace," "bless," "place" and even "this," and further set apart by the consonance of "peace" and "place" and the link of "bl" and "pl" in "bless" and "place," represents the brief intrusion of a per-spective contradictory to the rest of the poem. Without peace and silence, "nothing" is just that—a denial and negation of meaning and of life, and the view of nature presented throughout the poem, as an epiphany of humility, a paradigm of prayer, bowed down yet with the steadfastness of steel, is indeed "mad"—irrational, senseless. But through the blessing of peace[10] what would otherwise be perceived as the "madness" of contradiction is revealed as the creativity of paradox; through the love of silence an apparently barren emptiness is recognized as actually a fruitful nothingness. Here at last is the explanation for the imperatives used throughout the poem: the speaker is exhorting natural objects to serve as signs of contradiction to a naturalistic, ultimately nihilistic view of the world. Obviously the objects addressed are doing what they are doing irrespective of his "commands"—therefore the imperatives function not to change the actions but to frame the interpretation of these actions, to counter a perspective without peace and without silence that would find in the scene only "a mad place." The imperatives say: be a revelation of a dimension that is not perceptible to the senses: on one level a sacrament of the divine creative presence, on another a foreshadowing of the new life that will emerge in the spring—and the second, natural pattern is itself a sign of the first, spiritual one, as the final lines intimate further:

> O silence, golden zero
> Unsetting sun
> Love winter when the plant says nothing. (ll. 19-21)

This final sentence is simply an expansion of the immediately preceding line, as silence is once again called upon to love. But silence is now identified as "golden zero," echoing the "daily zero" of line 8, but replacing the temporal element with a modifier suggesting that emptiness, relinquishment is precious; the gold color also leads into the second identification of silence as "Unsetting sun"— a moment of timeless illumination, of bright emptiness[11]—that is nonetheless called to "Love winter when the plant says nothing." The temporal silence of winter becomes a channel to experience the deeper silence of God, and in that silence winter's "daily zero" is transfigured as "golden zero," an awareness that emptiness and wordlessness are not meaningless but a summons to wait in patient expectation for the "*kairos*" when the "unlettered" immobile water will dissolve and the "Secret / Vegetal words" will emerge from the depths of "A house of nothing" that is indeed discovered to be "the house of growth."

The final line is of course identical to the poem's title, but the imperative addressed here to silence functions differently without a vocative: it summons readers to learn, through the poem's meditation on its stark landscape,[12] to embrace the silence and emptiness of "winter" in their own lives, to descend into the secret darkness in the depths of their own spirits which seems to be a "house of nothing" and only in faith and through love is recognized and accepted as a "house of growth," and so to discover transcendent and transforming meaning in what would otherwise be merely "a mad place."

* * * * * * *

While the season has changed, the landscape has bloomed, and silent plant has metamorphosed into singing flower, in "Song for Nobody"[13] a continued focus on the "negative" dimension of contemplative awareness, already implicit in the title, links this poem thematically with the previous one, though the shift from "Nothing" to "Nobody" hints that here the poet, in an appropriately oblique way, will invite consideration of the relation of emptiness to subjectivity, of self-renunciation to self-transcendence. With its short, mostly two-beat lines, its verbal and formal patterns of repetition with variation, its spareness of diction (only a single word—"emptiness"!—has more than two syllables), the poem radiates a limpid and luminous simplicity that should not be too readily equated with an absence of tension and struggle. Probably written in June 1960,[14] at a time when Merton was wrestling with the implications of his own solitary vocation in a particularly intense way,[15] the poem is a meditation on the contemplative significance of authentic solitude, which is ultimately revealed to be not exclusive but all-embracing.

The opening stanza, a single laconic declarative sentence, may at first seem straightforward enough:

A yellow flower
(Light and spirit)
Sings by itself
For nobody. (ll. 1-4)

A moment's reflection, however, suggests that potentially there are two fundamentally incompatible ways of understanding this statement. The prepositional phrases concluding the sentence could have connotations of isolation and self-absorption, a narcissistic rejection of communal activity and of any relationship with an audience. Only the presence of the parenthetical "Light and spirit," placed in apposition to "flower" before the predicate is expressed, signals that the phrases are not to be read in a solipsistic way. These positive characteristics point toward the alternative interpretation of what follows: that the song is not dependent upon or reacting to external stimuli, but is a revelation of the flower's own nature; it is not merely instrumental, a means to some extrinsic end, nor is it intended to attract attention to itself, to impress or to influence or even to communicate information; there is no effort to calculate or even to observe an effect, no self-consciousness, no concern for how, or whether, others will respond; it is therefore an act of perfect innocence and integrity and beauty and simplicity, a model of spontaneous immediacy of action in which the entire being is engaged.

The juxtaposition of the matter-of-fact "yellow flower" with "Light and spirit" also suggests a deeper, mysterious dimension, the inner "*logos*" or ordering principle,[16] present in even the most ordinary object. "Light" is associated with the yellow color of the flower, but also with the property that makes vision possible, literally and figuratively, while "spirit" carries connotations of an animating principle, of vitality, and of a hidden transcendent dimension. So there is clearly more than meets the eye (or ear) here. Evidently, then, the poem is not merely about what is perceived but about the act of perception, on various levels, and implicitly about the one perceiving, even though he never draws attention to himself.[17] For in order to make this apparently simple statement, the speaker has to have been able to "hear" the flower's song, through which its identity with light and spirit is revealed, which he could do only by refusing to objectify the flower, to analyze it. Renouncing a perspective that would place himself as subject, as organizing consciousness, at the center of the scene, he has in effect become the "nobody" the song is "for." The flower can be described as "by itself," even though the speaker is present, because the speaker is not functioning as another distinct "self": in becoming "nobody" he has by an intuitive identification "become" the flower as well, and so participates in that light and spirit that he finds in the flower and its song. His self-effacement is the prerequisite for an awareness of what is truly happening. There is an implicit congruence between observer and observed, a "contemplative" awareness that transcends the distinction between subject and object, "a kind of knowledge by identification, an intersubjective knowledge, a communion in cosmic awareness and in nature, ... communion between subject and object, man and nature, upon which wisdom depends."[18]

In this context, it is perhaps significant also that the song is for "nobody" rather than "no one"—an indication that such perception cannot be reached through the bodily senses. The physical body is transcended without being negated: the original description of the "yellow flower" is material, sensuous, and this dimension is not cancelled out but deepened by "Light and spirit." There is therefore a valid but not absolute role for the senses. This becomes more evident in the reworked version of the same sentence that follows as the second stanza:

> A golden spirit
> (Light and emptiness)
> Sings without a word
> By itself. (ll. 5-8)

"A yellow flower" has now become "A golden spirit"—the suprasensual has moved from parenthetic appositive to subject; the deeper perception has now become part of the syntactic framework. The new adjective "golden" can be read both literally, as a synonym for "yellow," thus retaining a sensuous aspect of the flower, and figuratively, as "precious, valuable," and so an apt descriptor for "spirit." The main focus has thus shifted to the non-visible dimension, without excluding or eliminating the visible. In the parenthesis, "emptiness" is now paired with "light" in place of "spirit"; there might seem to be an implicit contrast between the two terms—"emptiness" could be more readily linked with "darkness" than "light," but in this context "emptiness" suggests the complete absence of any objects that would block the light, the void of absolute limitlessness, empty of all distinctions, empty of self, empty of desire—the "kenosis" of the Philippians hymn (2:5-11), the "sunyata" of the Buddhists that negates all dualities, even the distinction between subject and object; so that here both positive and negative terms point to the same ultimate reality beyond positive and negative. Thus this stanza deepens the perception, or at any rate the articulation, of the mystery: "spirit" is both "Light and emptiness," and because the flower is spirit, it too is emptiness as well as light.

The second pair of lines contains both a reordering and rephrasing of the comparable lines in the opening stanza. "For nobody" is replaced by "without a word" and "By itself" is moved (by itself!) into the fourth line. "Sings without a word" is of course literally accurate—the flower/spirit does not actually speak, but the deeper point is that the "song" transcends both the senses (no sound) and the reason (no speech). What is sung is not something to be comprehended, grasped by conceptual thought; to be aware of this "singing" is to have an intuitive identification with pure light and emptiness beyond words and ideas. No information is being communicated; rather, an experience of spirit, light, emptiness is being manifested, but for no ulterior motive, no purpose extrinsic to the act itself, which is its own end, its own fulfillment. Therefore the spirit sings "By itself"—not only alone but by a power that is intrinsic to itself, in the depths of its own ground. In its receptivity to this song, the speaker's own deepest self participates, without self-consciousness, in this same light and emptiness

The third stanza alters the pattern of the poem in both form and syntax, replacing the quatrains of the first two stanzas with a tercet (found as well in the two final stanzas) and shifting from declarative to imperative:

> Let no one touch this gentle sun
> In whose dark eye
> Someone is awake. (ll. 9-11)

The command not to touch (which may recall the *"noli me tangere"* of the risen Christ to Mary Magdalene in John 20:17) is a warning not to reduce the flower to the level of sense, to a merely material object to be grasped by the hand. Such physical contact results from a dualist mentality, an awareness of separation and an effort to overcome it in a sensual manner; it is also a possible preliminary to plucking the flower, acting on the desire to possess, to control (and ultimately to destroy) the object, antithetical to the speaker's response that lets the flower be—lets it be itself, and so more than itself, a sun, a source of light, of illumination, a "gentle sun" that does not burn.

The "sun" with its dark eye, on the level of the senses, identifies the flower as a black-eyed susan (a variety of daisy—or "day's eye") or perhaps as a sunflower, but the paradox (analogous to the dark spot at the center of the light in the Taoist yin-yang symbol) suggests the same non-logical, supra-rational unity as "light" and "emptiness"—but now with light (sun) and darkness (eye) brought together in a single reality beyond the duality of light and dark. The dark is at the center of the light, and as "eye" is a receptor of light. The eye is dark not because it is closed, since "Someone is awake" in the eye, at the center of the flower. The appearance of "Someone" at this point in the poem may seem disconcerting, inconsistent with the transcending of finite, limited identity, of distinctions between subject and object, basic to the two previous stanzas. But being "in the eye," this "Someone" can refer simultaneously to the one who sees and the one who is seen—in an implicit reversal of roles, both to the flower and to the observer/observed of the flower; and thus to a mysterious reality that both inheres in and transcends distinct identities of particular beings: it is ultimately an unrestricted Someone, a Someone present within the depths of everything and everyone, a divine and divinizing Someone, for the "*logoi* of things are in the *Logos*," the Word; "they are created in the *Logos*. The *logoi* of things are then the *Logos* in things,"[19] which can be recognized only through the "*logos* of a man, ...something hidden in him, spiritual, simple, profound, unitive, loving, self-less, self-forgetting, oriented to love and to unity with God" and with all God's creation.[20] Whereas toucher and touched represent duality, seer and seen (interchangeable roles reinforcing aware-ness of the correspondence between nature and spirit) represent union and participation in a reality that is somehow personal yet not limited or exclusive, a "Someone" that is inseparable from the "nobody" for whom the flower's song is sung, a Presence at the heart of all that is, not a being among other beings but the source and end of all being.

To insure that this "Someone" is not reductively identified with some empirical, finite reality, flower as only flower, human as only human, the tercet that follows, enclosed in parentheses as a kind of "aside" set apart from the main movement of the poem, contains an immediate and radical rejection of any kind of clinging to limited images and concepts, even those already used:

> No light, no gold, no name, no color
> And no thought:
> O, wide awake!) (ll. 12-14)

This constitutes a rejection not of the previous lines, but of an inadequate and misleading interpretation of these lines. Here is a radically apophatic embrace of void, of emptiness: the first pair specifically negates "light" (ll. 2, 6) and "gold" (l. 5); the second, more general pairing broadens to reject "name" (i.e. any definitive image: e.g. "flower," "sun," "spirit") and "color"—any and all particular characteristics, "accidents"; finally, "no thought"— no concepts, no ideas. All this must be stripped away in order to have a direct, unmediated encounter with reality. At this point "Someone" disappears (as a concept), the verbs disappear—only "wide awake" is left—no object, no subject, just pure consciousness, pure act—an enlightened "state" that is no state. To be *wide* awake is to transcend the narrowness of the partial and embrace the whole—at once infinite—limitless—emptiness and absolute fullness: the "*todo y nada*" of St. John of the Cross.[21]

Yet in the final tercet the images return, and the pattern of the first two stanzas recurs—though not precisely:

> A golden heaven
> Sings by itself
> A song to nobody. (ll. 15-17)

In particular, "gold" ("color") returns, and a new "name" appears: "heaven." Yet this is not a falling back into discrimination, a failure to sustain the emptiness/sunyata/kenosis of lines 12-14. Rather it is a recognition that once this insight, this awareness, has been received and experienced, images can again be safely employed without danger of misinterpretation. There is no need now for parenthetical descriptors because the "golden heaven" is the infinite reality that encompasses and transcends flower, spirit, sun— particularly the sun (on one level) and the spirit (on another). For a heaven to sing "by itself" thus clarifies the universality already implicit in the flower/spirit singing by itself: the flower's song is its own unique participation in the one song of the entire cosmos, the "golden heaven," which sings "A song to nobody" because there is nobody who is merely and exclusively the hearer of the song. Nothing and "nobody" is excluded from participating in the song of heaven "itself," understood as "Light and spirit," as "Light and emptiness"—a cosmic and supracosmic reality (with perhaps a suggestion of the music of the spheres in this context) to be identified with "Somebody" as well, with the One through whom and for whom the song of creation is ultimately sung. There is no listener who is not also a singer, for by letting go of a separate identity, by becoming "nobody," "no-self," one becomes "wide awake," aware of the song of "golden heaven" which only "nobody" can perceive, and joins this singing and this song. This is what has happened to the speaker, and what is offered as well to the reader. Only a radical simplicity that renounces the illusory autonomy of a self-sufficient identity can "hear" the song, can "resonate" with it, can in fact "sing" it, which is not only what the flower is described as doing but what the speaker himself is doing, and inviting the reader to do, in the very poem that is being read, itself, as its title indicates, a "Song for Nobody."

* * * * * * *

While the spiritual identification of the speaker with the natural world represented by the flower in "A Song for Nobody" is integral to the poem's meaning, it remains implicit. In "O Sweet Irrational Worship,"[22] probably written in mid-1962,[23] the nature and significance of such an identification becomes a problematic issue that resists a facile resolution. Only in the course of the poem's dialectical development does the unique human contribution to the hymn of creation, the "sweet irrational worship" of the title, come to be recognized by the speaker and revealed to the reader.

The poem opens simply with the naming of three natural objects, presented without any interpretation or description or subjective frame, without a verb—in their "suchness" as the Buddhists would say:

> Wind and a bobwhite
> And the afternoon sun. (ll. 1-2)

The "fulcrum" of the poem comes between these two lines and the rest of the poem, in which the speaker identifies with what he sees by the surrender of the discriminating ego:

> By ceasing to question the sun
> I have become light,[24]
> Bird and wind. (ll. 3-5)

This identification is made possible by transcending the gap that a question would imply. What the particular question might be is not the point—it represents a desire for knowledge that is an accumulation of data, of pieces of information, an analytic approach to life that privileges investigation over identification, observation over participation.[25] Letting go of questions allows one to "become" the light, to share in the being and activity of nature "from within" in a non-dualistic way.[26] The sense of oneness expands from the sun to the other two objects, bird and wind, and beyond, to objects not previously mentioned: "My leaves sing" (l. 6). Here the speaker is not merely one with a tree but with the tree's activity, described in a non-literal way: leaves can be said to "sing" as the wind blows through them, and so to echo, or harmonize with, the bird—thus uniting the various phenomena into a single continuum. (This act of singing, which recalls "A Song for Nobody," also foreshadows the theme of worship that will be the focus of the last part of the poem.)

In the line that follows, "I am earth, earth" (l. 7) (a refrain that will subsequently recur twice), identification is made not just with discrete objects but with their common ground, complementing the identification with light and incorporating the identification with all that grows from the earth, and so acknowledging both unity and multiplicity. "All these lighted things / Grow from my heart" (ll. 8-9),[27] he continues: their true significance is illuminated by this way of experiencing them, lit up by an enlightened perception; such a perception is intrinsically linked to the heart, to love, which makes identification possible.

At this point some problematic implications of this surrender of a separate identity become apparent:

> A tall, spare pine
> Stands like the initial of my first
> Name when I had one. (ll. 10-12)

These lines, which bring the first section of the poem to a conclusion, initially appear to describe the culmination of the speaker's self-renunciation and identification with nature, but implicitly signal a crisis in that identification. While the pine also grows from the earth/heart, the speaker does not say "I become the pine" as he has with the light, bird, wind and earth. Rather, awareness of the tree's shape (presumably resembling the letter "T") breaks into the experience of ecstatic, unselfconscious oneness of the previous lines to confront the speaker with an intrusive reminder of the distinct identity represented by his name;[28] even as he claims to have left behind that name, that limited identity, he finds it mirrored in the very landscape that has represented wholeness. In fact, however, the experience of unity he has described has not been of an undifferentiated mass, but of light, bird, wind, tree, earth, both many and one. The resemblance of the pine to the initial calls into question the nature of authentic self-renunciation: by "becoming" light and earth and the rest, which remain themselves even as they participate in a larger unity, does he cease to be himself? The subsequent lines,[29] expanding the temporal reference in line 12 in a series of parallel clauses, suggest the answer must not be a reductive or simplistic one:

> When I had a spirit,
> When I was on fire
> When this valley was
> Made out of fresh air
> You spoke my name
> In naming Your silence:
> O sweet, irrational worship![30] (ll. 13-19)

The first two clauses seem particularly ambiguous. The first echoes the phrasing of the preceding lines, placing "a spirit" in parallel to "my first / Name" but the implications are quite different: to have a spirit is not to be limited to a narrowly circumscribed social identity represented by a name—quite the contrary. If its connotations are to be taken negatively, as seems to be intended, at least initially, by the speaker, it must be as referring to a time when spirit and matter were experienced as separate, when spirit was something "I had" rather than an intrinsic dimension of one's identity. The following clause leaves the meaning of "fire" unexplained: it could refer to being aflame with love, human or divine, but in the context it is perhaps more likely to indicate a time when the speaker was dominated by ardent passions, a time when his primary identity was as a sinner, a deeper form of alienation than simply a dualistic division of body and spirit. In both these periods, which might well overlap but are probably not to be regarded as coterminous, one's "name" might be considered as representing a superficial, constricted sense of self. But the final temporal clause moves back beyond the recent past of personal experience to the primordial time when "this valley" now alive with light, bird, wind and trees was called into being by the Creator. In this context, reminiscent of paradise, and retroactively in the two clauses that precede it as well, which reflect the ambiguities of post-lapsarian existence, "my name" is perceived, in what turns out to be the words of a prayer, not as limitation or as artificial social identity but rather as divine gift. Not only at crucial stages in the speaker's own life, however they may be understood, but from the foundation of the world this divine act of naming has been taking place. Such a perspective seems completely incompatible with that of the preceding section, when he has apparently left his name behind, but the name spoken by God, one's authentic name, has an ontological, not merely a social dimension. While he no longer has a name in so far as, in a fallen, fragmented world, this represents a distinctive ego that objectifies the rest of reality, from a more transcendent perspective to be named by God is to be called into being and sustained in being and brought to deeper levels of being. Thus these lines significantly qualify, or rather clarify, the sense of the loss of self described earlier in the poem—it is not merely an undifferentiated merging of his identity with that of the objects he experiences, but a unity-in-distinction characteristic of Christian ontology. The name that is surrendered on one level is recovered on a deeper level where it does not conflict with the renunciation of duality that marks the first part of the poem.

But something even more mysterious is going on here, for it is "In naming Your silence" that "You spoke my name." His name, and by implication every name, is somehow an articulation of the infinite silence of God. Whereas in the first twelve lines the focus had been on the fundamental unity of all created reality, in these central lines another, infinitely deeper level of identification opens up. The lighted things arise not only from earth but from the divine silence, the ultimate source of both individual and universal being. Insofar as a name represents personal identity, then, there seem to be three aspects to it: if it is held on to as a way of elevating oneself above the rest of creation it is to be surrendered; as spoken by God it is to be accepted as gift; as it is the name of God's own silence it is to be recognized as sacred, an opening into the abyss of divine life, the word that is within the Word, the Logos that comes forth from silence, as Ignatius of Antioch describes the generation of the Son.[31] So these lines undermine an absolutist reading of line 12 as denoting a loss of all ontological distinction between observer and observed. Union with creation does not entail a loss of self on every level, even as union with God does not entail such a loss. Just as the pine rooted in and emerging from the earth is both one with and distinct from its ground, so the name rooted in and emerging from the divine silence is both one with and distinct from its ground: distinction is not equivalent to separation; rather separation means extinction.

One more question emerges from this central section of the poem, and that is how the final line relates to what has preceded it. Despite the colon at the end of line 18, "O sweet, irrational worship!" does not summarize what has just preceded it. Rather, having come to terms with the question of his own identity in the context of his relationship with God and with the rest of creation, the speaker experiences an unexpected epiphany—a sudden awareness of a further dimension of identification with the natural world that clarifies his own human role as "purely and simply *part of nature,* …the part which recognizes God."[32] What is this "irrational" worship? It is not the prayer he himself has just spoken, the acknowledgement of the divine source of his name; rather it describes the mode of worship of the rest of creation, the non-rational world. At this point, then, there is an insight that union with light, bird, wind, etc. is not merely an experience of unity of being but of that being oriented toward its source. To identify with the earth, with all creatures, is to recognize and participate in this spontaneous, non-rational, non-verbal adoration, the "liturgy" of natural life that worships God by being what it is, as memorably expressed in the early pages of *New Seeds of Contemplation*: "each particular being, in its individuality, its concrete nature and entity, with all its own characteristics and its private qualities and its own inviolable identity, gives glory to God by being precisely what He wants it to be here and now."[33] The culminating paradox of this central section of the poem is that the acknowledgement of his own name being spoken by God, thereby in some sense setting him apart from nature, makes possible the recognition of the worship that is taking place. His role is not to deny or reject his human distinctiveness but to bring it with him into this oneness. The relinquishing of the "discriminating intellect" is not a rejection of the divine act of calling him into being by speaking his unique name. The fact that this name was spoken at the moment of the valley's creation means that he has a particular role to play in creation's worship of the Creator. The perspective of the first 12 lines is therefore necessary but not sufficient—the prayer of lines 13-19 leads to the deeper perception that will be articulated in the final twelve lines, which balance out the first twelve like the two wings of a triptych.

Thus when he repeats "I am earth, earth" (l. 20) to begin this last section of the poem it is a repetition that recurs on a more profound level, as the following seven-line section makes clear:

My heart's love
Bursts with hay and flowers.

> I am a lake of blue air
> In which my own appointed place
> Field and valley
> Stand reflected.[34] (ll. 21-26)

The first pair of lines is a more dynamic restatement of lines 8-9, as the passive "grow from my heart" becomes the energetic "My heart's love / Bursts" and "these lighted things" are specified as "hay and flowers," a complementary pair of the useful and the beautiful. Identification with earth is now balanced by identification with the "lake of blue air," the first element complemented by both the figurative water and the literal air—the "fresh air" out of which the valley was created, analogous to his own consciousness in which the scene is reflected. The key phrase here is "my own appointed place," reflecting a sense of belonging to this particular field and valley—not in an exclusive, reductive way, but as an expression of the speaker's sacramental awareness of being responsive to and responsible for a specific locale filled with particular beings, rather than some vague generality. The "appointment" was already made at the moment of the valley's creation, which was also the moment of his own naming, so that identity and vocation are intrinsically bound up with one another.

The final repetition of the refrain "I am earth, earth" (l. 27) leads into the two couplets that conclude the poem:

> Out of my grass heart
> Rises the bobwhite.
> Out of my nameless weeds
> His foolish worship.[35] (ll. 28-31)

The first pair of lines essentially recapitulates the kind of identity found in the first 12-line section of the poem. The bobwhite[36] was already one of "these lighted things" that grow from his heart—here described as "my grass heart," the field that is his appointed place. Again his love for the landscape makes him experience it not as a detached observer but as its very ground. The final couplet, syntactically parallel to the previous two lines and sharing with them the verb "Rises," goes beyond them by focusing on the added dimension first recognized in line 19. The bird's "foolish" (i.e. "irrational": non-practical, useless, meaningless from the perspective of a reductive materialism) worship rises from the speaker's "nameless weeds," grasses apparently too insignificant to have a name.

But what comes forth is worship—the bird's song or the bird itself, or both. This worship is not merely observed by the speaker but through the deep love that unites him to the scene it comes forth in some sense from himself. He experiences it intuitively, with the bird. Nevertheless he can and does name it, as the bird cannot. This is what he has been appointed for—to participate in the worship of the creature but to articulate it as well, to make it manifest, to call it by its true name. He participates in a rational way in the ir-rational worship—that is, he retains his unique human role even as he identifies with non-human creation. He can say, as the bird cannot, that this is indeed worship, that it is directed to the Creator. He both shares the immediacy, the spontaneity of the worship that arises from his "nameless weeds"—from himself as one with the natural world (and therefore on that level nameless), and reflects on what it is—the distinctive human contribution of articulating is thus ultimately recognized as not only compatible with this identification beyond subject and object but as both enhanced by it—he has a much deeper awareness of what is happening than an objective observer would—and enhancing it—he can do more than the creation apart from human consciousness is able to do: perceive and explain the most profound significance of what is happening. It is a kind of "naming," a participation in the divine act, that is the vocation here—the vocation of the contemplative and the poet, who operates not on the plane of analytic knowledge but on the plane of wisdom, of participatory awareness, for only wisdom can recognize and name the sweet, irrational worship of the whole creation because only wisdom both takes part in this worship and in so doing articulates its true meaning: "the transfig-ured, spiritualized and divinized cosmos ...speaks through him, and through him utters its praise of the Creator."[37]

* * * * * * *

In "Night-Flowering Cactus,"[38] possibly one of the last poems written before the publication of *Emblems of a Season of Fury*,[39] the voice of the poet himself disappears altogether, or rather is able imaginatively to identify completely with the voice of the plant, the cactus of the title. It is as though, having confronted and resolved the issues relating to the human role in articulating the "sweet irrational worship" of the natural world, the poet can now allow nature to speak as it were directly through him. Conversely, as a desert plant that blooms briefly and unexpectedly in the dark, the cactus reveals itself as a vividly apt, multivalent symbol for contemplation. In itself it is a kind of sacrament, an embodied sign (emblem) both of self-transcending created being and of divine self-donation; in relation to its audience it is also a sign of con-tradiction, voicing a prophetic critique of the customary human failure to recognize the epiphany of divine love in creation and to appropriate it, to participate in it in one's own life, and ultimately a sign of hope, finally allowing for the possibility of being attentive to and transformed by such experience.

The opening lines of the poem have a tone both assured and enigmatic:

> I know my time, which is obscure, silent and brief
> For I am present without warning one night only.[40] (ll. 1-2)

The assonance of "time," "silent" and "night" gives these words particular prominence, while that of "know" and "only" at the opening and close of the couplet provides a further formal element of unity of the two lines. Here the specific detail of the second line, while providing some clarification for the mysterious declaration of the first, serves only to deepen and sharpen the sense of mystery: "my time" is to be understood as involving a heightened mode of presence, a fullness of being-there, that is evidently not to be equated with ordinary occasions—not *chronos,* quantitative "clock time," but *kairos,* the unmeasurable point of receptivity and transformation when time is open to eternity. What this means for the speaker is not yet evident, but its readiness to respond, to be present at the proper time, is asserted in the face of the difficulties and implied consequences of being unprepared, since the time is "obscure," occurring at night; "silent," providing no anticipatory notice; and "brief," limited to a single night. One might be remind-ed here of the parable of the wise and foolish virgins (Mt. 25:1-13), used to good effect by Merton in his early poetry,[41] in which the Bridegroom arrives suddenly in the middle of the night—from one perspective the speaker's readiness likens it to the wise virgins, while from another the suddenness of its presence resembles the Bridegroom's arrival, an ambiguity suggesting the dual role of the cactus as symbol both of divine manifestation, which cannot be predicted or calculated, and of creaturely response, which depends on remaining alert and aware, in implicit contrast to those who may easily overlook a "time, which is obscure, silent and brief" and arrives "without warning"—a contrast that will become explicit as the poem develops.

The following line, given its own separate section, presents a metamorphosis that deepens the enigma: "When sun rises on the brass valleys I become serpent" (l. 3).[42] From the perspective of *chronos*, in the "normal" light of everyday existence, the speaker is perceived, metaphorically at least, as a snake, perhaps in reference to the elongated shape of the cactus pads, or the potentially injurious quality of its sharp spines. In any case it is easily regarded as an unattractive and unremarkable, if somewhat dangerous, part of the desert landscape. But the comparison to the serpent signals the possible ambivalence of anyone encountering it: is it to be avoided as a threat, even equated with the tempter of Genesis 3, or might it be in fact the symbol of wisdom to be imitated according to the command of Christ to the disciples in Matthew 10:16? Might the image recall the rod of Aaron, which both is transformed into a serpent (Ex. 7:8-13) and later puts forth blossoms (Nm. 17:16-26)? The reference to "brass valleys" might even call to mind the bronze serpent of Numbers 21:5-9, which healed all who looked upon it, and which in John 3:14-15 is of course compared to the crucified Son of Man by Jesus himself, so that this apparently unattractive shape might actually be an oblique sign of the plant's symbolic power to heal those who can perceive in faith its hidden identity. But at this early stage of the speaker's self-disclosure its serpentine form simply adds to its mysteriousness.

In the lines which follow, the nature of the speaker's special mode of presence is both contrasted with this customary "disguise" and described more specifically:

> Though I show my true self only in the dark and to no man
> (For I appear by day as serpent)
> I belong neither to night nor day.[43] (ll. 4-6)

To be fully present is now equated with being, and showing, one's true self, of course a central term in Merton's spiritual teaching, the "inner self" described near the beginning of *The Inner Experience* as "like a very shy wild animal that never appears at all whenever an alien presence is at hand, and comes out only when all is perfectly peaceful, in silence, …[that] cannot be lured by anyone or anything, because he responds to no lure except that of the divine freedom";[44] it is "the mysterious, invisible self of the Spirit" that entails "a deepening of the new life, a continuous rebirth, in which the exterior and superficial life of the ego-self is discarded like an old snake skin [!]"[45] It is already implied, and will become more evident as the poem continues, that to be one's true self cannot be a private, individualistic experience. Despite the qualifications, the speaker does declare: "I show my true self," and in fact is doing so in the very act of self-revelation that constitutes the poem. But authentic self-disclosure can be made only with great care. Thus the true self appears in the darkness where it cannot be reduced to any neatly defined formula but retains its mystery; yet it does not "belong" to night any more than it does to day, because its identity is a participation in the fullness of being that transcends all categorizations, all dualities. It is revealed "to no man" not in an absolute sense, as the rest of the poem will make clear, but insofar as the other remains other, prone to analyze and objectivize, to profane the mystery, an "alien presence" unwilling to risk the same "continuous rebirth," the same shedding of ego-identity as the speaker. Only the poverty and self-abandonment represented by the darkness and the desert make possible the receptivity to revelation that can perceive this "true self":

> Sun and city never see my deep white bell
> Or know my timeless moment of void:
> There is no reply to my munificence.[46] (ll. 7-9)

Sun and city represent the partial, restricted perspective of rationality and busyness that are incompatible with "my timeless moment of void": an epiphany that identifies the true self as transcending all limitations, a total openness without boundaries, even the boundaries of time and space.[47] The darkness and desert open out into the "timeless moment of void" in a way that the light of day and the crowded city cannot do. The parallelism between "show my true self" and "see my deep white bell" makes evident for the first time, though still in metaphorical terms, that it is the blossoming of the cactus flower, that rare, hidden and brief epiphany, that is to be recognized as the fulfillment of the plant's identity, the full expression of its possibilities. The description of the flower as a "deep white bell" reflects its shape and color, but also suggests a relationship to a bell's purpose to summon, particularly to call to worship, an image that suggests that the speaker's rejection of a reductively instrumental interpretation of its identity is not to be equated with a disregard or disdain for the potential effect on others of its flower's blooming. The final line here suggests that in fact the self-offering of the flower is an act of supreme generosity, but one that evokes no awareness, no response. There is a tragic failure to appreciate or even to be aware of the gift that has been proffered because people prefer to disregard the realms of night and desert as empty, "void" of meaning and life.

In the following section the focus shifts from the failure to recognize and respond to this vision on the part of humanity, to the relation of the flower to its source, both divine and material:

> When I come I lift my sudden Eucharist
> Out of the earth's unfathomable joy
> Clean and total I obey the world's body
> I am intricate and whole, not art but wrought passion
> Excellent deep pleasure of essential waters
> Holiness of form and mineral mirth:[48] (ll. 10-15)

The bloom is now identified not just with bells that call the faithful to prayer and signal the most sacred moments of liturgy, but with the whiteness of the consecrated host itself; while this "transubstantiation" is to be understood analogously rather than literally, the "sudden" apparition of the beautiful flower can indeed be considered an epiphany of Christ the Logos, the source of its being, of its true self, for the "meaning of each natural thing," as Hans Urs von Balthasar interprets St. Maximus the Confessor, "is to be an Incarnation of the divine Word, …to cooperate fully *in the total realization* of the Word in the world."[49] To respond to the flower's revelation is thus to enter into communion with the Word. But the focus here on "lift[ing]" the Eucharist orients it primarily toward the Father in an act of adoration and thanksgiving, the etymological root of the word "Eucharist": the flower offers itself to the Creator in union with, and as a symbol of, the offering of the embodied Word, and of the natural elements from which that body and all earthly reality is made. For it is a manifestation of "earth's unfathomable joy," an expression of all creation rejoicing in its existence, a joy that is incomprehensible and immeasurable, a joy that is always present but recognized only in rare moments. To enact this cosmic liturgy, its own "sweet irrational worship," is to "obey the world's body," to be conformed to and to express its inner dynamism, and so to manifest the true orientation of all that is: the blooming of the cactus flower is a brief unveiling of the true nature of creation; it is joy made visible. This is a glimpse of the world as it was intended to be, "clean and total," a symbol of the unfallen, unfragmented cosmos, "intricate and whole," a simplicity that encompasses and synthesizes complex reality, in which all parts are integral to a single whole. It is "not art," not put together from outside itself, but "wrought passion," realizing the intrinsic dynamism of its own make-up, a passion identified with three dimensions, all aspects of the earth's joy: it is "the pleasure of essential waters," without which no life, even life in the desert, is possible; "mineral mirth," a delight shared by the various natural components taken from the soil that are needed to form the flower; but also "holiness of form," centered between the material elements of water and minerals and complementing them by transforming them into an organized wholeness that is also holiness, a reflection of the beauty of the Creator in the creature.

Yet this is a wholeness that is not static but ecstatic, an infinite desire for the Infinite, the "timeless moment of void," expressed in the separate line that follows, "I am the extreme purity of virginal thirst" (l. 16), which suggests that the passion that went into the flower's making is matched by a passionate desire for the transcendent, for fulfillment in a reality beyond itself. The pleasure of essential waters has not slaked the "purity of virginal thirst" (approximate rhymes that also link up with "mirth" in the previous line). While the cactus is "whole" and "total" in one context, it is also oriented toward a participation in a more all-encompassing wholeness from another. Self-realization does not exclude the drive toward self-transcendence, "virginal" in its purity and innocence as well as in its desire for completion in union with that which is beyond itself, as the Bride of the Song of Songs desires the divine Bridegroom. This is what St. Gregory of Nyssa called *epektasis*, "a desire that is perpetually fulfilled without ever exhausting its object and which therefore goes on in a progress that has no end."[50]

Only at this point, having oriented itself with respect to the earth from which it arises and the heaven to which it aspires, does the plant return for the remaining lines of the poem to its possible connections with the human world, a topic that is gradually developed in the three final sections of the poem. In the first of these, the relationship to others is broached again, but tentatively, obliquely, in passive voice:

> I neither show my truth nor conceal it
> My innocence is descried dimly
> Only by divine gift

As a white cavern without explanation.[51] (ll. 17-20)

The opening line here appears to be inconsistent with what was stated in line 4, which it echoes, but the rephrasing is actually a refusal to be bound by the binary oppositions of dualistic thinking or a utilitarian focus on practical results. The flower is simply called to be what it is, to express the truth of its own being, which is the truth of infinite Being in finite form. How, or whether, others may perceive this truth is beyond its control and thus outside its responsibility. If truth is recognized it is through the working of grace, not as a consequence of its own calculation or purposeful intent. The active "show" is set aside in favor of the passive "is descried," with no explicit mention of an observer, and "my truth" is glossed as "My innocence," another suggestion that what is to be glimpsed in the blossoming of the cactus is the paradisal world of creation as it was meant to be: but it can only be "descried dimly," in the darkness of faith, not as a "truth" that can be neatly defined in clear concepts, and as "a white cavern without explanation," an image of the hidden depths of reality, the abyss of being, that is not accessible to the rational understanding, not to be discovered by a systematic accumulation of discrete details but only through an immediate, intuitive awareness of the whole.

In the penultimate section an attentive, perceptive observer at last appears:

> He who sees my purity
> Dares not speak of it.
> When I open once for all my impeccable bell
> No one questions my silence:
> The all-knowing bird of night flies out of my mouth.[52]
>
> (ll. 21-25)

Just as the plant itself provides no explanation, so one who sees its blossoming is not to profane the experience by trying to reduce it to words, which would be to violate the very purity that constitutes its mysterious revelation. Nor should he question its silence—either pose a question about the silence, asking why there is no explanation; or pose a question to the silence, asking for some explanation. The only proper response is to enter into and participate in the silence, which is an expression of experience beyond the limits of language. Once again the flower is described as a bell, which opens "once for all," a phrase that commonly means "finally and definitively," but also has scriptural resonances, as Paul refers to Christ's death to sin "once for all" (Rom. 6:10), for all time but also for all humanity, so that the opening of the "impeccable bell," like the lifting of the "sudden Eucharist" in line 10, has redemptive overtones; "impeccable,"[53] a term generally connoting perfection, literally means "sinless," and so is properly applied only to Christ or to earth before the fall, in each case suggesting a silent proclamation of the world as it should be, the "purity" of Eden and of the eschaton, creation as an epiphany of the Creator. The final line here suggests that silence is not a failure of speech reflecting a lack of knowledge but a dark knowledge, the fullness of revelation beyond the capacity of words to articulate. The mysterious "bird of night" which had entered the white cavern and fed upon the sweet nectar in its depths now emerges from the flower's "mouth" as "all-knowing"—participating completely in its revelation, itself a kind of embodied "word" witnessing to the truth, and thus an emblem of the Holy Spirit, the Paraclete of whom Christ said, "He will teach you everything…. He will guide you to all truth" (John 15:26, 16:13).

By not speaking and not asking, by waiting in silence, this ultimate revelation of truth may become accessible to the poem's audience as well, which is addressed directly for the first time in the final three lines:

> Have you seen it? Then though my mirth has quickly
>   ended
> You live forever in its echo:
> You will never be the same again.[54] (ll. 26-28)

The "it" about which the speaker inquires here most aptly refers not to the "bird of night" of the previous line but to the cavern out of which the bird flies, the "impeccable bell" which will continue to echo long after the ephemeral bloom, the embodiment of the earth's joy and of its "virginal thirst" for divine fulfillment, has disappeared. Each listener must personally respond to the question the cactus poses. A revelation of infinite beauty in finite form, of eternity in "my time," is not automatic, not to be taken for granted. Like the cactus itself, the budding contemplative must be alert, attentive to the "*kairos*" when God appears "without warning" in unexpected places, whether it be the unlikely beauty of an easily overlooked desert plant or the dark and arid desolation of one's own seemingly unfruitful spirit. But the miracle of this desert epiphany does, in the plant's final words of assurance, serve as an emblem of hope that for those who see with the eyes of faith, such an experience is permanently transformative, and however brief the "timeless moment of void," any such contemplative realization echoes and enters into not just the "mirth" of this world but an "unfathomable joy" that will "live forever."

Endnotes

1. Thomas Merton, *Emblems of a Season of Fury* (New York: New Directions, 1963). For an overview of the volume's contents, see the entry in William H. Shannon, Christine M. Bochen and Patrick F. O'Connell, *The Thomas Merton Encyclopedia* (Maryknoll, NY: Orbis, 2002), 132-35.

2. Thomas Merton, *The Literary Essays of Thomas Merton*, ed. Patrick Hart, OCSO (New York: New Directions, 1981), 345.

3. Merton's publisher James Laughlin refers to the poem in a February 10, 1960 letter to Merton (see Thomas Merton and James Laughlin, *Selected Letters*, ed. David D. Cooper [New York: W. W. Norton, 1997], 151); the poem was first published in *The Catholic Worker* in June 1960.

4. *Emblems*, 51; Thomas Merton, *Collected Poems* (New York: New Directions, 1977), 353; for previous discussions, see: Alan Altany, "Thomas Merton's Poetic Incarnation of Emptiness," *The Merton Annual*, 10 (1997), 124; Michael Higgins, *Heretic Blood: The Spiritual Geography of Thomas Merton* (Toronto: Stoddart, 1998), 255-56; George A. Kilcourse, *Ace of Freedoms: Thomas Merton's Christ* (Notre Dame, IN: University of Notre Dame Press, 1993), 66; Ross Labrie, *The Art of Thomas Merton* (Fort Worth: Texas Christian University Press, 1979), 133; Ross Labrie, *Thomas Merton and the Inclusive Imagination* (Columbia: University of Missouri Press, 2001), 91-92, 242; Bonnie Thurston, "Wrestling with Angels: Some Mature Poems of Thomas Merton," *The Vision of Thomas Merton*, ed. Patrick F. O'Connell (Notre Dame, IN: Ave Maria Press, 2003), 192-94.

5. In three earlier drafts of the poem, now at the University of Kentucky's King Library, these lines constitute a considerably different opening section: "O little forests / Meekly cry alone / Striking the snow" (the first two lines combined into one in the second and third drafts); the image is perhaps intended to recall Moses striking the rock to bring forth water in Exodus 17:1-7 and Numbers 20:2-13 (the latter passage an ambivalent one that might have prompted the change).

6. The earlier drafts read "broken" rather than "covered"—an additional instance of assonance, but an image that is not integrated with the rest of the poem as "covered" is.

7. Thurston helpfully points out that "under their weight of snow, the trees of the forest are bowed down, almost 'forced' to pray ... like human

beings who only 'bend the knee' (pray) when facing crises—personal 'winters'" ("Wrestling," 194).

8. In the first draft this line begins the following section and is thus associated with the fire (initially typed as "Inverted fire" which is x'd out and followed by "Fire turned inward"—transformed into an imperative in second and third drafts).

9. In the first draft "mad place" is typed in following x'd out "wet growth," which is moved to the next line where it remains through successive drafts.

10. In the first draft this line is also addressed to "Silence"; "O peace" appears in the second draft.

11. Thurston suggests a possible pun on "Son" ("Wrestling," 194).

12. See Labrie, *Inclusive Imagination*, 92: "Nature here is portrayed as both emblem and model in its beckoning of the mind to contemplation."

13. *Emblems*, 35-36; *Collected Poems*, 337-38. For previous discussions, see: Altany, 118-19; Higgins, 249-50; Kilcourse, *Ace of Freedoms*, 65; Labrie, *Inclusive Imagination*, 89, 242; Thérèse Lentfoehr, *Words and Silence: On the Poetry of Thomas Merton* (New York: New Directions, 1979), 62-63, 139; Lynn Szabo, "The Sound of Sheer Silence: A Study in the Poetics of Thomas Merton," *The Merton Annual*, 13 (2000), 219-20; Bonnie B. Thurston, "The Light Strikes Home: Notes on the Zen Influence in Merton's Poetry," *Merton & Buddhism: Wisdom, Emptiness & Everyday Mind*, ed. Bonnie Bowman Thurston (Louisville, KY: Fons Vitae, 2007), 206-207.

14. In a journal entry for June 26, 1960, Merton writes: "Sat in the cool woods, bare feet in the wet grass, and my quails whirling near me for my comfort, and wrote a poem about a flower" (Thomas Merton, *Turning Toward the World: The Pivotal Years. Journals, vol. 4: 1960-1963*, ed. Victor A. Kramer [San Francisco: HarperCollins, 1996], 16); the poem was first published in the July 22, 1961 issue of *The Saturday Review*.

15. See for example the journal entry for Pentecost 1960 (June 5), in which he discusses solitude not "as a withdrawal, a refuge: but for the sake of understanding, wisdom, widening necessarily a certain commitment…. Honestly it is a search for perspective—and for commitment. But it is also a symptom of confusion" (*Turning Toward the World*, 8).

16. See Thomas Merton, *An Introduction to Christian Mysticism: Initiation into the Monastic Tradition 3*, ed. Patrick F. O'Connell (Kalamazoo, MI: Cistercian Publications, 2008), 121-35. (These notes are from the text of conferences given by Merton to newly ordained monks in 1961.)

17. Thurston notes that "the speaker …is so much in the background that a 'voice' is hardly discernable" ("Light," 207), which is certainly true, but revealing the reason for that truth is an integral, if implicit, aspect of the poem's thematic development.

18. *Literary Essays*, 108.

19. *Introduction to Christian Mysticism*, 131.

20. *Introduction to Christian Mysticism*, 128.

21. See Thomas Merton, *Mystics and Zen Masters* (New York: Farrar, Straus and Giroux, 1967), 269: "The self is 'void' indeed, but void in the sense of the apophatic mystics like St. John of the Cross, in whom the *nada*, or nothingness of the self that is entirely empty of fictitious images, projects, and desires, becomes the *todo*, the All, in which the freedom of personal love discovers itself in its transcendent Ground and Source which we are accustomed to call the Love of God and which no human name can ever account for or explain."

22. *Emblems*, 42-43; *Collected Poems*, 344-45. For previous discussions, see: Altany, 122-23; Sheila M. Hempstead, "Emblems of Birds: Birds as Symbols of Grace in Three Poems by Thomas Merton," *The Merton Seasonal*, 18.1 (Winter 1993), 23-24; Higgins, 250-53; Kilcourse, *Ace of Freedoms*, 65; Labrie, *Art*, 132-33; Labrie, *Inclusive Imagination*, 34-35; Thurston, "Wrestling with Angels," 196-98; George Woodcock, *Thomas Merton, Monk and Poet* (New York: Farrar, Straus, Giroux, 1978), 141-42.

23. On July 10, 1962, Merton wrote to John Wu: "I also enclose a poem, landscape, especially with a quail in it. The quail, as I seem to remember, is also a bird loved by Chuang Tzu. The quail is called, popularly, 'bobwhite' around here. I thought you might like this" (Thomas Merton, *The Hidden Ground of Love: Letters on Religious Experience and Social Concerns*, ed. William H. Shannon (New York: Farrar, Straus, Giroux, 1985), 623).

24. In an earlier version of the poem, a typescript with autograph alterations entitled "Song 9" (later cancelled) now at the King Library of the University of Kentucky, this line reads "I became light" and is followed by a line space and preceded by the x'd out line "I am made of Him" followed by "this light" also x'd out.

25. In an April 5, 1958 journal entry, Merton writes, "Man can know all about God's creation by examining its phenomena, by dissecting and experimenting and this is all good. But it is misleading, because with this kind of knowledge you *do not really* know the beings you know. You only know *about* them. That is to say you create for yourself a knowledge based on your observations. What you observe is really as much the product of your knowledge as its cause. You take the thing not as it is, but as you want to investigate it. Your investigation is valid, but artificial.... But people who watch birds and animals are already wise in their way. I want not only to observe but to *know* living things, and this implies a dimension of primordial familiarity which is simple and primitive and religious and poor. This is the reality I need, the vestige of God in His creatures. And the Light of God in my own soul.... Do no violence to things, to manipulate them with my ideas—to track them to strip them, to pick something out of them my mind wants to nibble at" (Thomas Merton, *A Search for Solitude:*

Pursuing the Monk's True Life. Journals, vol. 3: 1952-1960, ed. Lawrence S. Cunningham [San Francisco: HarperCollins, 1996], 190).

26. See Merton's description of "connatural" knowing as a "mode of apprehension" that "reaches out to grasp the inner reality, the vital substance of its object, by a kind of affective identification of itself with it" (*Literary Essays*, 347).

27. In the draft, these verses form a single line that reads: "All these things grow out of my heart" (heart *initially cancelled and replaced by* chest *interlined and cancelled, with* heart *then added on line*); two other lines then follow: "Grow out of my imagination [imagination *added in pen following* head *added in pen and cancelled, following cancelled* mind,] / Grow out of my eyes."

28. See the discussion of names in Thomas Merton, *The Inner Experience: Notes on Contemplation*, ed. William H. Shannon (San Francisco: HarperCollins, 2003), 5: "it is better to describe yourself with a name that is yours alone than with a noun that applies to a whole species. For then you are evidently aware of yourself as an individual subject, and not just as an object, or as a nameless unit in a multitude. It is true that for modern man even to be able to call himself by his own proper name is an achievement that evokes wonder both in himself and in others. But this is only a beginning, and a beginning that primitive man would perhaps have been able to laugh at. For when a person appears to know his own name, it is still no guarantee that he is aware of the name as representing a real person. On the contrary, it may be the name of a fictitious character occupied in very active self-impersonation in the world of business, of politics, of scholarship, or of religion. This, however, is not the 'I' who can stand in the presence of God and be aware of Him as a 'Thou.'"

29. It is significant that these lines do not form part of the initial typed text of the poem in the King Library draft but are added in the lower right hand corner of the page and marked with an arrow for insertion at this point.

30. In the draft, ll. 15-16 are originally a single line, subsequently divided into two, concluding "...made out of sun" [sun *cancelled and replaced by* air]; l. 18 originally reads: "In naming Yourself" [self *cancelled and followed by* silence]; two additional lines follow: "So You spoke my silence / "I hear You sing to ourself" (the second of which is cancelled).

31. *Magnesians*, 8; see also *Introduction to Christian Mysticism*, 45: "[For St. Ignatius, the] basic idea {is} of the hidden, transcendent and *silent* Godhead, in Whom is all reality, indeed Who is Himself the Real and the Father. As silence is to speech, so the Father is to the Son. *To hear and possess the silence of the Father* is the real objective of reception of the Word. 'Whoever truly possesses the Word of Jesus can also hear His silence, that he may be perfect, that through his speaking he may act and through his silence be known' (Ephesians, 15). *Christian perfection ...* is penetration into

this silence and this reality of the Word in the Father. He who penetrates to the inner silence of God can himself become a word of God."

32. *Turning Toward the World*, 312 [April 13, 1963]; see the revised version of this passage in *Conjectures of a Guilty Bystander*, which, as Bonnie Thurston points out ("Wrestling," 189), is central to what she calls Merton's "mature" poetic vision of the natural world: "How absolutely central is the truth that we are first of all *part of nature*, though we are a very special part, that which is conscious of God. In solitude, one is entirely surrounded by beings which perfectly obey God. This leaves only one place open for me, and if I occupy that place then I, too, am fulfilling His will. The place nature 'leaves open' belongs to the conscious one, the one who is aware, who sees all this as a unity, who offers it all to God in praise, joy, thanks" (Thomas Merton, *Conjectures of a Guilty Bystander* [Garden City, NY: Doubleday, 1966], 268-69).

33. Thomas Merton, *New Seeds of Contemplation* (New York: New Directions, 1961), 30.

34. In the earlier draft, the first line of this section is followed by a pair of lines that originally read: "Is a whole wet land under the sun / Deep as the summer hay"': "under the sun" is replaced first by "of grass and corn crops" with the two last words then replaced by "flowers"; "hay" is cancelled and replaced by "sky"—the original final word in the following line, which is cancelled and replaced by "air"; "appointed place" in the next line is added on line to replace "home fields".

35. In the draft version of the final couplet, "nameless weeds" replaces the cancelled "grass lake", and the final line reads "The golden heaven." replacing the cancelled "The [*illegible*] sun."

36. In a journal entry for December 13, 1958, Merton had identified the bobwhite as "my totem bird" (*Search for Solitude*, 238).

37. Thomas Merton, *Disputed Questions* (New York: Farrar, Straus and Cudahy, 1960), 20-21.

38. *Emblems*, 49-50; *Collected Poems*, 351-52. For previous discussions, see: Altany, 123; Kilcourse, *Ace of Freedoms*, 74-75; George Kilcourse, "'Pieces of the Mosaic, Earth': Thomas Merton and the Christ," *The Message of Thomas Merton*, ed. Brother Patrick Hart, CS 42 (Kalamazoo, MI: Cistercian Publications, 1981), 149; Labrie, *Inclusive Imagination*, 108-109, 161-62; Lentfoehr, 60-61; Szabo, 220-21; Thurston, "Wrestling with Angels," 195-96; Robert Waldron, *Poetry as Prayer: Thomas Merton* (Boston: Pauline, 2000), 111-31; Woodcock, 142.

39. Merton sent the poem to his friend Robert Lax early in July, 1963; Lax writes enthusiastically about it in a letter from Patmos on July 27 (Thomas Merton and Robert Lax, *When Prophecy Still Had a Voice: The Letters of Thomas Merton & Robert Lax*, ed. Arthur W. Biddle [Lexington: University Press of Kentucky, 2001], 248); it is of course possible that the poem

had been written a considerable time before and only now forwarded to Lax along with other pieces from *Emblems* not previously sent, though Merton generally passed on new works to Lax fairly quickly. Merton had already written in a journal entry for March 4, 1963 that New Directions "is now getting ready to publish" the volume (*Turning Toward the World*, 300), and receives the first copy on November 16 (Thomas Merton, *Dancing in the Water of Life: Seeking Peace in the Hermitage. Journals, vol. 5: 1963-1965,* ed. Robert E. Daggy [San Francisco: HarperCollins, 1997], 35).

40. There are two holograph drafts of the poem in the collection at the King Library of the University of Kentucky, the first untitled and heavily revised, along with a typed draft with autograph corrections. The opening sentence in the first version, after some cancelled false starts, reads: "I take my time but it is very short and I am / present without warning [*followed by cancelled* only] in one night only / and when day dawns I am gone." In the second draft the first two lines read: "I know [*interlined above cancelled* take] my time. It is obscure silent [*interlined with a caret*] + short / I am present without warning one night only." The typescript is identical to the printed text.

41. See for example "The Trappist Abbey: Matins," ll. 10-17, from his earliest published collection, *Thirty Poems* (Norfolk, CT: New Directions, 1944); *Collected Poems*, 46.

42. This line is not found in either of the holograph drafts, the second of which reads for this line: "When sun rises on the hot [*interlined above cancelled* dry world] valley [*interlined below followed by cancelled* dry stones] I am gone".

43. These lines in the first holograph draft read (after cancelled lines and fragments): "Though I show in the Dark I belong / Neither to night or day." The next draft includes an additional line, which provides a parallel set of alternatives related to the newly added second element of the initial line (which is retained in the final version although the added line is not): "Though I show myself only in the dark and to no man [*preceded by cancelled* one] / I belong neither to night or day / Neither [*added in left margin*] To [*followed by cancelled* wilderness or to man] man nor to wilderness."

44. *Inner Experience*, 5.

45. Thomas Merton, *Love and Living*, ed. Naomi Burton Stone and Brother Patrick Hart (New York: Farrar, Straus, Giroux, 1979), 199.

46. The earlier holograph reads: "Suns shall never see [*interlined above cancelled* The sun has never seen] my timelessness. / I am the void / There is no reply to my munificence" [*preceded by cancelled* majest]; further down the page, marked with an arrow for insertion between first and second lines here, are lines not included in the final version of the poem: "Speak! Speak! you have a blind minute / [*followed by cancelled line* In which you

recognize yourself in *followed by*] In which to utter [*interlined above cancelled* find] yourself / In my presence! / But [*added in left margin*] If you lie you will drop dead!" At least the first line of this material, and perhaps all of it, is marked with an arrow for insertion before the lines "Though I show ... / ...or day." The second holograph draft is identical to the final text, except that "or know" is added in the second line before "My" and the third line is divided in two after "reply".

47. See Merton's description of "The Zen intuition ...of the metaphysical ground of all being and knowledge as void. This void itself is infinite.... The infinite emptiness is then infinite totality and fullness.... [P]ure void is pure Being" (*Mystics and Zen Masters*, 39). This is "the great 'emptiness' of *Sunyata* which is described as emptiness only because, being completely without any limit of particularity it is also perfect fullness" (Thomas Merton, *Zen and the Birds of Appetite* [New York: New Directions, 1968], 85).

48. In the earlier holograph these lines read: "I am the eucharist [*followed by cancelled* of earth] hid in the earth's heart / Obeying the world's body. [*followed by cancelled* The huge] our [*interlined above cancelled* vir] virginal star / The [*preceded by cancelled* I am the mother's passion] extreme purity of [*followed by cancelled* mother *followed by cancelled* earth *followed by cancelled* life *followed by*] birth [*followed by cancelled line* I am the passion + sanctity of rain] / I am the passion of clean waters [*interlined below cancelled illegible word*] and the sanctity of rain". The second holograph draft reads: "When I come I show [*preceded by cancelled* bring *preceded by cancelled* bear] / My [*added in left margin before cancelled* A *followed by cancelled illegible word*] sudden Eucharist out of the earth's [*preceded by cancelled* dry] unfathomable [*interlined above cancelled* heart] passion / Obeying the world's body I am [*followed by cancelled* aware] all form / Perfection [*followed by cancelled* totality of for *followed by cancelled* I am all form in myself *followed by*] Deep pleasure of essential waters [*followed on new line by cancelled* A cosmic Earth + heaven Passion of the day of and in earth] / Sanctity, of dark + [of dark + *interlined above cancelled* born of] mineral mirth [*preceded by cancelled* dearth] / I am the extreme purity of virginal [*interlined above cancelled* mother] thirst [*followed by cancelled line* Reward, inscrutability, the one flower]. In the typescript, "lift" is added in the left margin to replace cancelled "show"; "joy" is added on line following cancelled "passion"; "Excellent" is added in left margin before cancelled "Perfection"; "form +" is added in left margin and marked for insertion to replace cancelled "dark and" with "formal" interlined below and cancelled.

49. Hans Urs von Balthasar, *Liturgie Cosmique: Maxime le Confesseur* (Paris: Aubier, 1947), 224, translated by Merton in *Introduction to Christian Mysticism*, 127.

50. Jean Daniélou, SJ, "Contemplation chez les Orientaux Chrétiens: III. La Contemplation de Dieu: D. Mystique de la Ténèbre chez Grégoire de Nysse," *Dictionnaire de Spiritualité*, vol. II, col. 1884, translated by Merton in *Introduction to Christian Mysticism*, 82.

51. The earlier holograph reads: "I am descried dimly [*followed by cancelled line* A cosmos {*interlined above cancelled* world} without explan] / Only in gift / a cosmos without evident purpose [evident purpose *interlined above cancelled* explanation] / a white cavern without explanation". The second holograph reads: "I neither show my face [show my face *interlined above cancelled* utter my name] / Nor conceal it [*two lines written in right margin and marked for insertion*] / I am descried dimly, by divine gift [*followed by cancelled* By In unbelievable I do not / And and by Only by divine gift] / As [*added in left margin*] A [*followed by cancelled* cosmos without purpose] white cavern without explanation."

52. The earlier holograph draft of these lines reads: "When [*preceded by cancelled lines* The all-knowing night I come and open the / I open my mouth for] I lay open the full perfection of my silence / I am completely gone [*followed by cancelled line* All knowing night is a bird] / The [*preceded by interlined and cancelled* When] all knowing bird of night flies out of my mouth:" The revised holograph reads: "He [*preceded by cancelled line* Speak Spe you dare not] who comes to my presence / Dares not speak. He who questions [*interlined above cancelled* names] my innocence / Sins [*added in left margin before cancelled* Lies], or [*followed by cancelled* perhaps even drops dead] is struck dead / When [*added in left margin before cancelled* But] I open one [*sic*] for all my [*interlined above cancelled* the fullness] bell full [*interlined with a caret*] of silence [*followed by cancelled line* I am {*added in left margin and cancelled*} And when the all] / The all-knowing bird of night flies out of my mouth".

53. In the draft typescript, "impeccable" is preceded by x'd out "big perfect bell".

54. The concluding lines of the earlier holograph read: "After [*preceded by cancelled* And I] that I [*followed by cancelled* cannot] am not found; / For I [*followed by cancelled* and] am never again absent." The revised holograph draft reads: "Have you seen it? Then [*preceded by cancelled* You] though I have gone / You can [*altered from* cannot *interlined below cancelled* will never] never [*interlined below*] be the same man [*interlined below and marked for insertion*] again." In the draft typescript, "quickly ended" is added on line after cancelled "dissapeared" [*sic*].

The Myth of the Fall from Paradise:
Thomas Merton and Walker Percy

John P. Collins

Introduction

"A starship from earth is traveling in the galaxy, its mission to establish communication with extraterrestrial intelligences and civilizations." This is the opening line from Walker Percy's Chapter 19 in his book titled *Lost in the Cosmos, The Last Self-Help Book.* Percy goes on to say that: "The time is the year 2050 C.E. (Common Era, so called because, though the era is post-Christian, it proved useful to retain the year of Christ's birth)." Eventually "excited earthlings" in the space ship establish communication with the inhabitants of the planet, Proxima Centauri or PC3, and both communicants agree upon a lexicon and syntax. The earth ship and PC3 work many weeks to develop successful communication and eventually the earth ship asks for permission to land. The following are excerpts from their two way communication:

Earthship: [We] [r]equest permission to land....
PC3: Not quite yet. You haven't answered our question about C[consciousness]–type.
Earthship:What do you mean by type of consciousness?
PC3: We are C1s. We wanted to know whether you are C1s or C2s or C3s.
Earthship: What is a C1?....
PC3: A C1 consciousness is a first-order consciousness, or what you would call a preternatural consciousness—according to the dictionary your computer transmitted.
Earthship: It is? Say again. Preternatural?

After a description of this Edenic or unfallen state there is a dialogue about the C 2 and C3 state of consciousness:

Earthship: What is a C2 consciousness?
PC3: A C2 consciousness is a consciousness which passes through a C1 stage and then for some reason falls into the pit of itself.
Earthship: The pit of itself?

PC3: In some evolving civilizations, for reasons which we don't entirely understand, the evolution of consciousness is attended by a disaster of some sort.... It has to do with the discovery of self and the incapacity to deal with it, the consciousness becoming self- conscious but not knowing what to do with the self, not even knowing what its self is, and so ending by being that which it is not, saying that which is not, doing that which is not, and making others what they are not.

Earthship: What does that mean?

PC3: Playing roles, being phony, lying, cheating, stealing and killing. To say nothing of exotic disordering of the reproductive apparatus of sexual creatures.... What concerns us is our experience with C2s whom we have allowed to land on PC3. They are usually polite at first, but always turn hostile [and] deceptive.... They are mainly concerned with self-esteem.

We are afraid of C2s. They do not know themselves or what to do with themselves. . . . What's your C-type? Are you C1, C2, or C3? You will not be given permission to descend until we establish that.

Earthship:(*after a pause*): What's a C3 consciousness?

PC3: A C3 consciousness is a C2 consciousness which has become aware of its predicament, sought help, and received it.... If a C1 meets with disaster, falls into the pit of itself, and becomes a C2, it must become aware of its sickness and seek a remedy in order to be restored to the preternaturality of C1.

The PC3 people go on to ask the Earthship inhabitants a series of questions about the planet Earth to determine its C status—1, 2, or 3. One question was about wars in the last hundred earth-years. The earth ship responds that there have been about a hundred million people killed in wars. After a series of other questions and answers PC3 replies:

"...your species is in trouble. You don't even know whether you have a civilization, and the chances are you do not." Then PC3 asks the earthlings if they have sought help for their debased condition. The earthlings reply in the negative but they do have an amorphous bundle of self help programs that include "meditation, caring, sharing interpersonal warmth, creativity." PC3 then sorrowfully states: "Permission denied [to land]. Please resume your mission or return."

Earthship (*frantically*): We can't return. There is nothing to return to.

PC3 recommends that they proceed to PC7, another C2 civilization which is "curious, inquisitive, [and] murderous… They are sentimental, easily moved to tears, and kill each other with equal ease…. Two superpowers, ideological combat but not yet a nuclear exchange. They like wars too, pretend not to, but get into trouble during an overly prolonged peace. Right now they are bored to death and spoiling for a fight….Good luck. You have one hour to vacate orbit. Over and out."

Thus we have Walker Percy's interpretation of the three states of created mankind played out in a satirical drama in space.[1] There is the C1 or preternatural or unfallen state; the C2, the fallen or violent state and C3, the restored state.

Although the Fall is the main focus of my paper, the preternatural and restored states will also be presented to provide the necessary context. The purpose of this paper will be to demonstrate a parallel development of the vision of the "Fall" by Thomas Merton and Walker Percy. In a previous publication, I established the foundation for similar concerns articulated by both writers about the "malaise" and "alienation" of our contemporary society. This paper will focus on the "Fall" primarily through Merton's book, *The New Man*, although other Merton texts will be referenced as necessary. I will attempt to demonstrate in parallel fashion the works of Walker Percy including his two novels, The *Last Gentleman* and *The Second Coming*. Percy's essays and interviews will be cited to provide background for the selections from the above mentioned works. In a word, the protagonist, Will Barrett of both novels by Percy symbolizes the first or fallen Adam, a parallel to the fallen Adam, as articulated in the first part of Merton's book, *The New Man*. Will emerges, however, as the redeemed or recovered Adam in *The Second Coming* and can be seen as the counterpart for Merton's second Adam or Christ, the redeemer for mankind in *The New Man*. The Redemption would restore the unity that was ruptured through the fall. This loss of unity interrupted man's contemplative vision because he "was created as a contemplative" according to Merton.[2] The conclusion of the paper will point to the final optimism of both writers as the new Adam, or the second Adam, heralds the way to an inner transformation and union with God, hopefully leading to the eventual renewal of a broader human society. All of us need this kind of optimism and hope in our contemporary world marked by violence, terror, and the casual indifference of Western man in regards to his eternal salvation.

As proper context for the development of the paper it would be well to review the brief relationship between Thomas Merton and Walker Percy. Why was Merton so interested in Percy's work? He had demonstrated his admiration for Percy's novel, *The Moviegoer*, in correspondence to Walker Percy dated January, 1964.[3] In fact, the two men exchanged letters between the years, 1964-1967.[4] Moreover, Percy admired Merton, as evidenced in his 1984 interview with Victor and Dewey Kramer.[5] Percy and Merton met for a brief meeting at Merton's hermitage, albeit the meeting was disappointing and not productive other than small talk.[6] Merton's interest in Percy's novels is underscored by George Kilcourse when he states: "The evidence of [Merton's] personal reading habits suggests that he nurtured his mature contemplative life by reading a diverse spectrum of novelists" which included Walker Percy.[7] As Merton integrated his spirituality with his reading of imaginative writing, he realized that the contemplative and the novelist are, at times, on the same wave length in their ability to diagnose the spiritual malaise in our society.[8] In a letter to his publisher, James Laughlin, Merton declared that, "perhaps the most living way to approach theological and philosophical problems . . . would be in the form of creative writing and lit. criticism."[9] Kilcourse states that Merton volunteered the term "'sapiential', the highest level of cognition," which explains how the novelist or any artist, for that matter, has a commonality with the contemplative. Merton describes the mission of the contemplative is "'to keep alive a sense of sin' as ontological lapse" resulting from the fall from paradise and the subsequent alienation of man. The ontological lapse, of course, is a violation a "person's very being."It is through "imaginative literature that Merton finds sapientially dramatized the deepest levels of human freedom and the discovery of . . . human authenticity."[10] One of Walker Percy's essays is titled, "Diagnosing the Modern Malaise," in which he compares the role of novelist to a medical doctor, that is; "Something is wrong. What is it? What is the nature of the illness? Where is the lesion? Is it acute or chronic, treatable or fatal? Can we understand it? Does the disease have a name or is it something new?"[11]

On May 22, 1966, Thomas Merton wrote Robert Giroux, his editor:

Walker Percy is one of the few novelists whose books I am able to finish. This is in fact a haunting, disturbing, funny and fantastic anti-novel structured like a long dream and relentlessly insisting that most of reality is unconscious. It ends up being one of the most intelligent and sophisticated statements about the South and about America, but one which too many people will probably find so baffling that they will not know what to make of it. Even then, if they persist in reading it, they cannot help being affected by this profoundly wacky wisdom of the book. Precisely because of the wackiness I would call it one of the sanest books I have read in a long time.[12]

I would conjecture that Merton's characterization of the novel, *The Last Gentleman*, as "wacky," could be linked to Percy's view of man as a looney denizen of the world where looniness is the norm. In an interview with Zoltan Abadi-Nagy in 1986, Percy declared, "I think it is fair to say that [man] doesn't know who he is, what he believes, or what he is doing. This unprecedented state of affairs, is, I suggest, the domain of the 'diagnostic novel.'"[13] On another occasion, Percy states that Will Barrett "was really sick" and he was lost while being in a fugue state of amnesia—he would come and go with these fugue states.[14] In the context of interpreting Percy's writings, Robert Rudnicki writes that the fugue state in the broadest sense is the "cultural transmission of the doctrine of Judeo-Christianity—the story of the Fall, or exile of man from God—which accounts for the alienated condition of man."[15]

Merton evidently detected in Percy's novels a sense of the general malaise prevalent in contemporary American society which in turn was closely aligned to one of his own main themes throughout his writings, that is, man's alienation from himself and from others.[16] Malaise and alienation are a result of the fall and I became interested in both writers as Percy's indirect communication[17] through his novels seem to be a gloss for Merton's more direct communication.

The Merton interface for the three states of consciouness described by Percy, is taken from the book, *The New Man*, which is described as a series of meditations based St. Paul's letter to 1 Corthinians 6:17—"But he who cleaves to the Lord is one spirit with him."[18] William Shannon states that, "these meditations, cover three main topics: (1) the primal state of humankind before the fall ;(2) the fall and its consequences, and (3) the new creation in Jesus Christ which reestablishes communion between God and humankind. ... [an] 'existential communion' given, lost, restored."[19]

Although the focus of my paper is the Fall, I will first present Merton's interpretation of the Unfallen State as well as insights from Walker Percy. Following the section on The Fall, I will conclude the paper with a discussion on the Restored or Recovery State.

The Unfallen State of Man

In his book, *The New Man*, Thomas Merton has two chapters devoted to the unfallen or primal state of man, "Image and Likeness," and "Free Speech: Parrhesia."

Adam received the gift of love and wisdom from God who intended to preserve his bodily life while increasing Adam's spiritual life which was the main reason for his existence. In Paradise, therefore, there "could be no violence [nor] alienation."[20] William Shannon declares that Merton writings about contemplation often reference the theme of paradise which represents "a place of unity, harmony, and contemplative joy.... There was perfect communication between [human creatures] and God."[21] Perhaps it would be helpful to spend a brief moment to understand Merton's interpretation of Paradise. He has this to say about Paradise in his book, *Zen and the Birds of* Appetite:

> Now this concept [of Paradise] must be properly and accurately understood. Paradise is not 'heaven.' Paradise is a state, or indeed a place, on earth. Paradise belongs more properly to the present than to the future life. In some sense it belongs to both. It is the state in which man was originally created to live on earth. It is also conceived as a kind of antechamber to heaven after death—as for instance at the end of Dante's *Purgatorio*. Christ, dying on the cross, said to the good thief at His side: 'This day thou shalt be with me *in Paradise*,' and it was clear that this did not mean, and could not have meant, heaven.[22]

Thomas Merton found paradise, the fall and return, a very powerful myth within the Christian message. Patrick O'Connell describes myths in this context as "imaginative patterns that convey a truth transcending literal facts."[23] Merton further explains that a myth is not a lie but "an imaginative synthesis of facts and intuitions about them, forming an interpretative complex of ideas and images." Therefore these ideas and images becomes a "complex of values"which is "central in a meaning-system."[24] Understanding the myth of the fall and return to paradise in this context, hopefully, will inform the following discussion.

In his unalienated condition Adam was placed in paradise subordinated to the angels and superordinate to the beasts and "inanimate beings." Adam was, in fact, a "mediator between God and His world," without malice or any destructive inclinations. It was only after the fall through division, and a loss of unity that destruction and violence befell our planet and a general malaise set in.[25] As a mediator or interpreter, and a contemplative, Adam was appointed as the overseer of the garden of Paradise or Eden. But Adam was also an activist in this role as he praised God through "the work of his hands and of his intelligence"[26] and therefore the traditional antithesis between action and contemplation was not present in Paradise. Merton cites St. Augustine in the interpretation "that if Adam worked even in Paradise, work is by no means to be regarded by us as an evil." Work was part of "the existential communion with the reality of nature and of the supernatural by which he was surrounded." In fact, work was a "conversation with God"—a form of worship.[27]

As a contemplative in Paradise, Adam constantly met with God in "flashes of mystical intuition" which obviated any form of rebellion, but rather, enabled him to have a perfect self-knowledge.[28] Merton uses the Greek word "parrhesia" to mean free speech symbolizing the "perfect communication" of man's "intelligence with God by knowledge and contemplation." Through this condition, "being with Being" Adam experienced the freedom of "spiritual communion." This internal contemplative moment, "being with Being", is the "existential communion" of Adam's "reality around him" and the internal awareness of the "Reality of God."[29]

Another level of mystery and contemplation was realized with the creation of Eve as Adam progressed in a level of "existential communion" from his first moment of creation in the image and likeness of God to realizing he had a partner who enriched his existence through the form of human love.[30] This human love allows man not only to love but to be loved—a vocation to charity. This companionship of love or life of the "other" is a means of giving further "glory to God." "His one Nature and Three Persons" is a refraction and multiplication of the many natures of men united "with one another in society" emanating from the first union or society of Adam and Eve.[31]Merton states:

> Already, in the woman he saw before him, and in the love that united him to her, Adam also saw the charity and the self-sacrifice that would enable human beings to love one another spiritually and to live as one body in Christ.[32]

In an interview with Linda Whitney Hobson Walker Percy renders his construct of the unfallen state or the C1 Consciousness:

> Arnold Gesell describes the difference between a four- year old and a seven-year-old this way: the four- year old is a C1 consciousness…. He is in an Edenic state; he's celebrating the world. By the time he's seven, something has happened. He is 'fallen.'He is worried to death about his sexuality, about being naked; it's like Adam and Eve discovering their nakedness.[33]

Later in the interview, Percy refers to Sigmund Freud "who would never have talked of God or a fallen state." Percy claims that through his analysis with a patient, Freud is attempting to create an "Edenic community."[34]

In his novel, *The Last Gentleman*, Percy gives us a view of the unfallen state through the character Valentine Vaught, Jamie's sister. She is a nun in a remote area of southern Alabama who is working with children deprived of communication and her work is satisfying because "when they finally do speak, they come into the world, see it for what it is and themselves as part of it, just as fully as Adam and Eve in the Garden.[35] Valentine asserts:

> They are like Adam on the first day. What's that? They ask me.That's a hawk, I tell them, and they believe me. I think I recognized myself in them. They were not alive and then they are and so they'll believe you. Their eyes pop out at the Baltimore catechism (imagine). I tell them that God made them to be happy and that if they love one another and keep the commandments and receive the Sacrament, they'll be happy now and forever. They believe me. I'm not sure anybody else does now.[36]

Another paradisiacal image described by Linda Whitney Hobson is the three month stint spent by Will in a florist's shop in Memphis "just to be near green, growing things and perhaps recover part of Eden".[37]

The above passages by both Thomas Merton and Walker Percy foreshadow the fallen state of man. Merton, however, is explicit in his description of man destined to be a contemplative and after the fall man is attempting to be restored to his former state. Percy, on the other hand, describes the unfallen state through C1 consciousness in his book, *Lost in the Cosmos*. A further example of the Edenic community is the innocence of Valentine's children in the scene from *The Last Gentleman* cited above.

The Fall

Walker Percy's novel, *The Last Gentleman*, describes Will Barrett, a modern day Adam, in his search for redemption. The novel, according to Bernadette Prochaska, is about Will Barrett, the journey of a soul, "Adam encountering the unbearable punishment for sin, yet hoping for redemption."[38] When asked by interviewer, Zoltan Abadi-Nagy, how he got started with his novel, *The Last Gentleman*, Percy stated: "I wanted to create someone not quite as flat as Binx in *The Moviegoer*, more disturbed, more passionate, more in love and, above all, *on the move*. He is in pilgrimage without quite knowing it."[39]

Martin Luschei characterizes Will as "an incapacitated pilgrim" on a pilgrimage.[40] He travels from ground zero, in Central Park to Santa Fe. Early in the novel Will befriends the Vaught family and he agrees to accompany them on the journey to Santa Fe and to be a companion for the youngest son, Jamie, who is dying. As he travels, Will recognizes in the landscapes, the "Fallen world of suffering and death, the home that he shares with others."[41] In route he is convinced by Jamie's sister, Valentine Vaught, to have Jamie baptized to fulfill God's promise of salvation. The baptismal scene represents, on one hand, the effects of the fall through the stench of death and on the other hand, the "hope of resurrection when Father Boomer, reading the ritual for the dying, says to Jamie:'Today you shall see God'."[42] Michael Kobre in his book titled *Walker Percy's Voices* claims that: "As a trained physician, Percy is mercilessly accurate in describing the rigors of Jamie's illness. His prose has never been more exact and powerful than in those scenes in which we see the final decay of Jamie's body".[43] Martin Luschei asserts that, in fact, *The Last Gentleman,* "is structured on the impending death of Jamie Vaught," a powerful scene, indeed.[44] Search as he may, however, Will Barrett still does not get it. In an interview with John C. Carr in 1971, Walker Percy gives us some insight into the memorable scene when Will is trying to understand what happened as he confronts Sutter, Jamie's irascible older brother. Percy states:

> [Will] knows that Sutter's on to something. Sutter's got something he wants to know, and Barrett has this radar.... [He] fastens on Sutter, because he has to find out what it is. Sutter leaves him this diary which has all kinds of clues and such, but he still doesn't know exactly what Sutter's getting at. So he finally catches up with Sutter, and in the death scene a baptism takes place, with a very ordinary sort of priest, a mediocre priest. And here again, Barrett has eliminated Christianity. That is gone. That is no longer even to be considered. It's not even to be spoken of, taken seriously, or anything else.... And he is aware of something going on between the dying boy Jamie and Sutter there across the room and the priest. And he is aware that Sutter is taking this seriously. So after the boy dies, they leave and Barrett catches up with Sutter and...he asks Sutter, 'What happened there? Something happened. What happened?' And Sutter brushes him off as usual. 'What do you think happened? You were there.'... [Percy explains:] He *misses* it![45]

Martin Luschei underscores the fact that Will has missed it and that the "derisive Sutter" knows what is going on. Further Will has missed it because he is a good postmodern Christian and as Percy stated above Will has eliminated Christianity and, in fact, it is gone and not "even to be considered."[46] Hence the meaning of the epigraph at the beginning of the novel which is prescient of the post Christian Age as articulated by Romano Guardini in his book, *The End of the Modern World*:

The epigraph reads:

> We know now that the modern world is coming to an end... at the same time, the unbeliever will emerge from the fogs of secularism. He will cease to reap benefits from the values and forces developed by the very Revelation he denies.... Loneliness in faith will be terrible. Love will disappear from the face of the public world, but the more precious will be that love which flows from one lonely person to another...the world to come will be filled with animosity and danger, but it will be a world open and clean.[47]

Percy echoes Guardini's statement that the modern world known as Christendom has ended. This is a world fueled by the optimism of the Western culture including the breakthroughs in science and "rational humanism." With two World Wars and other tradegies of the past century, this optimism waned. Percy goes on to say that literary traditions that attempt to revive the symbols of Christendom have all but disappeared and "contemporary novelists have moved into a world of rootless and isolated consciousness for whom not even the memory and nostalgia exist" but rather the focus is on "existential self."[48]

John Desmond in his book, *Walker Percy's Search for Community*, states that Percy diagnosed "the debilitated state of modern American culture, trapped in its self-absorbed individualism, consumerism, violence, racism." This has signaled "the death throes of the collapse of Western culture [and]...the end of the modern world" according to Percy.[49] The epigraph in *The Last Gentleman* is a link to Percy's novel, *The Second Coming*, but actually it " expresses the prevailing view in Percy's fiction regarding contemporary post-Christian society," according to Ross Labrie.[50] We will meet Will Barrett again in this novel which is a sequel to *The Last Gentleman*. But more about that later.

Thomas Merton, too, realized that we were living in a post-Christian society when he stated:

> Whether we like it or not, we have to admit we are already living in a post-Christian world, that is to say a world in which Christian ideals and attitudes are relegated more and more to the minority. It is frightening to realize that the façade of Christianity which still generally survives has perhaps little or nothing behind it, and that what was once called 'Christian society' is more purely and simply a materialistic neopaganism with a Christian veneer.... Not only non-Christians but even Christians themselves tend to dismiss the Gospel ethic on nonviolence and love as 'sentimental.'[51]

The propensity of man for violence which resulted from the fall severed the existential flow of communication between Adam and God in the Garden of Eden. Adam, now false and subject to illusion was, therefore, "stripped of his sincerity" and he could "no longer face [God] without a disguise."[52] What does Merton say about the causes of the Fall? In his book, *The New Man*, Merton declares that a rupture of exisistential communion caused Adam's fractured relationship with God, with himself, and with other men. Cain became the symbol of violence and disunity. The sin according to Merton was "an attitude of mind," a condition leading to the eating of the fruit from "the forbidden tree." According to Merton, the sin was really a change of attitude on the part of Adam who had been, heretofore, mystically united with God. Adam wished to expand his "experiential knowledge of all that was good" to an "experiential knowledge of evil" which was unknown even by God.[53] Merton cites St. Augustine explanation of the fall as Adam's withdrawal from "God into himself...[causing] multiplicity and confusion of exterior things."[54]

Consequently, we see the effects of the original sin from the smell of death in Jamie's hospital room in Percy's novel to the crucifixion of Christ as described by Merton. In his book, *New Seeds of Contemplation*, Merton delineates the effects of the fall in a chapter titled, "A Body of Broken Bones." He describes how the mystical Body of Christ "is drawn and quartered from age to age by the devils in the agony of that disunion which is bred and vegetates in our souls, prone to selfishness and to sin." He goes on to detail the "unceasing divisions" among men causing "huge wars...[m]urder, massacres, revolution, hatred...slaughter...the destruction of cities by fire, the starvation of millions, the annihilation of populations and finally the cosmic inhumanity of atomic war."[55]

Redemption: The Restored State

Walker Percy's pessimism about the post-Christian society is redeemed, however, when he states:

> I have referred to the age as 'post-Christian' but it does not follow from this that there are not Christians or that they are wrong. Possibly the age is wrong. Catholics—who are the only Christians I can speak for—still believe that God entered history as man, founded a Church, and will come again. This is not the best of times for the Catholic Church, but it has seen and survived worse.[56]

Percy further speaks of the characters in his novels moving "toward God" through "religious 'transcendence,'" although the movement is blurred, incomplete, and the reader is puzzled when Will Barrett's destiny in unclear at the end of *The Last Gentleman*.[57]

However, in his fifth novel, titled, *The Second Coming*, Walker Percy expresses a more optimistic view when he describes his new novel as having an unambiguous ending unlike his other novels. He claims that it may be the first unalienated novel since Tolstoy. However, Marc Kirkeby states that: "[a]lienation, and Percy's longstanding concern with the hazy line between sanity and insanity, haven't disappeared in *The Second Coming*, but the violence and sense of foreboding that pervaded his last two novels, *Lancelot* and *Love in the Ruins*, are gone." Will Barrett, "callow protagonist," returns in *The Second Coming* as a "prosperous but confused" middle aged man who meets a much younger Allison Huger who has recently escaped from a mental institution.[58] I will return to this novel after I present Thomas Merton's new Adam as explicated in his book, the *New Man*.

For Merton, alienation was the result of the fall from Paradise and therefore the Redemption represents "a return to the paradisal state, a recovery of lost unity," according to George Kilcourse.[59] The Resurrection of Christ after His death on the cross is the "central mystery of our Redemption" and, in fact, the "center of all spiritual freedom."[60] The natural head of humankind was the first Adam, and Christ is the new Adam, or the second Adam, through the Redemption.[61] Merton asserts, "All men were united in Adam. All were 'one image' of God in Adam. 'Adam is in us all.' We all sinned in Adam. Adam is saved and redeemed in us all."[62] Merton strikes the theme of unity as he calls upon John Ruysbroeck and his mystical doctrine concerning a "unity of spirit" within man's interior self, "with God and with other men."[63]

Our life was given to us from the first Adam as an outgrowth of the "natural union with God as our Creator." The life given to us by Christ, or the second Adam, is "totally spiritual." We might say that Adam presided over "the first creation" and Christ was sent by God to preside over "an entirely new spiritual Creation."[64] Because of the fall of Adam, Christ, the second Adam, found confusion and chaos imbedded in the hearts and minds of man causing an alienation of man from himself, from other men, and from God.[65] The irresponsible first Adam "brought death, illusion, error, destruction into the life of man."[66]

The mission of Christ, therefore, was to clear the way for God to reunite all of creation including mankind and the quest for salvation. Through Christ "the original existential communion with God" was restored. The gates of Paradise have been once again opened by the second Adam who "restored peace to the soul of man."[67] The sufferings of Christ through the crucifixion was a unifying force allowing each individual the potential of being part of His Mystical Body.[68] There will come a day when through "a mystical transformation" we will be "perfectly conformed to the likeness of Christ." He "will live entirely in us [and]…[w]e will be 'the New Man.'"[69] Merton concludes the chapter, titled "The Second Adam" with the theme of unity when he states: "We see that we ourselves are Adam, we ourselves are Christ, and that we are all dwelling in one another, by virtue of the unity of the divine image reformed by grace…. We are His new Paradise." [70]

In his novel, *The Second Coming*, a sequel to *The Last Gentleman*,[71] Walker Percy presents his readers with a theme of restoration. Linda Whitney Hobson strikes an optimistic note about this novel. She claims:

> That Eros appears to win at the close of *The Second Coming* is an emblem for how one may yet turn back the tide of violence, apathy, and boredom; seize once again the sovereignty for his own life away from 'experts'; and turn the massive potential for an apocalypse—personal, national, and global –toward the equal potential for love. [72]

Caroline Gordon, the novelist, had read drafts of Percy's early unpublished novels and at one point admonished Percy according to Patrick Samway. He states:

> For the record, Gordon made her credo very clear: all novels must be about love; and love between a man and a woman is an analogue of divine love. She stated explicitly that this love is rooted in the incarnation of Jesus, the Christ. 'Your business as a novelist is to imitate Christ. He was about His Father's business every moment of His life. As a good novelist you must be about yours: Incarnation. Making your word flesh and making it dwell among men.'[73]

Bernadette Prochaska interprets Walker Percy's book, *The Second Coming*, as an intergration of the characters into *communitas*, a road to salvation.[74] The *communitas* is Barrett's intention to marry Allison and have a child. Barrett will also garner several unhappy older residents of a convalescent home and build houses on large plots of land. In addition the building of the village, forming a corporation, and sharing the profits with the older residents who are participants "is essentially the integration of the person in the communitas."Hence, "Will has moved from alienation to participation...[and a] [c]ommunitas...[has become] his most valued vehicle of salvation."[75] Prochaska recounts the event in Genesis before the fall when God was conversing with Adam and Eve, in the evening, while walking in the Garden of Paradise—this is Communitas. Will Barrett had encountered the effects of the fall with Jamie's death in *The Last Gentleman* and now Will, as the new Adam, "is consoled by resurrection" or rebirth. Examples of the rebirth are found in the character of Allison who experienced a rebirth through her escape from Valleyhead Sanatorium. Will is, also, reborn with his fall into the greenhouse from the cave. Throwing his guns into the gorge and his resolve not to commit suicide like his father is another sign of rebirth.[76]

John Desmond in his book, *Walker Percy's Search for Community*, presents a poem by Percy written when he was "celebrating his companionship with a small group of friends" in Covington, Louisiana. The title of the poem is "Community." The last five lines are:

> Twenty years of solitariness and success at solitariness,
> Solitary with his family like the Swiss family
>   on their island,
> Then all at once community.
> Community? What, friends out there in the world?
> Yes.[77]

According to Desmond the poem expresses Percy's joy and affirmation of finding community amidst his natural proneness to the solitary life. The search for community is a theme found in Percy's novels, as Desmond notes "alienation and separateness, hope and the possibility for communion reflect the spirit of Percy's obsession with community throughout his career as a writer."[78] Redemption from their fallen state was the condition of Percy's characters according to Desmond. Driving Percy's theological belief was the Eucharist, "the real presence of God-in-Christ," which was a manifestation of the "mystical community." Therefore "the central truth of community" is "[b]elief in the divine Word made flesh."[79] Like Guardini, Percy saw the collapse of the modern world as "hope for the renewal of genuine community, of true relations between human beings based on love and truth and honesty."[80] Gary Ciuba asserts that Will Barrett's love for Allison in *The Second Coming* is an "apocalyptic comedy...a romance for the end of the world in which human love serves as a sign of the divine love at its source."[81] Further, Cuiba states: "Having looked for signs of God throughout the novel, in the last pages Will keeps glimpsing the divine image through its human embodiments: Allie, Father Weatherbee, and a puzzling pair of orderlies at St. Mark's."[82] Cuiba states that: "Will's final revelation is that although the Second Coming has not yet reached its conclusion, it has already begun in the daily arrival of the divine presence."[83] Ciuba suggests that Percy's title to the novel, *The Second Coming,* is an ever occurring event –"God is always coming" and an echo of the "Karl Rahner's meditation on the Parousia in affirming that the divine approach is neither 'past nor future, but the present, which has only to reach its fulfillment."[84]

Thomas Merton also echoes Rahner when he asserts that man "cannot rest unless he rests in God" and this resting and departure from "anguish" is through the mystical experience[85] or contemplation—man's original destiny. In the last chapter of *The New Man,* titled "Called Out of Darkness," Merton describes the *Exsultet,* the traditional Catholic hymn of praise sung by the deacon during the Easter Vigil, as a summoning of "Heaven and earth" to join the triumph of Christ. Merton claims that the *Exsultet* is the zenith of Catholic liturgy in its expression of spirituality. In my opinion, Merton's description of this beautiful liturgical hymn as a unifying theme around the positive and negative in God's creation is one of his best rhetorical writings. Couched within the context of the Resurrection, Merton states: "The Exsultet... becomes...a hymn in praise not only of light but also of darkness. So profound is the meaning of the Resurrection that everything, even the purest negation, that is touched by its light, acquires something of a positive orientation." Merton goes to say that evil and sin "seen by the light of the sacramental fire, becomes capable of helping the work of God." The sin of Adam becomes a "happy fault,"perhaps, a "necessary" fault to fulfill God's plan of proving His love through "Christ's death on the Cross."[86] This love is a unifying love, bereft of division, strife, violence and the general malovence of mankind.

Walker Percy, of course, is not as direct as Thomas Merton in his articulation of the fall and the subsequent Redemption through Christ as a harmonizing force. Through his many interviews, we learn that Percy was wary of using religious words such as God, sin, salvation , baptism, and the fall.[87] However, Percy gifted us with the three stages of mankind in his book, *Lost in the Cosmos,* and we followed the journey of Will Barrett as the pilgrim, lost and found again through the redemptive effects of *communitas* and community in *The Second Coming*. Ted R. Spivey cites the influence of Soren Kierkegaard on Percy's thinking and underscores, in particular, his remarkable essay, "On the Difference Between a Genius and an Apostle." Although a discussion of the essay is beyond the purview of this paper, Spivey conjectures that, "[t]he emergence of the apostle is necessary for both true religious renewal as well as cultural renewal." Percy claimed he had very little knowledge of a real apostle, however, he knew something about the cultural renewal represented by both science and art. Percy believed "that the role of the scientist—philosopher—artist in our time is to prepare for the coming of the apostle."[88] Science and art representing the analytical and the imaginative can be the elements of a communication modality creating a renewal of unity and harmony in our cosmos.[89] Spivey illustrates the "withdrawal from cosmic unity" and the "restoration with Being" in Percy's novel, *The Second Coming*.[90] Will had been living a rather superficial life when he discovers the pain of his father's attempt to kill him and then subsequently commits suicide. Upon recovery and through the help of grace, Will assists Allison who has also suffered pain and has "withdrawn into a mental cocoon." Through the restoration of this communication process, aided by the analytical and imaginative powers, "Percy sees hope for the eventual restoration of harmony within men."[91] Spivey concludes that although Percy chronicles the "decline and fall of the American dream...he presents us with a vision of the possibility of that dream's renewal."[92]

Conclusion

My paper is a modest attempt to interpret the fall from paradise through the works of Thomas Merton and Walker Percy. As a prelude to the fall, Paradise or the unfallen state was primarily exemplified through Percy's book, *Lost in the Cosmos*, as the inhabitants of the planet, Proxima Centauri explained the C1 consciousness stage to the crew of the Earthship. Paradise, the primal state of man, was explicated by Thomas Merton in his book, *The New Man*. Merton's two chapters titled, "Image and Likeness", and "Free Speech:Parrhesia" describe Adam as a contemplative experiencing "flashes of mystical intuition" with God. Through the fall, however, the mirror of "existential communion" was shattered and we find Will Barrett, the protagonist, in Walker Percy's *Last Gentleman*, trying to fathom the Christian message in the memorable deathbed scene with Jamie. Since Will has eliminated Christianity and he is in a fallen state, "he misses it." In his book, *The New Man*, Thomas Merton interprets the shattered mirror as "a rupture of existential communion" between Adam and God which led to division and disunion among mankind.

Finally however, we experience Walker Percy's optimism through his novel, *The Second Coming*, a sequel to *The Last Gentleman*. Linda Whitney Hobson describes the success of Eros in *The Second Coming* in overcoming the violence of our society. Percy evidently heeded Caroline Gordon's admonition that novels should be about human love, an "analogue of divine love." Thomas Merton calls us out of darkness in his explanation of the *Exsultet* and it is, perhaps, a symbol of the restored or redemptive state whereby we experience God's love as a unifying love for mankind.

And so we have it, with Will Barrett, a fallen Adam restored as the second Adam, a hopeful Adam, an Adam with a vision of love and harmony. We have learned through Gary Ciuba's interpretation of *The Second Coming* that Will Barrett's human love for Allison mirrors a divine love for God who is not past or future but a God who resides in all of us waiting for fulfillment—an echo of the love espoused by Romano Guardini; that is; the precious love which will flow "from one lonely person to another." So too, Thomas Merton's second Adam, Christ, provides by grace and a transformation, the unity of all of us dwelling in one another through the Mystical Body of Christ, a return to Paradise—"We are His new Paradise."

Endnotes

1. Walker Percy, *Lost in the Cosmos, The Last Self-Help Book* (New York: Washington Square Press, 1983), pp. 198-213.

2. Thomas Merton, *The Inner Experience* (ed. and Introduction by William H. Shannon; San Francisco: HarperSan Francisco, 2003), p.35.

3. Thomas Merton, *The Courage for Truth: The Letters of Thomas Merton to Writers* (ed.Christine M. Bochen; New York: Farrar, Straus & Giroux, 1993), pp. 281-282.

4. *Correspondence: Thomas Merton and Walker Percy* (The Thomas Merton Center Archives, Bellarmine University Brown Library).

5. Lewis A. Lawson and Victor A. Kramer (eds.), *Conversations with Walker Percy* (Jackson: University Press of Mississippi, 1985), p.316.

6. Lawson and Kramer (eds.) *Conversations*, pp. 310-313.

7. George Kilcourse, Jr., *Ace of Freedoms: Thomas Merton's Christ* (Notre Dame: University of Notre Dame Press, 1993), p.128.

8. Kilcourse, *Ace of Freedoms*, pp. 130-131.

9. David D. Cooper (ed.), *Thomas Merton and James Laughlin, Selected Letters* (New York: W.W. Norton & Company, 1997), p.301.

10. Kilcourse, *Ace of Freedoms*, pp.134-135.

11. Walker Percy, *Signposts in a Strange Land* (ed. Patrick Samway, SJ; New York: Farrar, Straus &Giroux, 1991), p.205.

12. Patrick Samway, S.J., *Walker Percy, A Life* (Chicago: Loyola Press, 1997), pp. 251-52.

13. Lewis A. Lawson and Victor A. Kramer (eds.), *More Conversations with Walker Percy* (Jackson: University Press of Mississippi, 1993), pp.141-142.

14. Lawson and Lewis (eds.), *Conversations*, p. 66.

15. Robert W. Rudnicki, *Percyscapes* (Baton Rouge: Louisiana State University Press, 1999), p.31.

16. Note. Merton describes alienation in this way. "Humanity, which was one image of God in Adam, or, if you prefer, one single 'mirror' of the divine nature, was shattered into millions of fragments by that original sin which alienated each man from God, from other men and from himself. But the broken mirror becomes once again a perfectly united image of God in the union of those who are one in Christ. Thus, in Christ, 'God reunites His whole creation, including matter, but especially man, in a new economy of salvation.' " Thomas Merton, *The New Man* (New York: Farrar, Straus and Giroux, 1961), p.149. Walker Percy in his novel, *The Moviegoer*, describes the malaise through the protagonist, Binx. "What is the malaise? you ask. The malaise is the pain of loss. The world is lost to you, the world and the people in it, and there remains only you and the world and you are no more to be in the world than Banquo's ghost. Walker Percy, *The Moviegoer* (New York: Vintage Books, 1998), p. 120. On alienation Percy states: "[A]lienation, after all, is nothing more than a very ancient, orthodox Christian doctrine. Man is alienated by the nature of his being here. He is here as a stranger and a pilgrim, which is the way alienation is conceived in my books." Lewis A. Lawson and Victor A. Kramer (eds.), *Conversations with Walker Percy*, pp. 28-29.

17. Note. Regarding indirect communication Percy has this to say. " [A] reason for reticence is that novelists are a devious lot to begin with, disinclined to say anything straight out, especially about themselves, since their stock–in-trade is indirection, if not guile, coming at things and people from the side to speak, especially the blind side, the better to get at them. If anybody says anything straight out, it is apt to be one of their characters, a character, moreover, for which they have not much use. *Percy, Signposts in a Strange Land*, p. 304.

18. Thomas Merton, *The New Man* (New York: Farrar, Straus and Giroux, 1961), p. 67.

19. William H. Shannon, Christine M. Bochen and Patrick F. O'Connell (eds.), *The Thomas Merton Encyclopedia* (New York: Orbis Books, 2002), p. 322.

20. Thomas Merton, *The New Man*, p. 53.

21. William Shannon, *Thomas Merton's Paradise Journey* (Cincinnati, Ohio: St. Anthony Messenger Press, 2000), p.3.

22. Thomas Merton, *Zen and the Birds of Appetite* (A New Directions Book: New York, 1968), p.116. Note. Merton continues about his concept of paradise:"We must not imagine Paradise as a place of ease and sensual pleasure. It is a state of peace and rest, by all means. But what the Desert Fathers sought when they believed they could find 'paradise' in the desert, was the lost innocence, the emptiness and purity of heart which had belonged to Adam and Eve in Eden.... What they sought was paradise within themselves, or rather above and beyond themselves. They sought paradise in the recovery of that 'unity' which had been shattered by the 'knowledge of good and evil.' Merton, *Zen and the Birds of Appetite*, pp. 116-117.

23. *The Thomas Merton Encyclopedia*, p.349.

24. Thomas Merton, *Faith and Violence* (Notre Dame: University of Notre Dame Press, 1968) p. 274.n.

25. Merton, *The New Man*, p. 57.

26. Merton, *The New Man*, p. 59.

27. Merton, *The New Man*, p. 78-79.

28. Merton, *The New Man*, pp. 73-74.

29. Merton, *The New Man*, pp. 73-76. Note. The phrase "existential communication" occurs repeatedly throughout the book and was, in fact, the original title of the book. *The Thomas Merton Encyclopedia*, p. 322.

30. Merton, *The New Man*,p.89. Note.The image of God is in nature. The likeness of God is through grace. Source unknown. Merton alludes to the image and likeness in the following: After the fall "human nature in its essence was not ruined, only weakened, by original sin. St. Bernard sees the fall not as a descent from the supernatural to the natural, but as a collapse into ambivalence in which the historical 'nature' in which man was actually created for supernatural union with God is turned upside down and inside out, and yet *still retains its innate capacity and 'need' for divine union*. The human soul is still the image of God, and no matter how far it travels away from Him into the regions of unreality, it never becomes so completely unreal that its original destiny can cease to torment it with a need to return to itself in God, and become, once again, real." Merton, *The New Man*, p. 112.

31. Merton, *The New* Man, p.91.

32. Merton, *The New Man*, pp. 93-94.

33. Lawson and Lewis (eds.), *More Conversations*, pp.89-90. Note. Arnold Gesell (1880-1961) was a noted child psychologist, especially, during the 1940's and the 1950's. He was widely regarded as the nation's foremost authority on child rearing and development. Gesell remains an important pioneer in child development. *Encyclopedia of Psychology*. Internet.

34. Lawson and Lewis (eds.), *More Conversations*, pp 93-94.

35. Linda Whitney Hobson, *Understanding Walker Percy* (Columbia: University of South Carolina Press, 1988), pp.52-53.

36. Walker Percy, *The Last Gentleman* (New York: Farrar, Straus and Giroux, 1966), pp.301-302.

37. Hobson, *Understanding Walker Percy*, p. 52.

38. Bernadette Prochaska, *The Myth of the Fall and Walker Percy's Last Gentleman* (New York: Peter Lang Publishing, Inc. 1992) p.ix.

39. Lawson and Lewis (eds.), *More Conversations*, p.143.

40. Martin Luschei, *The Sovereign Wayfarer* (Baton Rouge: Louisiana State University Press, 1972), p. 114.

41. Allen Pridgen, *Walker Percy's Sacramental Landscapes* (Selinsgrove: Susquehanna University Press, 2000), p. 79.

42. Prochaska, *The Myth of the Fall and Walker Percy's Last Gentleman*, p. ix.

43. Michael Kobre, *Walker Percy's Voices* (Athens: The University of Georgia Press, 2000), p.108.

44. Luschei, *The Sovereign Wayfarer*, p.111.

45. Lawson and Lewis (eds.), *Conversations*, pp. 67-68. Note.The dialogue is quotation marks in slightly different than the dialogue in his book, *The Last Gentleman*. Perhaps, Walker Percy was doing the quote from memory rather than the actual text.

46. Luschei, *The Sovereign Wayfarer*, p.166.

47. Walker Percy, *The Last Gentleman*, Epigraph.

48. Walker Percy, *Signposts in a Strange Land*, pp. 208-209.

49. John F. Desmond, *Walker Percy's Search for Community* (Athens: University of Georgia Press, 2004), pp. 6-7.

50. Ross Labrie, *The Catholic Imagination in American Literature* (Columbia: University of Missouri Press, 1997), p.147.

51. Thomas Merton, *Peace in the Post-Christian Era* (ed. and with an Introduction by Patricia Burton, New York: Orbis Books, 2004), p.xxi.

52. Thomas Merton, *The New Man*, p. 77.

53. Thomas Merton, *The New Man*, pp.105-106.

54. Thomas Merton, *The New Man*, p.114.

55. Thomas Merton, *The New Seeds of Contemplation* (New York: A New Direction Book, 1961), p. 71.

56. Walker Percy, *Signposts in a Strange Land*, p. 388.

57. Walker Percy, *Signposts in a Strange Land*, p. 388-389.

58. Lawson and Lewis (eds.), *Conversations*, p. 190.

59. Kilcourse, *Ace of Freedoms*, p.135.

60. Thomas Merton, *The New Man*, p·232.

61. Merton, *The New Man*, p.131.

62. Merton, *The New Man*, p.133.

63. Merton, *The New Man*, p.141.

64. Merton, *The New Man*, p.148.

65. Merton, *The New Man*, p.149.

66. Merton, *The New Man*, p 151.

67. Merton, *The New Man*, pp. 151-152.

68. Merton, *The New Man*, p.154.

69. Merton, *The New Man*, p.158.

70. Merton, *The New Man*, p.161.

71. Note. Paul Elie states: "No novel ever demanded a sequel less than the *Last Gentleman*; it is doubtful that even Percy himself had wondered what had happened to Will Barrett and Kitty Vaught." Elie goes on to describe the characters in *The Second Coming*. He states further: "Percy was openly repeating himself [about the characters in the book]. The question is why. He was just writing along . . . when a middle –aged character turned into Will Barrett. He [Percy] may have found once again that he could not imagine new characters. He may have honestly seen a sequel as a new way forward, a classic Kierkegaardian return, a visit to old territory as a different person and a different writer." Paul Elie, *The Life You Save May Be Your Own* (New York: Farrar, Straus and Giroux, 2003), p. 447.

72. Hobson, *Understanding Walker Percy*, p. 131.

73. Samway, *Walker Percy, A Life*, p.164.

74. Prochaska, *The Myth of the Fall and Walker Percy's Last Gentleman*, p.115.

75. Prochaska, *The Myth of the Fall and Walker Percy's Last Gentleman*, pp.120- 121.

76. Prochaska, *The Myth of the Fall and Walker Percy's Last Gentleman*, pp.122-123.

77. John F. Desmond, *Walker Percy's Search for Community*, p. 2.

78. Desmond, p.3.

79. Desmond, p. 5.

80. Desmond, p.7.

81. Gary M. Cuiba, *Books of Revelation* (Athens: University of Georgia Press, 1991), p.202.

82. Cuiba, p.243.

83. Cuiba, p. 246.

84. Cuiba, p.234.

85. Thomas Merton, *The New* Man, pp.113-114.

86. Merton, *The New Man*, pp.244-245.

87. Lawson and Lewis (eds.), *Conversations*, p. 79.Note. Although the word "fall" is not used in a series of words quoted by Walker Percy who stated: "In my view you have to be wary of using words like 'religion,' 'God,' 'sin,' 'salvation,' 'baptism,' because the words are almost worn out." *Conversations*, p. 79. In a Percy interview, Peggy Castex states: "The Fall...?" She continues with her dialogue with Percy, "[The Fall]. But that's a dirty word. You can't use that word in a novel. If you do, everybody will close the book." Through further dialogue Percy assents to the statements by Castex. *More Conversations*, p.56.

88. Ted R. Spivey, *The Writer as Sharman* (Macon: Mercer University Press, 1986), p.169.

89. Spivey, *The Writer as Sharman*, pp.187-188.

90. Spivey, *The Writer as Sharman*, p.172.

91. Spivey, *The Writer as Sharman*, pp.172-173.

92. Spivey, *The Writer as Sharman*, p.188.

Standing to the Side and Watching:
An Introduction and Remembrance about Interviewing Walker Percy

Victor A. Kramer with Dewey Weiss Kramer

I first had the pleasure of meeting Walker Percy in October 1972 when we were both invited to participate in the Dedication for the "James Agee Room" of the Simmons Library at St. Andrew's School in Monteagle, Tennessee. Quiet, diffident, soft-spoken and witty, Percy seemed a bit bemused that he was there at an event honoring Agee up "on the mountain". Percy's family, and his famous "Uncle", William Alexander Percy, had been, for years, visitors to the well known Monteagle Campgrounds, and that place, near Sewanee and St. Andrew's had been one of the assembly places for many Southern Writers for decades. Allen Tate and Andrew Lytle were then living close to Sewanee, and Lytle was one of the Agee Event Speakers. These were significant Southern writers who had made names for themselves, but Percy seemed a kind of outsider and he stood beyond that defined circle. Interestingly, he and I actually conducted our conversation standing on the front steps of the library distanced from the event.

Later through the editorship of Will Campbell for *Katallagete* both Percy and Merton served together on the Editorial Board of that ecumenical journal, exchanging materials by mail, and as Percy put it in 1983 when we went to Covington, Louisiana, to give him a copy of the *Reference Guide* for Andrew Lytle and Peter Taylor, the Southern writers, as well as for Percy's work, which I had compiled and edited, it was inevitable that he would talk about writers like Tate and Lytle, Agee and Caroline Gordon, his "mentor." But again, as we spoke, Percy still seemed to both of us to remain a bit on the outside. So it was no surprise when he professed this also to have been so when he experienced his only actual meeting with Merton.

They had come together for the Board Meeting of *Katallagete*. They had only corresponded a little bit before, but Merton knew *The Moviegoer*. They had also corresponded about material which went into the third novel too, *Love in the Ruins*. Thus, while it was not easy to talk, this interview demonstrates, as Paul Elie relates

173

in his study of these two scholarly writers, that he and Merton were cut of the same cloth and shared a lot of similar experiences as converts. This is what Merton stressed in the interview.

In my own recent talk for the Percy Panel for The International Thomas Merton Society General Meeting in Memphis in 2007, I related some important remarks which Percy made to us on that afternoon, May 1, 1983, about being in Germany in the summer of 1934. He talked about his wandering about the German countryside observing Nazi Brown Shirts who were moving about in an almost crazy manner. This was before he wrote *The Thanatos Syndrome* with its similar fictionalized recollections. Percy remembered that summer as a season of madness and how it made such a vivid impression on him. This was, in a sense, the same Germany which Merton passed through in the middle 1930's, and I therefore think it may be correct to say what was witnessed by both of these perceptive young men at that time planted the "seeds" which led to their conversion and to their creating parallel work as Christian writers and witnesses. It would be good to write an essay about "their" arguments with the Gestapo. Both Merton and Percy learned in their ways to distance themselves from the madness, the craziness of contemporary culture. Both sought ways instead to focus on the transcendent love of God.

What Percy said to us on that May Sunday afternoon in 1983, as transcribed here, yet also before the tape recorder was turned on for a full two hours preceding, demonstrated his total Christian commitment and concern for the society of which we are all part. Percy's books, especially the six novels, demonstrate a growing compassion for all persons as demonstrated in his awareness of the Sacramentality of every moment.

Before Percy let us turn on the tape recorder, he was musing about his own life of grace, and Merton's and the fact both were given the insight to enter the Church. He clearly didn't mean this in any prideful way. He simply meant he and Merton had been quite fortunate to have been able to recognize God's grace and accept it. Maybe that appreciation is why both Percy and Merton cultivated the roles of solitary observer. By distancing themselves they were able to see the bigger picture and pray.

When we did this interview Percy would not admit that the book imagined in *The Moviegoer*—on the character Kate's psychiatrist's bookshelf—with its burlap cover so resembling a first edition of the 1949 *Seeds of Contemplation*—was an indirect reference to Merton's very popular book of the 1950's and the need for contemplation. But we know, and knew then and later, that Father Smith of *Love in the Ruins* and *The Thanatos Syndrome* is to some degree an indirect portrait of Merton—a compliment to both of these wise and quiet writers.

An Interview with Walker Percy about Thomas Merton.

Conducted by Victor A. Kramer and Dewey Weiss Kramer in May 1983.
Edited by Paul M. Pearson

Question: What was your association with Thomas Merton?

Answer: Well, I met him only once and the connection was unusual. I had been asked to be on the advisory board of an obscure journal called *Katallagete*, which means in Greek "let us be reconciled." It was organized, edited, and published by two friends of mine, one being Will Campbell, a Baptist preacher, theologian, civil rights activist, and his friend Jim Holloway who was the editor. So, Will asked me to be on the board. He said he had all sorts of Protestants and blacks but he didn't have a Catholic. So I was his token Catholic, I guess, and he had Merton. I don't know why he needed me if he had Merton. I guess he needed a broken-down lay novice Catholic. I didn't mind doing that because being on the advisory board meant you didn't have to do anything -- I had no particular duties. I only went to one meeting and the only reason that I went to that was that Will called me and said that "We are going to meet at Gethsemani Abbey this year. We are going to meet at Merton's place." So that was a chance to meet Merton which turned out to be very fortunate because I think that was either the year or the year before he died, before he went to Thailand. So, we all converged on Gethsemani. I think I flew up to Louisville and was met by somebody, maybe Will, and we drove to the Abbey. We drove up the hillside to Merton's little cinder-block cottage about a half-a-mile or so from the Abbey.

Question: So you went directly to the Hermitage?

Answer: We went directly to the Hermitage. I'd been curious about what the connection was between Merton and the Abbey and the Abbot -- you heard the strangest things about Merton. One that he was schizophrenic, and another was that he had left the Church or he had broken his vows or he was living with a couple of women and all sorts of things. I was amazed at the number of intellectuals who admired Merton and who could not tolerate the idea that he could be an observant Trappist monk for twenty years. But I wanted to see for myself what he was like. I think I corresponded with him several times. I think he wrote me about *The Moviegoer*. He had read *The Moviegoer*, and he was interested in *The Moviegoer*. But I just remember finding ourselves sitting on the front porch of this rather rude, but pleasant, cinder-block cottage overlooking a little swale, a little meadow. And Merton surprised me. He was much more robust than I expected. Now that I look back on Furlong's book, she talks about him being sick all the time. You would think after reading the book that he was an invalid. He was always complaining about this or that, usually a gastrointestinal thing. But, maybe, it was true. But he looked like he was very husky. He was dressed in jeans and I have a recollection of something like a Marine skivy-shirt, and a wide belt. And as I say very, very healthy looking and a pretty tough-looking guy. Very open, outgoing, nice and hospitable. And he fixed everybody a drink, he poured me a nice bourbon and water. Well we were right in bourbon country, you know. In fact driving from Louisville, I remember seeing all these huge places where they stored the liquor.

Question: Can you describe Merton's face? Can you remember?

Answer: He had a ruddy complexion and a healthy, unlined, not a particularly distinguished face; I mean, if you met him in a crowd, or on the street you wouldn't pick him out as being extraordinary looking. I think maybe thinning hair. But, a sturdy, outgoing, well-met fellow.

Question: Had you read many of his books?

Answer: I had read most of them. Not his poetry particularly, I don't read much poetry. I don't have a gift for it. But I'd read most of his prose works.

Question: And so when you were there at that meeting did you talk about the magazine mostly? Or did you have a chance to talk about other things?

Answer: Well, I don't remember. It was very casual. There was a lot of bantering, kidding around, you know, not very serious talk. I remember I was left alone with him for maybe a half hour. And I was a little uneasy, you know, about what to do, and I think he was uneasy with me. What do two writers say to each other?

What do you say to Thomas Merton? There were a lot of things that I wanted to ask him. I remember thinking what to call him. So I called him Fr. Louis. He didn't say otherwise. I would have wanted to ask him things like: "What's going on here? I mean, what's your relationship with the Abbot?" Maybe I should have, maybe he would have answered. Well, obviously, I didn't do it. So we made polite conversation.

We had had a meal. We had gone down to the refectory with the other monks. We ate there; it was good, it was very nice and the monks were very nice. And we went back up the hill, but I don't remember Merton being with us when we ate with the monks. I don't remember whether he came down there or not.

But I remember asking him what he thought of the future of the monastic movement in this country. I wasn't particularly, really interested in that; I wanted to ask him about himself but, I mean, I didn't. Oh incidentally, he had a camera. Griffin had been up there right before then. In fact, there were photographs by Griffin of Merton—big, big, almost poster size—showing Merton just as I saw him in his jeans, that's exactly how I saw him, the way Griffin photographed him. Griffin had just been there, we just missed him was my impression. And Griffin had gotten him interested in photography. He was taking pictures. I remember him, we looked across the meadow and there were deer right at the foot of the meadow. So I asked him something about the future of monasticism in the U. S. It's amazing how little we found to talk about, how much I wanted to ask him, but didn't feel free to ask him. He said something about, "Well he didn't think that the big monastery or the big abbey was a thing of the future." He thought that there were going to be small communities, maybe in cities. He talked about a few men living in a house, you know, somewhere maybe in Louisville or something . It was a rather standard reply which a lot of people were thinking in terms of in 1967. There were maybe half a dozen of us, one was a black guy from Atlanta, and I've forgotten his name. He would have been on the Board of *Katallagete*, a black activist. (VAK: Julius Lester?) I think that's who it was.

Question: Would you like to say something about the magazine?

Answer: *Katallagete* was a very remarkable magazine, it went quite a ways back and mainly reflects the thinking of Will Campbell and Jim Holloway. But it was one of the earlier expressions of ecumenism in a particular sense, Will Campbell being a drop-out from the National Council of Churches. He disagreed with the social orientation of the National Council of Churches very much believing in Christian orthodoxy or rather Anabaptist anarchy. And yet at the same time with a very strong feeling for, maybe the main orientation, was racial reconciliation. In the early sixties, this was not as commonplace as it is today. I'm impressed by early issues having articles by Jacques Ellul. Ellul was an admirer of *Katallagete*. And Merton, Ellul, and other people. I don't think the magazine ever had a circulation of over a thousand or so. It was chronically broke and you never knew when it was coming out. But it was unique of its kind.

Question: You said that you had read several of Merton's books, do any of those books stick out in your mind?

Answer: Well, *Seven Storey Mountain* meant a great deal to me. It was about the time it came out that I became a Catholic so it had a good deal of influence on me. We were coming from the same place —shall I call it Columbia University agnosticism? I was interested in the fact of Merton's own reaction to it, I think he came to dislike the book himself. Life is never as simple as you think it's going to be, and I think he came to regard his monastic vocation, his first idea of it, much more romantically than in fact it turned out. *The Seven Storey Mountain* was a very compelling and attractive book and it came at just the right time both for me and maybe for my generation—postwar, a postwar feeling of uprootedness and dislocation. I had powerful reasons for connecting with it like, I guess, many people did. His background was quite similar to mine. We had both been to Columbia and I knew people that he had known. So I was fascinated with his idea of just leaving Columbia and striking out for the wilds of Kentucky.

Question: Were you surprised when he first wrote to you to say that he'd read *The Moviegoer*?

Answer: Yes, I was astonished, because I had heard from him and Flannery O'Connor about the same time. And I was much flattered, and I wrote him back. I think we corresponded a half a dozen times.

Question: I think maybe one of those letters of his indicates he sent one of those abstract drawings of his to you?

Answer: I've got them somewhere. I didn't understand them, I didn't know what he was trying to do.

Question: Some of those were printed in a book called *Raids on the Unspeakable*. Do you remember that book?

Answer: No.

Comment: It's a book of essays and it has a prose elegy in it for Flannery O'Connor.

Answer: I wonder if he corresponded to any degree with Flannery?

Comment: There's no record of it.

Answer: Really? You would think that he would have. Come to think of it, I don't remember any correspondence from her in her collected correspondence. I don't recall anything about Merton.

Comment: She mentions him a couple of times but she really wasn't excited about what she read. If you go through the index, his name is there a couple of times but she didn't spend much time with Merton.

Answer: She was on good terms with the monks at Conyers, wasn't she? Didn't she go over there?

Question: Oh, yes. Then also, because of the Robert Giroux connection, she was very aware of what Merton was doing. And you may know, Sally Fitzgerald wrote a little piece which was given up at Columbia University where she compares Merton and O'Connor. Have you read that?

Answer: No.

Comment: She talks about O'Connor and Merton as having similar temperaments and living a monastic life and being disciplined and so on. When I met Bob Giroux I talked with him about Merton and he made some of the same connections. Mr. Giroux said that when he would go to see O'Connor she would ask questions about Merton and the same thing when he would go see Merton, more questions would be raised about O' Connor. So, he was kind of the intermediary.

Question: Were you already Catholic or were you thinking about Catholicism before you had read *The Seven Storey Mountain*, or did it just help you find your way as a Catholic?

Answer: I think it did. I don't exactly remember the timing. I think my wife and I both became Catholics in 1948. So it I read it with great enthusiasm and much interest.

Question: You mentioned Columbia and your being a student at Columbia during the same time Merton was. Would you want to say a little bit about Columbia and New York City at that time?

Answer: I was in medical school which was up at 168th Street and he was down at Columbia College. He knew people like Giroux, and his friend, Robert Lax, and Mark Van Doren, and I knew none of those. I had not the slightest interest in English or English departments or writing. I was a medical student at P & S. [Columbia University College of Physicians and Surgeons]

Question: So you had no suspicion at that point that you would become a writer?

Answer: Not the faintest. In the interval I had interned at Bellevue Hospital, had done all the autopsies on tuberculosis patients and had contracted T.B. Not a bad case, but enough. In those days you went to a sanatorium. So I was out of it for a couple of years and I read a good deal.

Question: You know when Merton finally decided to go to Gethsemani he was so relieved to leave New York City. What do you think it was about New York City that he found was so oppressive?

Answer: I don't know. I think he must have mentioned that. He had a political period there. He was very funny talking about his first novel, I think he said he wrote a novel, he said it was a very pessimistic and ominous novel, from a left wing point of view, about Nazi bombers flying over the waterfronts of Hoboken or something. Sounded like a very bad novel. And he said it was. I think he got tired of the standard secular liberal orthodoxy around Columbia University. He was on his own spiritual quest.

Question: Do you have any ideas about why Merton became such a popular writer?

Answer: It had to do more with his talent. He was a very skillful writer and a very appealing writer and a very prolific writer. And also, in the late forties and fifties there was a tremendous spiritual awakening or hunger in this country and in the postwar generation. A friend of mine, Father Charles, had been a friend of Merton's and he had read the book and he had been a tail-gunner on a B-24 that got shot-up on the Ploesti raid. I think there were a whole genera-tion of people who had been through the war and been through that experience. Imagine going from being a tail-gunner to a Trappist monk in Conyers. It wasn't a unique experience.

He was interested in Eastern monasticism which is one of the reasons he went to Thailand. And, I wanted to ask him more about that and didn't. It's a shame. I don't know whether it's an American trait, or a trait of writers but they don't really like to talk to each other much. But I had the feeling that if I could have spent the weekend with him or maybe had six drinks or something I think I would have been able to say a lot more and ask him a lot more. But there was a sense of a great deal left unsaid and a great deal that I would have liked to ask him about.

Something else, I was always curious about and wanted to ask about, and didn't feel like it—how did it work for him, for the abbots to ask him to write, produce these books? When you go to the bookstore at Conyers or the bookstore at Gethsemani and there is a big display, it looks like a Doubleday display of Merton's works. I've often wondered how he felt about that. On the one hand, he liked to write. Maybe it wasn't a bad idea. Writers often need somebody to tell them to go ahead and write. Like Dickens wrote under duress, you know.

Comment: I think Merton realized that. I mean on the one hand, he would say that he would prefer not to write. And on the other, and there are records of this, he knew full well that he profited by being told to go ahead.

Answer: Yes. I had that feeling that it might not have altogether been a bad deal. The popular idea is "poor Merton" having to crank out all this stuff just to help the Trappists. But I'm sure it wasn't that simple.

Comment: No, I think he enjoyed it, I really do. And I think he found that he could, through the writing, find what the next step would be. And he learned more and more to be very disciplined. I talked with Fr. Flavian, the man who was his abbot in the last year of his life, and he said that Merton was so disciplined that finally he could just stop doing one thing, maybe counseling as Novice Master, stop talking, go to his room, sit down, and just turn on the valve and write. He would write for a half hour and then he would stop. And that takes a lot of discipline.

Answer: It takes a lot. And something, not all of us do either. Some of it sounds like that. Although I'm not a critic of poetry, it doesn't strike me much of his poetry is really first rate.

Comment: Part of the problem there is that the *Collected Poems* is such a fat volume. He never would have republished all that stuff.

Answer: One thing that surprised me about Merton was that I made a retreat at a Jesuit Retreat House near New Orleans and they have a room with different tapes. I noticed that they had a series of tapes of Merton's—"Talks to the Novices." He was Novice Master. They are really impressive, he really had a gift for that.

Comment: In fact he spoke to the Community on Sunday afternoons and they started taping so that the lay brothers could hear it also. And they did it for about five years. They've got, well, over two hundred tapes. He would speak to the Community about all kinds of subjects and there are some interesting talks there about literary theory.

Answer: What was admirable about it was the spontaneity, I mean, and the humor. It's funny. I would think he would have been an excellent Novice Master.

It was hard in my own mind to square this impression of him talking in this way to the novices with the portrait that Furlong paints of a rather tortured soul.

Comment: I think that's true. I think that she didn't talk to enough people. We had a man named Jim Finley come to Atlanta and speak at a conference we did on Thomas Merton, and he was a novice of Merton's. Finley told the nicest story. He said when he had gone to Gethsemani, he was a young novice of seventeen and he was supposed to go in and talk with Fr. Louis. He said he went in several times and he was just so nervous he didn't know what

to say, he just felt he wasn't getting anywhere with the spiritual direction. About the fourth time he went in Merton realized that this young man was very, very nervous. So Merton asked, "What's your job here at Gethsemani?" He said, "Well, Fr. Louis, I'm in charge of feeding the pigs." So Merton started laughing and Jim Finley started laughing, and Merton said, "Now look, from here on when you come here for your weekly conference, I want you to tell me something very specific about the pigs, tell me something that happened with the pigs that week." Jim had to go back the next week and he said, "Well, I was feeding the pigs and this one big pig, kind of, pushed this little pig over…" and they both started laughing, and then they laughed a lot. Jim Finley said that was exactly what he needed, and then Merton was his Novice Master for the rest of the time, and it was a real success.

Answer: I'm just remembering the only thing that I recall him saying about the Abbey. It was a rather hostile remark about the Trappist Monastery. He was talking about non-violence, he was very strong on non-violence, and he was saying how the Trappists, even the Trappists, violated this principle. And either I, or somebody, said, "Well, what do you mean? How do they do that?" He said, "Well, look at the way they exploit these brothers, these monks…." I remember the expression was "They got to break their ass carrying all this cheese around." I said, "I didn't really buy that, I didn't really think that was doing violence to people carrying cheese around."

He didn't like that, he thought that was a form of commercial exploitation.

Comment: I was speaking with a monk, Fr. Phillip, a Holy Cross Brother for twenty-five years before he became a monk, and he was a novice of Merton. We were talking about this very subject of cheese. And Fr. Phillip said, "You know we really have a problem here because if some of the younger monks actually knew how much money was being made, they might leave." And he kind of laughed. And so it is a problem, it really is. Although the monastery is very aware of their responsibility and so on.

Answer: Do they need the money to be self-sustaining, I wonder?

Comment: Well they give their excess money away. And in fact, at Gethsemani they employ people from that neighborhood on full-time and a part-time basis. And I think the younger monks are pretty aware of their responsibilities within the community so I don't think it's really a problem. I don't think anybody's getting rich.

Answer: Maybe I ought to say that I went there with some curiosity about the relationship between him and his hermitage and the Abbey. And I came away with the feeling that there was no disaffection, that they were on good terms. I mean maybe I expected to find him grousing in the woods and putting down Gethsemani Abbey. But, the only unfavorable thing he said was the crack about cheese.

"Our Transformation in Christ": Thomas Merton and Transformative Learning

Fred Herron

It has often been remarked that reading Thomas Merton rewards and requires a liberal arts education. Those who knew him and those who were his students were taken by his ability to be filled with and to share his enthusiasms for new ideas from a variety of sources. One of his monastic confreres referred to this as his capacity for "eruption." Abbot Flavian Burns remarked on Merton's ability to integrate a wide variety of insights into his writing, teaching, and preaching. When asked how Merton was able to do this, Merton responded, "Read, read, read."

More than most, Thomas Merton was able to discern and articulate the inner dynamic of the soul's journey to God in the modern and emerging post-modern world. He did this with one foot firmly planted in the rich tradition of the Catholic or sacramental imagination and the other fixed in the spiritual pilgrimage of a new age. He was formed in Christian faith and became an evangelizer for that faith. He helped reshape the vision of monastic life from one of a kind of isolation and spiritual passivity in which each individual came to the monastic community in search of individual growth to one in which the community lived their life of prayer in service to the world as a vibrant evangelizing community.[1]

The monastic experience of formation, consequently, came to be an extension of his understanding of the monk's service to the world. All that reading was not simply an aspect of individual growth and navel-gazing. Merton, and those who studied with him, came to understand it as a part of what allowed them to pray and to teach. John Kavanaugh described the object of that mission in this way: "The great project of education--which is that of human self-understanding in all its forms-- a project of human emancipation. It is also, in that very fact, an affirmation of human dignity. The meaning and purpose of education is justice itself. Human dignity is its premise. Human freedom is its goal."[2] This experience demands both mindfulness and intentionality. It requires an intentionality which understands that to live and teach the gospel--to evangelize--is to be purposefully conscious of our experiences and worldview and how these call us to incarnate human dignity and justice.

The object of this paper is to critically consider transformative learning theory as a "comprehensive...description of how learners construe, validate, and reformulate the meaning of their experience."[3] I hope to show that Thomas Merton serves as a useful exemplar of many of the key elements of this vision of adult learning. This theory provides both a language and a framework for understanding the spiritual growth which human beings experience throughout their lives. At the same time I intend to argue that Merton's insights into this experience may help to deepen and enrich transformative learning theory as well. It would appear that there is a profoundly sacred and sacramental reality at play in the business of real transformative learning which puts us in touch with the mystery of divine activity in our everyday lives. Consequently Thomas Merton can serve as a valuable guide for all those involved in the task of adult faith formation today.

Transformative Learning Theory

Jack Mezirow argues that, in order for people to change their "meaning schemes (specific beliefs, attitudes, and emotional reactions)," they need to become involved in critical reflection on their experiences. That reflection, in turn, leads to a transformation of perspective.[4] He described this perspective transformation as "... the process of becoming critically aware of how and why our assumptions have come to constrain the way we perceive, understand, and feel about our world; changing these structures of habitual expression to make possible a more inclusive, discriminating, and integrating perspective; and, finally, making choices or otherwise acting upon these new understandings."[5]

This is more, however, than simply adding or integrating information into an already existing scheme or approach. Perspective transformation explains how the meaning structures that people acquire over a lifetime become transformed. Edward Taylor describes these meaning structures as frames of reference that are based on the person's cumulative cultural and contextual experiences which influence how they act and interpret events.[6]

Perspective transformation which leads to transformative learning happens much less often than simple change in meaning schemes. Mezirow maintains that it happens as a result of a "disorienting dilemma" which is triggered by a life crisis or a major transition. It may result also from a kind of cumulative "tectonic" shift in meaning schemes over a period of time.[7] Mezirow argues that transformative learning takes place when people change frames of reference as a result of critically reflecting on their assumptions and beliefs. The result of this reflection is a conscious decision to make and implement plans that bring about new ways of defining their worlds.

This shift has sometimes been called a movement toward "emancipatory learning." Mezirow describes the process of emancipatory learning this way: "The emancipation in emancipatory learning is emancipation from libidinal, linguistic, epistemic, institutional or environmental forces that limit our options and our rational control over our lives but have been taken for granted or seen as beyond human control."[8] Put another way, it involves "…critical reflection through which we are able to recognize inherent distortions, limitations, and narrowness of vision."[9] Patricia Cranton describes emancipatory learning as "becoming free from forces that limited our options, forces that have been taken for granted or seen as beyond our control."[10]

This process of transformative learning can be described in four movements, each closely related to the others: (1) questioning the existing perspective, (2) exploring a variety of alternatives, (3) applying the newly transformed perspective, and (4) reintegrating and grounding the new perspective.[11]

The first step involves an experience that challenges the present world of meaning and acts as a catalyst for transformation. This event or series of events exposes the inadequacies of the present assumptions. This challenge may be dramatic-the death of a loved one, a traumatic event- or gradual. It may be the result of a cumulative set of experiences that undermine or challenge the present assumptions.

This critical event or series of events demands renewed critical attention be paid to the content, process and premise of the experience. It requires that we endeavor to name the values and assumptions that provided the foundation for our prior perspective and demands that we begin to revise them. We begin to move from what Jurgen Habermas described as nonreflective learning which "takes place in action contexts in which implicitly raised theoretical and practical validity claims are…taken for granted…" and begin a process of critical reflection that focuses on the foundations of our prior learning and understanding of experience.[12] This resembles Paulo Freire's understanding of conscientization which focuses on the basis on which a question is expressed or defined.[13] Jane Regan and others rightly note that this process happens best when people are in conversation with others.[14]

Having stepped back from our tacitly held meaning perspective and examined its assumptions, the third step in this process involves drawing out and living out the implications of this new meaning perspective. This new perspective focuses attention in some areas and sheds light on areas that were not well seen before. Mezirow suggests that when this new perspective represents a true advance over earlier ones, it is "more inclusive, discriminating, integrative and permeable... than less developed ones."[15] We will need to return to the question of adequate criteria for true advances later.

Finally, at the conclusion of this moment, "the person has reached an equilibrium in which a new set of meaning perspectives provides a context for interpreting new experiences.[16]

This approach is not without its critics. While the model proposed by Jack Mezirow focuses on a transformation which takes place as a result of critical reflection and rational discourse, others focus on the profound place of the imaginative and the affective in this shift. Robert Boyd and J. Gordon Myers point to the place of imagination in serving as foundation for this shift.[17] Others argue that the starting point for transformative education is not to be found in the kind of cognitive dissonance which Mezirow describes but in "... profound emotional experiences that force us to grieve the loss of what used to be a meaningful state of being before we move onto another state that is deeper and wiser and more in tune." with the larger complexities of reality.[18] Jane Regan puts it simply: "There is also an affective, intuitive, creative, and imaginative dimension to transformative learning to be recognized and nurtured in the process of enhancing transformation."[19] We shall argue later that there is reason to go beyond the cognitive/ affective discussion and to ask more fundamental questions regarding the foundations of transformative learning.

Certainly a specifically Christian vision of this sort of transformation would need to take account of those "amazing grace" moments which make up the experience of conversion.[20] Those moments like Paul's on the road to Damascus and those which involve a kind of on-going conversion involve elements of a true "leap of faith." James Loder provides a kind of metaphysical foundation for an understanding of this transformation when he argues that such shifts are not just about a person's understanding of the world, but also serve as essential elements of a person's experience of the "Holy" and the "Void." It is such moments that David Tracy refers to when he discusses the impact of "limit experiences" on a person's religious convictions.[21] I will suggest later that Thomas Merton offers significant insights from the Christian tradition which provides a substantial grounding for an understanding of these experiences.

Valerie Grabov argues that these two views- a rational approach and an emotional/intuitive approach- have much in common. She notes that they share a dedication to "humanism, emancipation, autonomy, critical reflection, equity, self-knowledge, participation, communication and discourse."[22] In fact, Edward Taylor comes to the conclusion that not all learners are predisposed to transformative learning and that not all teachers of adults may feel comfortable with a goal of transformative learning. Further, not all situations may lend themselves to transformative learning.[23]

Others have criticized Mezirow's approach to transformative learning, arguing that it fails to recognize the multiple contexts in which people make meaning. Particularly, they suggest, it fails to account for the relationship between individuals and socio-cultural, political, and historical contexts in which they live and choose.[24] Lillie Albert makes this point in discussing the spirituality of teachers. She argues for the need to adopt an approach suggested by Russian developmental theorist Lev Vygotsky who argued that there is a powerful interweaving of individual learning and developmental and collective learning and development.[25]

Finally, some suggest that Mezirow's transformational learning theory is insufficient because it lacks an adequate theory of social change and consequently does not deal with the question of political and social action that would appear to be demanded by emancipatory education.[26] Jane Regan proposes Paulo Freire's insights as a corrective to these deficiencies.[27] This involves a praxis epistemology that moves back and forth between reflection and action in the world. A praxis approach to knowing involves actions and reflections through which we see the world more clearly and the future that we are approaching. It calls us to a critical awareness of the situation in which we live and leads us to evaluate the prevailing presumptions and to project these into the future. The focus is social transformation-not personal transformation-through which our reality is transformed and liberated.[28]

The challenge here would be to include both personal and social transformation in this understanding and to see an essential connection between the two. James Fleming S.J. suggests, "consciousness-raising education needs intentionality, and if such education is taken for granted, it is likely not to take place. Our hopes are not that people simply understand justice, but that they live justly."[29]

Thomas Merton's Transformative Learning

One productive way in which we might examine Mezirow's approach is to apply the four stages in the transformative learning experience to the life and experience of Thomas Merton. Specifically I shall look at the period between the publication of *Seeds of Contemplation* in 1949 and *New Seeds of Contemplation* in 1962. It was during this critical period that Merton, "who in 1948 was essentially a world-denying and triumphalist monk, a contemplative-out-of-the-world," was transformed into "... a world-affirming and broadly ecumenical person, a contemplative-at-the-heart-of-the-world...."[30] This larger shift came as a result of a dynamic interaction with other more discrete shifts in perspective.[31] Our object is to look at two discrete shifts which took place during this time. The first is more clearly associated with Merton's famous experience at the corner of Fourth and Walnut Streets in the shopping district of Louisville, Kentucky in March of 1958. The second, building upon many of the insights of that powerful year, marked Merton's definitive entry into the struggle against war in October of 1961. Each event bears the marks of a transformative learning experience and helps us to understand such a theory in "a marrowbone" while providing some insights into a critical vision of that theory as well.

A. Fourth and Walnut

It is ironic perhaps that Thomas Merton, a monk of the abbey of Gethsemani, experiences a profound insight into his vocation of solitude while in the middle of Louisville. But he wrote on March 19, 1958 about a powerful experience he had there the day before: "Yesterday, in Louisville, at the corner of 4th and Walnut, I suddenly realized that I loved all the people and that none of them were, or, could be totally alien to me. As if waking from a dream-the dream of my separateness, of the 'special' vocation to be different. My vocation does not really make me different from the rest of men or put me in a special category except artificially; juridically. I am still a member of the human race-and what more glorious destiny is there for man, since the Word was made flesh and became, too a member of the Human Race!"[32]

This passage has been written about many times as a highlight in Merton's life and a critical window into the Christian life. It is sometimes described as a kind of Pauline experience which came to Merton from out of the blue. Yet, as Merton scholar William Shannon and others have noted, the soil had been tilled for some time in preparation for this event. Shannon quotes the Zen saying: "When the pupil is ready, the teacher will come" and reminds us that there is meaning in the waiting.[33] A closer look at this experience allows us to see the stages that transformative learning theorists talk about in a concrete spiritual experience.

(1) Questioning the Present Perspective: What Is the Monastic Mission?

It began to happen almost immediately after his grand farewell to the world, reflected in his remark in *The Seven Storey Mountain*, when Merton commented, "Never since I have entered religion have I ever had the slightest desire to go back into the world."[34] By 1958 Merton knew a great deal more about the world than he had known in the 1940s. He dealt with a large variety of correspondence which demanded substantial replies. Over time he began to respond to the problem of what it meant for him to be in a monastery for others. Merton came gradually to see that "mission can never be the goal of the contemplative, yet it can be, and perhaps ought to be, its fruit."[35]

(2) Exploring Alternatives: The Threat of "Spiritual Narcissism"

As early as December 29, 1949 Merton reflected on the possibility of "… spiritual narcissism in our lives." He explains that he is thinking about a "narcissistic solitude… that is really a substitute for the responsibility of living with people." The opposite of this, he argues, is "a craven activism that delights in company and noise and movement and escapes the responsibility of living at peace with God." He sees the need for balance between "narcissistic solitude" and "crass activism" which requires that our lives become "a dialectic between community and solitude." Noting other places where Merton pointed out the link between this dialectic, William Shannon suggests that Merton "...believed what he said without yet understanding all that it meant."[36] This was a new question which Merton was confronting. The question of mission was an inevitable overflow of contemplation.

Merton began to give more explicit shape to this struggle in November, 1958 in a letter to Pope John XXIII: "It seems to me that, as a contemplative, I do not need to lock myself into solitude and lose all contact with the rest of the world." Instead, he argues, "this poor world has a right to a place in my solitude." He proceeds to articulate what one commentator has termed "Merton's mission statement" for his future: "I have to think in terms of a contemplative grasp of the political, intellectual, artistic and social movements in this world-by which I mean a sympathy for the honest aspirations of so many intellectuals everywhere in the world and the terrible problems they have to face. I have had the experience of seeing that this kind of understanding and friendly sympathy, on the part of a monk who really understands them, has produced striking effects among artists, writers, publishers, poets, etc. who have become my friends without having to leave the cloister."[37]

(3) Applying a Transformed Perspective: "There Are No Strangers"

This experience shattered forever Merton's notion of a separate holy existence that went with living in a monastery. Merton continues his journal entry, describing this Louisville experience, by linking it to Proverb, a young Jewish girl about whom he dreamed in late February, 1958 and to whom he wrote in his journal on March 4, 1958.[38] He writes to tell her that he saw her yesterday "in a different place, in a different form, in the most unexpected circumstances. I shall never forget our meeting yesterday. The touch of your hand makes me a different person. To be with you is rest and truth. Only with you are these things found...."[39]

Merton comes to dramatically reinterpret the meaning of solitude as a result of this experience. It becomes clear to him that "when I am alone they are not 'they' but my own self. There are no strangers."[40] Describing his vision he says, "then it was as if I suddenly saw the secret beauty of their hearts, the depths of their hearts where neither sin nor desire nor self-knowledge can reach, the core of their reality, the person that each one is in God's eyes."[41]

Using a phrase which he borrowed from Louis Massignon to express what he saw as the deepest reality of the human person, *le point vierge,* Merton wrote: "At the center of our being is a point of nothingness which is untouched by sin and by illusion, a point of pure truth, a point or spark which belongs entirely to God... this little point of nothingness and of *absolute poverty* is the pure glory of God in us." [42] This point is "a pure diamond," and is "in everybody, and if we could see it we would see these billions of points of light coming together in the face and blaze of a sun that would make all the darkness and cruelty of life vanish completely."[43]

(4) Reintegrating the New Perspective: "I Remain a Contemplative"

Merton's experience fostered his "mission statement" to Pope John XXIII, a correspondence with Russian writer Boris Pasternak, and a renewed dedication to his mission to intellectuals. Within the next year he initiated fruitful contacts with Polish writer Czeslaw Milosz and with Japanese Zen scholar D.T. Suzuki.[44] Ernesto Cardenal, reflecting on that time when Merton was his novice master, recalls Merton asking him about his life in Nicaragua. At first Cardenal felt cheated, as if he had wasted time that should be spent on spiritual guidance. "Gradually," he said, "I began to understand that he was giving me spiritual guidance." He came to Gethsemani in order to renounce everything, his writing and his interest in politics. Finally, "Merton made me see that I didn't have to renounce anything." That is, "Merton saw no conflict in the contemplative life and the life of action."[45] In an introduction to a projected series of his complete works, to be published in Spanish beginning in 1958, Merton points to the need to find a contemplative spirit in the church's mission: "Without contemplation, without the intimate, secret pursuit of truth through love, our action loses itself in the world and becomes dangerous. Yet, if our contemplation is fanatic or false, our action becomes much more dangerous. We should lose ourselves to win the world; we should humble ourselves to find Christ everywhere and to love him in all beings."[46]

B. War and Peace

Merton's "return to the world," sparked by the events of 1958, led to an increased concern with issues of social justice. The issue of violence in society and the possibility of nuclear war drew his particular attention and concern. One can hardly imagine a topic which a Catholic readership, familiar with his best-selling autobiography lauding a withdrawal from the world, might find more unsettling than this. Writing to Dorothy Day in August, 1961 he expresses a concern that the Trappist order's censors might not accept some writings on the subject since "a Trappist should not know about these things, or should not write about them." Yet he tells her that he feels "obligated to take very seriously what is going on, and to say whatever my conscience seems to dictate."[47]

Merton scholars generally agree that his definitive leap into the struggle against war can be located in October, 1961.[48] But there are moments in the years and months before which set the stage for this dramatic step.

(1) Questioning the Present Perspective: "The Catholic Way of Looking at War"

The common notion of just war was a fundamental assumption for Merton. Shannon argues that "Merton seems to have been hung up on the theory of the just war as something that had been so long a part of Catholic tradition that it could not be set aside." That is, it simply was "the Catholic way of looking at war."[49] At best this position would allow for an argument to a kind of practical pacifism based on just war principles. Merton based his application for non-combative status before World War II on a *jus in bello* argument which accepts the legitimacy of the war but resists the methods of waging war. He wrote in *The Seven Storey Mountain*: "To my mind, there was very little doubt about the immorality of the methods used in modern war.... Methods that descend to wholesale barbarism and ruthless indiscriminate slaughter of non-combatants practically without defense are hard to see as anything else but mortal sins."[50]

Merton's reading of Mohandas Gandhi played an important part in his developing interest in nonviolence. In 1931, when Merton was a student at Oakham School in England, Gandhi came to London for a conference to negotiate home rule for India. More than thirty years later Merton recalled his sixteen-year-old self staunchly defending Gandhi and the Indian desire for home rule. He vividly recalled arguing this case with the captain of the football team who was also head prefect.[51] It is clear that the adult Merton was reading Gandhi by 1955. He found Gandhi's perspective congenial at least in part because he found in him an understanding of the contemplative dimension of reality which was similar to the Christian mystical tradition and to his own experience of contemplation

(2) Exploring Alternatives: "Something Must Be Said"

Three short but important works helped to pave the way for Merton's war and peace writings. The first was a poem, "Chants to Be Used in Processions around a Site with Furnaces," which dealt with the gas chambers at Auschwitz.[52] The second, *Original Child Bomb*, was written in midsummer of 1961 and took as its subject the dropping of the first atomic bombs.[53] Merton describes his attitude toward these events using irony and understatement. His "objectivity" as a narrator draws readers into the events he describes.

The third work is a letter-essay which he wrote to Pablo Antonio Cuadra, a Latin American poet. In contrast to the objective stance of *Original Child Bomb*, this piece is most notable for Merton's passion and indignation.[54] The letter is biting and violent. It is so violent, in fact, that Merton biographer Michael Mott reports that Merton felt it necessary to question why it had gotten "so violent and unfair."[55] He describes this letter as being "about the merciless stupidity of the Great Powers and power politicians." Merton is upset with the pharisaism of the West and the Russians-he refers to them as Gog and Magog- and believes that "something must be said."[56] Merton describes this in a letter dealing with "the international situation and the deplorable attempts of the great powers to threaten one another and the world with nuclear weapons." He looks instead to the Third World for the restoration of sanity: "It is my belief that all those in the world who have kept some vestige of sanity and spirituality should unite in firm resistance to the movements of power politicians and the monster nations, resist the diplomatic overtures of power and develop a strong and coherent third world that can stand on its own feet and affirm the spiritual and human values which are cynically denied by the great powers."[57]

(3) Applying a Transformed Perspective: "The Root of War Is Fear"

An article entitled "The Root of War is Fear" which first appeared in the *Catholic Worker* in 1961 marked Merton's official entrance into the peace movement. Actually it was a chapter in a book, *New Seeds of Contemplation*, which was an extensive rewriting of the earlier *Seeds of Contemplation*.[58] Merton added three significant paragraphs to the revised edition of this chapter, with the intention of situating "these thoughts in the present crisis."[59] So powerful were these three paragraphs that William Shannon argues "… that it is hardly an exaggeration to say that they sum up in brief fashion a whole program for opposing war and working for peace."[60]

Merton begins by arguing that the world has been swept up in a war fever. Singling out the United States for particular scorn, he goes on to discuss the duty of the Christian in the present situation. Christians need to avoid a fatalistic attitude and the saber-rattling which he sees as "the great and not even subtle temptation of a Christianity which has grown rich and comfortable." He insists that it is the duty of every Christian to work for the total abolition of war. Regarding the church, Merton argues that "she must lead the way on the road toward *non-violent settlement of difficulties* and toward the gradual abolition of war as the way of settling international or civil disputes."[61] He concludes: "we may never succeed in this campaign, but whether we succeed or not, the duty is evident. It is the great Christian task of our time. Everything else is secondary, for the survival of the human race itself depends upon it."[62]

(4) Reinterpreting the New Perspective: The Cold War Letters

Following the appearance of this article there appeared literally a barrage of articles dealing with this subject in the next six months. Indeed most of Merton's writing on this subject was done between October, 1961 and April, 1962. It was in that month that the abbot general of the Trappists ordered Merton to stop writing in this area. But during that brief period he published articles in *Commonweal, Jubilee, Fellowship, Blackfriars* and the *Catholic Worker*. He also began to organize a plan for a book of letters, written to a variety of people, but all dealing with some aspect of the war and peace question. This book would come to be called *The Cold War Letters*.[63]

He writes in January, 1962 that "the great peril of the cold war is the progressive deadening of conscience."[64] On February 6, 1962 he warns against the inevitable presence of hidden aggressions in people dedicated to nonviolence.[65] An article appears in *Commonweal* on February 9, 1962 entitled "Nuclear War and Christian Responsibility." He suggests the need for negotiating multilateral disarmament and argues for the renewal of a moral sense and a resumption of genuine responsibility. He challenges the *Commonweal* readers to form their consciences regarding participation in the political and military efforts that threaten to lead to universal destruction. Merton highlights much of what he came to believe about this question in the last of the Cold War Letters (# 106) in November 1962: "Our first task is to liberate ourselves from the assumptions and prejudices which vitiate our thinking on these fundamental points, and we must help other men to do the same. This involves not only clear thinking, lucid speech, but very positive social action. And since we believe that the only effective means are non-violent, we must learn non-violence and practice it. This involves in its turn a deep spiritual purification."[66]

Transformative Learning and Conversion: "The Providential Designs of God"

A consideration of transformative learning theory in the light of Merton's monastic experience strongly suggests that something more is happening beyond a mere change in perspective regarding war and peace or even the nature of humanity itself. Certainly we can trace the shift which transformative learning theory describes in both of these cases. But as important as these insights are, it would appear that focusing too much on these might cause us to miss the forest for the trees. Merton was able to look at the changes in his life and to see in them the activity of the divine.

A careful reading of *The Seven Storey Mountain* suggests that Merton saw his conversion to Catholicism as part of a process and not simply as a one time event, no matter how powerful. He remarks that he could read "the providential designs of God" in his coming to Columbia University.[67] This was a place, he wrote, where "God brought me and a half dozen others together." Reflecting a profoundly sacramental or incarnational vision of reality, he realizes that salvation "begins on the level of common and natural and ordinary things.... Books and ideas and poems and stories, pictures and music, buildings, cities, places, philosophies were to be the materials on which grace would work." Transformation, then, at it its most profound level, is never simply a movement from one perspective to another. Merton's recommendation to Flavian Burns is more than a suggestion about a way to perform one task better. It was a challenge and a reflection on his own insight, shaped in a rich monastic tradition of prayer and study, which views real transformation as a commitment to a lifelong journey.

Merton's commitment to a "conversion of manners," is a radical embrace of a commitment to inner transformation. This transformation involves a constant awakening and attentiveness to his true self, his true identity in God.[68] How are we to determine whether or not our transformative experiences are matters of true growth or simply a matter of shifting perspectives? What is it that can truly pass for growth? Mezirow argues that "a developmentally progressive meaning perspective is more inclusive, discriminating, integrative, and permeable...than less developed ones."[69] A monastic vision of development would be hard pressed to criticize such a vision. The challenge which James Loder and others might offer to this perspective would focus on the metaphysical foundations of that emancipatory process. Merton might suggest that those concerned with transformative learning that might foster a truly adult faith need to recall that "we are not 'converted' only once in our life but many times, and this endless series of large and small 'conversions,' inner revolutions, leads finally to our transformation in Christ."[70] Merton later explains that he is talking about a profound "interior revolution" in which what seems to be the "self" is "gradually destroyed and exchanged for another self, the Spirit of Christ."[71]

At the heart of this process of transformation is the self in dialogue with the loving God, encouraging the transformation of the self from the false self to the true self, reflecting the image of the divine. A monastic spirituality turns the discussion of transformation on its head precisely because it changes the conditions of the discussion. No longer are we speaking about an isolated soul involved in a journey of discovery. Instead we are speaking about a person's journey, both as an individual and in community, in response to a loving God who calls us not to discover ourselves but to remember our truest selves.

This is the image of memory which poet Seamus Heaney highlights in his reflections on Dante:

> So I live now, for the things I saw depart
> And are almost gone, although a distilled sweetness
> Still drops from them into my inner heart.

> Because, by returning to my memory some-
> What, and being celebrated in these tercets
> Your overallness will be more brought home.[72]

William Shannon highlights one aspect of Merton's experience of transformation which provides those who study it with reason to pause and reflect. Pointing to the seemingly mundane events of our quotidian realities and remarking that he does not mean to suggest

"... that events that appear to be insignificant have no meaning," Shannon reminds us that "moments of great significance may be hidden in the seemingly meaningless events that make up ordinary life."[73] The sense that nothing much is happening may belie the working of the Holy Spirit, suggesting that "...because nothing spectacular is happening, nothing is happening at all." "Life is full of moments of conversion," Shannon remarks, "however small they may appear to be and however unnoticed they may pass. For they are (or can be) steps in the gradual buildup to a decisive conversion experience that marks a new and distinctly recognizable moment of grace in our lives. We need to realize that it was indeed these little conversions, which went almost unnoted, that helped to make possible the decisive experience."[74] The key word here is *grace*. The impetus for growth and change is God's grace, a hidden ground of love for us. Our transformation is ongoing but it is willed by a loving God.[75] It does not happen alone but in the *"I-Thou"* relationship we share with that God.[76]

In the context of that relationship none of us are ever truly lost along the way. Merton helps to remind us that we are called to a life-long transformation and that we are lost only when we try to seek one unchanging "abiding place." Having lived through a period of dramatic spiritual transformation, Merton remarked in 1961 that "the way toward the Homeland becomes more and more obscure. As I look over the stages which were once more clear, I see that we are all on the right road, and though it may be night, it is a saving night."[77] It is Merton's fundamental insight that we are never truly rooted in one dear perpetual place but that we are pilgrims on a journey. He writes of Gethsemani, though it is a place where he found great happiness, "My monastery is not a home. It is not a place where I am rooted and established in the earth."[78] Gethsemani became for him not a home but a sign or sacrament pointing him towards eternity and reunion with his true self in a loving God.

Endnotes

1. In this regard Merton anticipated a variety of approaches which came to be spoken of as "trinitarian spiritualities." See Catherine M. LaCugna, *God for Us: The Trinity and the Christian Life* (San Francisco: Harper Collins, 1991).

2. John F. Kavanaugh, "Jesuit Education and Social Justice in Theory and Practice," in R.E. Bonachea, (ed.), *Jesuit Higher Education* (Pittsburg,

Pennsylvania: Duquesne University Press, 1989), p.173.

3. Patricia Cranton, *Understanding and Promoting Transformative Learning: A Guide for Educators of Adults* (San Francisco, California: Jossey-Bass, 1994), p.22.

4. Jack Mezirow, *Transformative Dimensions of Adult Learning* (San Francisco, California: Jossey-Bass, 1991), p.167.

5. Mezirow, *Transformative Dimensions of Adult Learning,* p. 167.

6. Edward W. Taylor, *The Theory and Practice of Transformative Learning: A Critical Review,* Information Series #374. (Columbus, Ohio: Eric Clearinghouse on Adult, Career, and Vocational Education, Center on Education and Training for Employment, College of Education, Ohio State University, 1998).

7. Jack Mezirow, "Transformative Theory of Adult Learning," in Michael R Welton, (ed.), *In Defense of the Lifeworld* (New York: SUNY Press, 1995), p.50.

8. *Transformative Dimensions of Human Learning,* p.87.

9. Jane Regan, *Toward an Adult Church: A Vision of Faith Formation* (Chicago: Loyola University Press, 2002), p.79.

10. Patricia Cranton, *Professional Development as Transformative Learning: New Perspectives for Teachers of Adults* (San Francisco, California: Jossey-Bass, 1996), p.2.

11. Cranton, *Understanding and Promoting Transformative Learning,* pp. 69-76.

12. Jurgen Habermas, *Legitimization Crisis* (London: Heinemann, 1966), p.16.

13. Paulo Freire, *Pedagogy of the Oppressed,* revised edition (New York: Continuum, 1993).

14. Regan, *Toward an Adult Church,* 92 and Edward Taylor, "Analyzing Research on Transformative Learning Theory," in Jack Mezirow (ed.), *Learning as Transformation: Critical Perspectives on a Theory in Progress* (San Francisco, California: Jossey-Bass, 2000), pp.306-309. See also Addie Lorraine Walker, "Dialogue As a Strategy for Transformative Education," http://www.bc.edu/research/cjl/meta-elements/sites/partners/ecrp/ CJC Walker. htm (Accessed June 27, 2005)

15. Mezirow, *Transformative Dimensions of Adult Learning,* p.193.

16. Regan, *Toward an Adult Church,* p. 95.

17. Robert D. Boyd and J. Gordon Myers, "Transformative Education," *International Journal of Lifelong Education* 7 (October-December, 1988), pp. 261-284.

18. S. M. Scott, "The Grieving Soul in the Transformative Process," in Patricia Cranton, (ed.), *Transformative Learning in Action: Insight from Practice* (San Francisco: Jossey-Bass, 1997), p.45.

19. Regan, *Toward an Adult Church,* p. 97

20. For one useful approach see Walter Conn, *Christian Conversion: A Developmental Interpretation of Autonomy and Surrender* (New York: Paulist, 1986) and Idem, *Conversion: Perspectives on Personal and Social Transformation* (New York: Alba House, 1978).

21. James E. Loder, *The Transforming Moment: Understanding Convictional Experiences* (San Francisco, California: Harper and Row, 1981) and David Tracy, *Blessed Rage for Order: The New Pluralism in Theology* (Chicago, Illinois: University of Chicago Press, 1975), p.105.

22. Valerie Grabov, "The Many Faces of Transformative Learning Theory and Practice," in *Transformative Learning Theory in Action,* p. 90.

23. Taylor, *The Theory and Practice of Transformative Learning.*

24. Taylor, *The Theory and Practice of Transformative Learning* pp. 25-28.

25. Lillie R. Albert, "The Call to Teach: Spirituality and Intellectual Life, *Conversation* 18(Fall, 2000), pp. 38-42.

26. Susan and Michael Collard, "The Limits of Perspective Transformation: A Critique of Mezirow's Theory," *Adult Education Quarterly* 39(1989), pp.99-107

27. Regan, *Toward an Adult Church*, pp. 99-103.

28. Thomas Groome, *Christian Religious Education: Sharing Our Story and Vision* (San Francisco, California: Harper and Row, 1981).

29. James Fleming, S.J., "The Emerging Role of Service Learning at Jesuit Universities," *Explore* (Spring, 1999), p.8.

30. Donald Grayston, *Thomas Merton: The Development of a Spiritual Theologian* (New York: Edwin Mellen Press, 1985), p.12.

31. Fred Herron, *No Abiding Place: Thomas Merton and the Search for God* (Lanham, Maryland: University Press of America, 2005), pp. 3-32.

32. Lawrence Cunningham, (ed.), *A Search For Solitude: Pursuing the Monk's True Life. The Journals of Thomas Merton,* volume 3: 1952-1960, (San Francisco, California: Harper San Francisco, 1996), pp.181-182.

33. William H. Shannon, *Silent Lamp: The Thomas Merton Story* (New York: Crossroad, 1992), p.8.

34. Thomas Merton, *The Seven Storey Mountain* (New York: Harcourt Brace, 1948), p.383.

35. Shannon, *Silent Lamp*, p. 33. I am grateful to William Shannon for many of the key insights which follow.

36. Shannon, *Silent Lamp,* p. 33.

37. William H. Shannon, (ed.), *Hidden Ground of Love: The Letters of Thomas Merton on Religious Experience and Social Concerns* (New York: Farrar, Straus and Giroux, 1985), p. 482.

38. Cunningham, *Search for Solitude,* p. 176.

39. Cunningham, *Search for Solitude,,* p.182.

40. Thomas Merton, *Conjectures of a Guilty Bystander* (Garden City, New York: Doubleday, 1966), p.158.

41. Merton, *Conjectures*, p. 158.

42. Merton, *Conjectures*, p. 158.

43. Merton, *Conjectures*, p. 158.

44. Robert E. Daggy, (ed.), *Encounter: Thomas Merton and D.T. Suzuki* (Monterey, Kentucky: Larkspur Press, 1988)

45. Paul Wilkes, *Merton By Those Who Knew Him* (New York: HarperCollins, 1984), p. 36.

46. Thomas Merton, *Honorable Reader: Reflections on My Work* (New York: Crossroad, 1989), p.42-43.

47. Merton, *Hidden Ground of Love*, p.139.

48. Shannon, *Silent Lamp*, p. 210.

49. Shannon, *Silent Lamp*, p. 239.

50. Merton, *The Seven Storey Mountain,* p. 312.

51. Thomas Merton, *Seeds of Destruction* (New York: Farrar, Straus and Giroux, 1964), p. 222.

52. Thomas Merton, *The Collected Poems of Thomas Merton* (New York: New Directions, 1977).

53. Thomas Merton, *Original Child Bomb* (New York: New Directions, 1962) and *Hidden Ground of Love*, p. 18.

54. *The Collected Poems of Thomas Merton,* p. 375.

55. Michael Mott, *The Seven Mountains of Thomas Merton* (Boston: Houghton Mifflin, 1984), p. 365.

56. *Hidden Ground of Love*, p. 132.

57. Merton, *Hidden Ground of Love,* pp.50-51.

58. Donald Grayston, *Thomas Merton's Rewriting: The Five Versions of Seeds/New Seeds of Contemplation as a Key to the Development of his Thought* (New York: Edwin Mellen Press, 1985).

59. Merton, *Hidden Ground of Love*, p. 140.

60. Shannon, *Silent Lamp,* p. 212.

61. A similar position echoed Merton's argument when Enda McDonagh and Stanley Hauerwas came to propose "An Appeal to Abolish War" at a conference sponsored by the Center for Ethics and Culture at the University of Notre Dame on October 28, 2002. Their goal was to "start a discussion about war that would make war as morally problematic as slavery." Stanley Hauerwas, "Reflections on the 'Appeal to Abolish War' or What Being a Friend of Enda's Got Me Into," in Linda Hogan and Barbara FitzGerald, (eds.), *Between Poetry and Politics: Essays in Honour of Enda McDonagh* (Dublin:Columba Press, 2003), pp. 135-147. See also Enda McDonagh's discussion of this appeal and Stanley Hauerwas's reflection, "Abolitionism: A Christian Response to War?" http://ethicscenter.nd.edu/archives/videos/shtml/ (Accessed August 8, 2005).

62. Thomas Merton, *New Seeds of Contemplation* (New York: New Directions, 1962), p. 7.

63. William H. Shannon (ed.), *Witness to Freedom: The Letters of Thomas Merton in Times of Crisis* (New York: Farrar, Straus and Giroux, 1994). In this volume all one hundred and eleven letters are placed in chronological order and 58 of the letters are included. See Patricia Burton, *Index to the Published Letters of Thomas Merton* (Rochester, New York: Thomas Merton Society, 1996). See also Thomas Merton, *Cold War Letters* (Maryknoll, New York: Orbis, 2006).

64. Merton, *Hidden Ground of Love*, p. 326.

65. Merton, *Hidden Ground of Love*, p. 326.

66. Merton, *Hidden Ground of Love*, p. 575

67. Merton, *The Seven Storey Mountain*, p.177.

68. Anne Carr, *A Search for Wisdom and Truth: Thomas Merton's Theology of the Self* (Notre Dame, Indiana: University of Notre Dame Press, 1988).

69. Mezirow, *Transformative Dimensions of Adult Learning*, p. 193.

70. Thomas Merton, *Life and Holiness* (New York: Herder and Herder, 1963), p. 159.

71. Merton, *Honorable Reader*, p. 99.

72. Seamus Heaney, "The Light of Heaven: Dante, *Paradiso*, Canto XXXIII, lines 49-145," in *Between Poetry and Politics*, pp. 12-13.

73. Shannon, *Silent Lamp*, p.7

74. Shannon, *Silent Lamp*, p. 8.

75. Cardinal Christoph Schonborn, "Evolution and Design in Nature: The Issues," *Origins* 35 (August 4, 2005), pp.166-167.

76. Martin Buber, *I and Thou* (New York: Free Press, 1971) and Aubrey Hodes, *Encounter with Martin Buber* (New York: Pelican, 1971).

77. Patrick Hart, (ed.), *The School of Charity: The Letters of Thomas Merton on Religious Renewal and Spiritual Direction* (New York: Farrar, Straus and Giroux, 1990), pp.139-140.

78. Merton, *Honorable Reader*, p. 65.

Thomas Merton and St. John of the Cross: Lives on Fire

Nass Cannon

The streets were empty that cold day as we shivered in our spring clothes. In January, no one is in Ubeda, not even American tourists! We were there almost by happenstance as a convenient place to spend the night on the long drive back to Madrid from Grenada. My family chose a trip to southern Spain, foolishly thinking it would be warmer than other European destinations. (My unsolicited advice would be that if you plan to take a trip to southern Spain in January, take your ski clothes!). Our trip included a rail excursion to Toledo and a self-drive trip through Andalusia including Seville and Grenada.

As we set out to explore the town, my middle son, an insatiable explorer, stumbled across a museum with the name of Juan de la Croix and asked whether I had heard of him? The museum was the monastery where St. John died. After touring the restored cell in which he lived, we viewed his relics and the table on which they treated his gangrenous leg. Unaware, I had traced his movements in Southern Spain (where he tirelessly journeyed to establish and serve in monasteries) and awakened to the reality of our own "pilgrimage" one day before departing Spain. It is this reawakened interest in the writings of St. John of the Cross coupled with the long term assistance provided by that spiritual guide, Thomas Merton, which prompts this essay.

In this paper, I wish to share some observations about Thomas Merton and St. John of the Cross as persons on fire with the love of God. I will to do this using St. John of the Cross's concept of contemplation as an encounter with the fiery presence of God. I intend also to reflect on the end effects of such a contemplation expressed by Merton as "the unity of a person" or "final integration" and St. John as "The Living Flame of Love."

Both Thomas Merton and St. John of the Cross encountered the God Moses described in Deuteronomy as a consuming fire (Dt 4:24). The analogy of God as fire permeates most of St. John's writings, especially in *The Dark Night of the Soul* and *The Living Flame of Love.*

St. John views the contemplative process as the transformation of the soul by this consuming fire. The source of this fire-- the Spirit— afflicts, transforms, and causes the soul to blaze in loving union with the Father and the Son. Merton also experienced this fire, as illustrated through his description of himself as a burnt man, his reference to "the living experience of divine love and Holy Spirit in the flame of which St. John of the Cross speaks" and believing that this spark resides in our heart.[1] Like St. John, Merton viewed contemplation as the action of the Spirit within the heart of every person. God's embrace of contemplatives such as Thomas Merton and St. John of the Cross cause them to be burnt, purged, and erupt into flames. Although both roared into flames, their writings reflect an individual, personal, and unique expression of their union with God.

In his writings, Merton quotes extensively from the texts of St. John and acknowledges his debt to him as a spiritual forbear and guide. Early in his monastic life, Merton comments on his relationship to St. John: "I say that St. John of the Cross seems to me to be the most accessible of the saints that is only another way of saying that he is my favorite saint."[2] Merton saw St. John as accessible because he revealed his inner depths and the intimacy of his relationship with God for all to see.

> Nevertheless it is true, if you consider that few saints, if any, have ever opened up to other men such remote depths in their own soul. St. John of the Cross admits you, in the Living Flame, to his soul's "deepest center", to the "deep caverns" in which the lamps of fire, the attributes of God, flash mysteriously in metaphysical shadows; who else has done as much?[3]

I think many of us would answer: Thomas Merton, who undressed himself, his thinking, his reflections and contemplative journey, in full public view.

These men, who were possessed by God and dispossessed in so many other ways, had many similarities during their earthly pilgrimage but also some striking differences. Both had splintered families at an early age. Juan de Yepes y Alvarez was born in Fontiveros, Spain, in 1542, the son of an affluent father who was disowned for marrying beneath his station. He died shortly after John's birth, forcing John's mother to support the family by silk weaving. Like John, Merton lost a parent at a young age. He was six when his mother died of stomach cancer.

St. John had a reputation of piety from youth and at age 17 attended a Jesuit College while working at the Plague Hospital de la Concepcion. After being ordained in 1567 in the Carmelite order, he later joined St. Teresa as her confessor and spiritual director at the Convent of the

Incarnation. St. Theresa introduced John to members of her convent as a saint. By contrast, devoted readers are quite familiar with the more Augustinian youthful life of Thomas Merton, particularly while at Cambridge, which may have been influenced by the bohemian lifestyle of his artistic father. At age seven, Merton was traveling in the company of his father and his father's love interest, including her husband, to Bermuda. (In Wikipedia, a biographer asserts that Merton referred to this as the "Bermuda Triangle").

Both St. John's and Merton's spiritual lives thrived in the desert. In 1576, the Calced Friars arrested John and confined him to a small cell in their monastery in Toledo because of his reform efforts. During this time of physical confinement and abuse, he composed the Spiritual Canticle, reflecting a spirit on fire. In the confinement of a Trappist monastery, Merton became a two-fisted monk. He took to being a monk the way he formerly took to the bars: He went at it. He left nothing behind, taking with him all of his gifts-- writing, scholarship, and a mind that would follow the truth wherever it took him. Within the monastery, Merton became an explorer of himself, society, other cultures, and the no-face of God.

Both experienced rejection. Although St. John held many offices in the Discalced Province and tirelessly journeyed on foot in their service, he was rejected by his own order which threatened to send him to Mexico near the end of his life. Shortly afterwards, when St. John's leg became infected, he chose to go to the monastery at Ubeda where his humility moved a hostile prior to became a champion of St. John's cause for beatification. Likewise, Merton was rejected by many as he spoke out for social justice, the peace movement, and immersed himself in Eastern thought; however, to my knowledge there is not a movement promoting Merton's cause for beatification.

While their lives were similar in some respects and very different in others, it is in the writings of their experience of the Spirit that their kinship is most striking. Both were great spiritual writers, guides and passionate men who sought God with great desire. Thomas Merton experienced the purgation reflected in St. John of the Cross's metaphor of the soul being like a log of wood heated by an external flame before slowly igniting and roaring into flames. St. John described this process in the *Dark Night of the Soul:*

> For the greater clearness of what has been said, and of what has still to be said, it is well to observe at this point that this purgative and loving knowledge or Divine light whereof we here speak acts

upon the soul which it is purging and preparing for perfect union with it in the same way as fire acts upon a log of wood in order to transform it into itself; for material fire, acting upon wood, first of all begins to dry it, by driving out its moisture and causing it to shed the water which it contains within itself. Then it begins to make it black, dark and unsightly, and even to give forth a bad odour, and, as it dries it little by little, it brings out and drives away all the dark and unsightly accidents which are contrary to the nature of fire. And, finally, it begins to kindle it externally and give it heat, and at last transforms it into itself and makes it as beautiful as fire.[4]

In his *The Ascent to Truth*, Merton uses a similar fiery analogy:

It is into this abyss of blazing light, so infinitely bright as to be pure darkness to our intelligence that the mystic enters not only with his eyes, his imagination, and his mind but with his whole soul and substance, in order to be transformed like a bar of iron in the white heat of a furnace. The iron turns into fire. The mystic is "transformed" in God.[5]

Merton also alludes to this purgation at the end of *The Seven Storey Mountain* when he uses the literary device of quoting the Spirit who is speaking to him:

Everything that touches you shall burn you, and you will draw your hand away in pain, until you have withdrawn yourself from all things. Then you will be all alone. Everything that can be desired will sear you, and brand you with a cautery, and you will fly from it in pain to be alone. Every created joy will come to you as pain, and you will die to all joy and be left alone. You will be praised, and it will be like burning at the stake.[6]

Merton concludes the revelation on why he was brought to Gethsemani: "That you may become the brother of God and learn to know the Christ of the burnt men."[7]

Becoming the brother of God led him into some strange places and activities as he became the brother of every person. After his epiphany on the streets of Louisville in 1958, he reached out to his brothers everywhere including celebrities, social activists, Buddhist and Zen monks. He also experienced the Christ of the burnt men, in himself, his neighbors, those who immolated themselves during the Vietnam peace protest, and in his Zen-like death by electrocution. But most of all, he knew the Christ of the burnt men purged by the fire of contemplation. Purged by that fire, Merton's soul roared into flames. In one of his last written and mature testimonies, *Contemplative Prayer,* he wrote:

> The living experience of divine love and Holy Spirit in the flame of which St. John of the Cross is speaking is a true awareness that one has died and risen in Christ. It is an experience of mystical renewal, an inner transformation brought about entirely by the power of God's merciful love, implying the "death" of the self-centered and self-sufficient ego and the appearance of a new and liberated self who lives and acts "in the Spirit".[8]

St. John described what that liberated self who lives and acts in the Spirit experiences.

> This flame of love is the Spirit of its Bridegroom, which is the Holy Spirit. The soul feels Him within itself not only as a fire that has consumed and transformed it but as a fire that burns and flares within it, as I mentioned. And that flame, every time it flares up, bathes the soul in glory and refreshes it with the quality of divine life.[9]

Experiencing this flame, Merton wrote, "Love sails me around the house…. I have only time for eternity which is to say for love, love, love…it is love and it gives me soft punches all the time in the center of my heart."[10] Merton attained a liberated self who lives and acts in the Spirit or "a living flame of love" in St. John's verbiage.

Although both were burnt by the same Spirit, their fruition differed towards their spiritual journey's end. While Merton chose to emphasize the Spirit's effect on leading a person to integration and wholeness, St. John focused on the intensity of the Spirit's flame. From Merton's perspective, the contemplative as a living flame of love recovers the true self, obtains final integration and has a realization of oneness with God and all that is. Merton states such a person embraces all of humanity, transcending the accidents of culture and recognizes the one truth shining out in all of its manifestations:

> The one who has attained final integration is no longer limited by the culture in which he has grown up."He has embraced all of life."… He passes beyond all these limiting forms, while retaining all that is best and most universal in them, "finally giving birth to a fully comprehensive self". He accepts not only his own com-munity, his own society, his own friends, his own culture, but all

mankind. He does not remain bound to one limited set of values in such a way that he opposes them aggressively or defensively to others. He is fully "Catholic" in the best sense of the word. He has a unified vision and experience of the one truth shining out in all its various manifestations, some clearer than others, some more definite and more certain than others. He does not set these partial views up in opposition to each other, but unifies them in a dialectic or an insight of complementarity. With this view of life he is able to bring perspective, liberty and spontaneity into the lives of others. The finally integrated person is a peacemaker, and that is why there is such a desperate need for our leaders to become such persons of insight.[11]

However, Merton is no stranger to the divine love operating within the soul. He writes that the fruit of contemplation results in a new man in union with the Spirit of Christ and therefore one with the Father and Spirit. He states that our oneness with Christ consists of being united to His Spirit.

We cannot get too deep into the mystery of our oneness in Christ. It is so deep as to be unthinkable and yet a little thought about it doesn't hurt. But it doesn't help too much either. The thing is, that we are not united in a thought of Christ or a desire of Christ, but in His Spirit.[12]

He perceives contemplation, like St. John of the Cross, as the very act of this living flame, the Spirit, bringing us to union with the Father through purifying our hearts. The fruit of this purgation is love.

That is to say he loves with purity and freedom that spring spontaneously from the fact that he has fully recovered the divine likeness and is now his fully true self because he is lost in God and hence knows of no ego in himself. All he knows is love.[13]

Near the end of his life, the yearning of that Spirit flared from the depths of his heart as he spontaneously uttered the closing prayer at a conference in Calcutta.

We are creatures of love. Let us join hands, as we did before, and I will try to say something that comes out of the depths of our hearts. I ask you to concentrate on the love that is in you, that is in us all. I have no idea what I am going to say. I am going to be silent a minute, and then I will say something... O God, we are one with you. You have made us one with you. You dwell in us. Help us to preserve this openness and to fight for it with all of our hearts. Help us to realize that there can be no understanding where there is mutual rejection. Oh, God, in accepting one another wholeheartedly, fully, completely, we accept You, and we thank You, and we adore You, and we love You with our whole being because our being is in Your being, our spirit is rooted in your Spirit. Fill us then with love, and let us be bound together with love as we go our diverse ways, united in this one spirit which makes You present in the world, and which makes You witness to the ultimate reality that is love. Love has overcome. Love is victorious. Amen.[14]

Although both men's writings testify to similar qualities in their experience of union with God's Spirit, it does not appear to me that Merton communicates (or chooses to communicate the intensity of the Spirit's wounding love that St. John calls a cautery. St. John notes that a soul in union with God can experience an even hotter flame.

This cautery, as we mentioned, is the Holy Spirit. For as Moses declares in Deuteronomy, Our Lord God is a consuming fire [Dt. 4:24], that is, a fire of love which, being of infinite power, can inestimably consume and transform into itself the soul it touches. Yet He burns each soul according to its preparation. He will burn one more, another less, and this He does insofar as He desires, and how and when He desires. When He wills to touch somewhat vehemently, the soul's burning reaches such a high degree of love that it seems to surpass that of all the fires of the world, for He is an infinite fire of love. As a result, in this union, the soul calls the Holy Spirit a cautery. Since in a cautery the fire is more intense and fierce and produces a more singular effect than it does in other combustibles, the soul calls the act of this union a cautery in comparison with other acts, for it is the outcome of a fire so much more aflame than all others. Because the soul in this case is entirely transformed by the divine flame, it not only feels a cautery, but has become a cautery of blazing fire.[15]

It is true that Thomas Merton is no St. John of the Cross. But then again, St. John of the Cross is no Merton. Each man was shaped by his embrace of God to become uniquely himself. Merton's personality flared toward openness, tolerance, inclusiveness, and wholeness. His intellect questioned and integrated. He stretched boundaries and saw "the one truth shining forth in all of its manifestations." He saw beyond irreconcilable differences and viewed the disparate as complimentary.

Buddhism, Zen, Sufism, existential literature, art, photography and all objects of his contemplative gaze as well as his lived experiences complemented his journey as a Christian contemplative. To my thinking, one of his major accomplishments was to achieve final integration in himself as a prophetic sign pointing the way to a potential deeper union of humankind, which may be attainable despite all our disparate cultures and belief systems.

St. John's temperament and mission differed. A reformer, confessor, and spiritual guide during his lifetime, St. John's mission was to poetically communicate the soul's embrace by God. He was uniquely gifted to view, experience and communicate the Spirit's effect on his own soul to the furthest extent possible and still remain on earth. A spiritual guide to St. Teresa of Avila and Merton, he beckons to those who leave all paths as they are consumed by the fire of the Living God.

Separated by time, culture, and mission, both contemplatives, in the Spirit, share with us their journey to God. For a fractured world bent on destruction, Merton radiates hope with his message of "the unity of a person" and "final integration" whereas St. John explains the timeless process of transforming union in which God and man become one "Living Flame of Love".

In conclusion, I propose that Thomas Merton like St. John of the Cross became a living flame of love. Purged by the Spirit of God, both penetrated into the center of their being to become a roaring conflagration as only occurs in those brought to union with the Living God. Burnt by this fire, both wrote of its effect. Merton's concept of the person, "a unity which is love" and his concept of the person's "final integration" arose from this encounter as did St. John of the Cross's perception of the perfected person as a "living flame of love."

Finally, for both men, contemplation is the means to this encounter. Merton states, "Contemplation is a supernatural love and knowledge of God, simple and obscure, infused by Him into the summit of the soul, giving it a direct and experimental contact with him."[16] St. John indicates that contemplation perfects the soul so that it may experience the indwelling of the Holy Trinity. An effect of this indwelling for Merton is the final integration of the person: "He has a unified vision and experience of the one truth shining out in all its various manifestations."[17] Similarly, St. John relates that a perfected soul "knows creatures through God and not God through creatures."[18] St. John would agree with Merton that "the one love that is the source of all, the form of all, and the end of all is one in him and in all."[19] Both encountered that love and became living flames spewing embers catching others on fire.

Notes

1. Thomas Merton, *Contemplative Prayer.* (New York: Image Books, 1996) p. 88

2. Clare Booth Luce, Ed., *Saints for Now.* (New York: Sheed & Ward, 1952) p. 274

3. Luce, Ed, *Saints for Now.* p. 274

4. St. John of the Cross, The *Complete Works of St. John of the Cross.* E. Allison Peers, Ed. (Westminster, Maryland: Newman Press 1964) pp. 402-03.

5. Thomas Merton, *The Ascent to Truth.* (New York: Harcourt Brace, 1981) p. 261

6. Thomas Merton, *The Seven Storey Mountain.* (New York: Harcourt, Brace, & World, 1948) p. 462

7. Merton, *The Seven Storey Mountain.* p. 462.

8. Merton, *Contemplative Prayer.* p. 88.

9. St. John of the Cross, *The Collected Works of St. John of the Cross.* Kieran Kavanaugh and Otilio Rodriquez, Eds. (Washington, D.C: Institute of Carmelite Studies, 1971) p. 580.

10. Thomas Merton, *Thomas Merton Reader.* Thomas P. McDonnell, Ed. (NY: Image, 1974) p. 190.

11. Thomas Merton, *Contemplation in a World of Action.* (New York: Doubleday, 1965) p. 207.

12. Thomas Merton, *The Hidden Ground of Love.* (New York: Farrar, Straus, Giroux, 1985) p. 360.

13. Merton, *Thomas Merton Reader.* p. 487.

14. Thomas Merton, *The Asian Journal of Thomas Merton.* Naomi Burton Stone, Patrick Hart & James Laughlin, Eds. (New York: New Directions, 1968) pp. 318-319.

15. St. John of the Cross, *The Collected Works of St. John of the Cross.* p. 596.

16. Thomas Merton, *The Inner Experience.* William H. Shannon, Ed. (New York: HarperCollins, 2004) p. 73.

17. Merton, *Contemplation in a World of Action.* p. 207.

18. St. John of the Cross, *The Collected Works of St. John of the Cross.* p. 645.

19. Thomas Merton, *Love & Living.* Naomi Burton Stone & Brother Patrick Hart, Eds. (New York: Farrar, Strauss, & Giroux, 1971), p. 17.

A Vow of Conversation:
Past, Present & Past-Present
Thomas Merton Bibliographic Review 2007

David Joseph Belcastro

Introduction

Stephen Miller's *Conversation; A History of a Declining Art* draws our attention to a critical problem that, while noted by intellectuals, has gone unnoticed and unaddressed by the public:

> In the twentieth century the possibility of conversation has been questioned by many novelists and thinkers (from psychologists to postmodernists), who say that we are all solipsists and that what we say is shaped mainly by subconscious passions or by ideas that enter our psyche subliminally. "There is no such thing as conversation," the novelist and essayist Rebecca West argues. "It is an illusion. There are intersecting monologues, that is all."[1]

Concerned about this present state-of-affairs, Miller notes recent publications that lament the death of conversation by the murderous atmosphere of unrelenting contention. While each book, article and essay provides a different perspective on the situation, the general message is the same. We have become a society hell-bent on arguing. Everyone is seemingly angry about something or another. For reasons yet unclear, ranting and raving have become national pastimes promoted by networks and widely enjoyed by the general public as evidenced by Nielsen ratings. Perhaps the intensity that conflict provides has become necessary to sustain attention, that is to say, sufficient attention to offset the impulse to change channels, check messages, or move onto other convenient distractions. Whatever the reasons, quiet reflection on issues, thoughtful consideration of questions, and civil exchange of ideas have been replaced by mindless wrangling between individuals interested only in hearing themselves talk. All of this, Miller believes, has eventually led to "conversation avoidance mechanisms"[2] whereby artless soliloquies are free to proceed uninhibited by interruptions from others or, for the faint-hearted, when troublesome subjects are accidentally raised, potential conversations may be graciously avoided. So prevalent is this behavior that few, if any, would doubt Miller's opinion that conversation is a dying art in American culture.

The loss of conversation is not without serious consequences. As forewarned by George Orwell in his novel *1984* and by Aldous Huxley in *Brave New World*, the elimination of conversation inevitably erodes the human spirit. Neil Postman in his book entitled *Amusing Ourselves to Death; Public Discourse in an Age of Entertainment* has presented a persuasive argument to this effect.[3] For Postman, the demise of conversation in the West was more accurately forecasted by Huxley than Orwell. While Orwell had it right with regard to the Soviet Union, it was Huxley who understood that a dramatic change was taking place with regard to Western modes of public conversation. While no *Mein Kampf* or *Communist Manifesto* announced its coming, change in the way persons converse with one another none-the-less represents an ideology that imposes a particular way of life that is counter to the spiritual and intellectual well-being of those who seek freedom of heart and mind.[4] This totalitarian state is more difficult to discern and oppose than that which happened in Russia for it is seldom experienced as an imposition. On the contrary, it takes place not by the threat of pain but by "the infliction of pleasure."[5] This ideology is attractively marketed for citizens (perhaps more accurately identified as customers trained to produce and consume) seeking security, prosperity, and amusement. For this reason, Postman directs our attention to Huxley's *Brave New World* as a portent of things that have come.

> What Huxley teaches is that in the age of advanced technology, spiritual devastation is more likely to come from an enemy with a smiling face than from one whose countenance exudes suspicion and hate. In the Huxleyan prophecy, Big Brother does not watch us, by his choice. We watch him, by ours. There is no need for wardens or gates or Ministries of Truth. When a population becomes distracted by trivia, when cultural life is redefined as a perpetual round of entertainments, when serious public conversation becomes a form of baby-talk, when, in short, a people become an audience and their public business a vaudeville act, then a nation finds itself at risk; cultural death is a clear possibility.[6]

There was one, however, who situated himself outside the walls of our civilized world. Like Savage in *Brave New World*, Winston in *1984* or, we could add, Berenger in Ionesco's *Rhinoceros*, Merton resisted the workings of this prevailing ideology by refusing to become a one-dimensional man whose voice could be used to lull the public into a meaningless and pacifying spirituality. In protest, he chose to become a stranger in this world. Nonetheless, he kept in touch by publishing his crimes against the state. Interested in finding others of like mind and spirit who had also moved to the margins of society, he read Czeslaw Milosz's *The Captive Mind*.[7] While Milosz had focused his attention on the dangers of totalitarianism present in Communism, Merton found the book just as relevant with regard to life in America. With this in mind, he wrote to Milosz in September of 1959:

> If there is one ambition we should allow ourselves, and one form of strength, it is perhaps this kind of wholehearted irony, to *be* a complete piece of systematic irony in the middle of the totalitarian lie—or capitalist one. And even the official religious one.[8]

Merton sensed the emergence of the world of which Miller now writes and recognized the seriousness of the problem of which Postman warns. We need to look no further than *War and the Crisis of Language* to find evidence of this. Commenting on Gunnar Ekelof's *Sonata For Denatured Prose*, Merton wrote:

> It is an angry protest against contemporary, denatured language. Ironically, it declares that ordinary modes of communication have broken down into banality and deception. It suggests that violence has gradually come to take the place of other, more polite, communications. Where there is such a flood of words that all words are unsure, it becomes necessary to make one's meaning clear with blows; or at least one explores this as a valid possibility. The incoherence of language that cannot be trusted and the coherence of weapons that are infallible, or thought to be: this is the dialectic of politics and war, the prose of the twentieth century.[9]

Merton's interest in language extended beyond the problem of violence. It was a preoccupation that defined in many ways his vocation as a monk. While *Contemplation and Dialogue*[10] focuses on interfaith dialogue, Merton's inclusion of Marxism in the discussion significantly extends the boundaries of this essay far beyond the borders of traditional religions. Furthermore, we are reminded of Merton's conversation with others like Albert Camus whom he referred to as the "Algerian Cenobite" or Lenny Bruce whom he called a "monk running in reverse." Merton's capacity for and interest in conversations knew no boundaries. Equally important, as *Contemplation and Dialogue* shows, he was of the opinion that the contemplative life was essential for meaningful dialogue providing as it does common ground for conversations that seek to transcend traditional boundaries and barriers by looking to new horizons. Merton, however, was aware that contemplation, like conversation, had become a lost art.

> Unfortunately, we must also admit that it can almost said to be a "lost art." And for this loss there is certainly in the world today a definite nostalgia, not unmixed with vague hopes for the recovery of this awareness. But the nostalgia and the desire do not of themselves suffice to make the nostalgic one a contemplative.[11]

Recognizing that the contemplative life was in danger of becoming a mere longing for a spirituality that pacifies rather than one that addresses the present state of affairs, Merton called for a reconnecting of monastic wisdom and public conversation in an effort to offset the destructive seeds of one-dimensional thinking that had given shape to modern technological society.[12] While *Contemplation and Dialogue* clarifies Merton's thoughts on the subject, his letters, journals and essays provide a record of his conversation with the world. This is especially true for the journal entitled *A Vow of Conversation*. Here we see the importance of the contemplative life for authentic conversation that is open and honest and thereby offers new possibilities for life to flourish. Naomi Burton Stone, after reading an early draft, referred to the manuscript as *Vow of Silence*.[13] On the one hand, this mistake reflects the modern world's disconnect between silence and conversation. To think of a hermit in conversation with the world is a contradiction too complicated for many to grasp. On the other hand, as Stone points out in her preface to the journal, "the hermit who stays in his abode and receives visitors is definitely in the tradition." The monastic vow of conversion of manners became for Merton a vow to re-establish the tradition of which Stone refers by restoring the relationship between silence and conversation. This he works out initially in the monastery and later in the hermitage where he rediscovers his place within the world and from which he is able to engage in authentic conversation. It is here that he confronts the solipsism that Miller and others recognize as an obstacle to meaningful conversation.

> One thing the hermitage is making me see is that the universe is my home and I am nothing if not part of it. Destruction of the self that seems to stand outside the universe. Get free from the illusion of solipsism.[14]

While Stone rightly points out that Merton's life of silence has provided us with "a feast of ideas and insights into contemporary and non-contemporary thought and writings,"[15] there is, however, something of greater value to be found in his work. The feast of which Stone writes has become something of a moveable feast to which writers and readers continue to turn for conversations that open us to deeper dimensions of the human spirit; to what Merton elsewhere identifies as "infinite capaciousness" that resolves the fears that drive humankind to hide from one another behind alienating walls.[16] In this way, Merton provides the antidote for the virus solipsism that is destroying our ability to effectively communicate and thereby rediscover authentic human community in the twenty-first century. While recognized as a notable spiritual writer, his role as spiritual director is no less significant. His writings not only inform readers but transform "intersecting monologues" into conversations among those who pick up his books, read, and talk with others about what they have read. Merton clearly understood this as an essential aspect of his vocation as a monk in the Twentieth century as evidenced by his notes for a paper on monastic experience and East-West dialogue to be delivered in Calcutta on October of 1968.

> The point to be stressed is the importance of serious communication, and indeed of "communion," among contemplatives of different traditions, disciplines, and religions. This can contribute much to the development of man at this crucial point of his history. Indeed, we find ourselves in a crisis, a moment of crucial choice. We are in grave danger of losing a spiritual heritage that has been painfully accumulated by thousands of generations of saints and contemplatives. It is the peculiar office of the monk in the modern world to keep alive the contemplative experience and to keep the way open for modern

technological man to recover the integrity of his own inner depths.[17]

This essay is an effort at discerning lines of conversation initiated by Merton; a conversation that presently engages the voices of writers, reviewers, and readers who are, in turn, engaged with one another in an allusive inquiry for which there will never be an end but only openings of those engaged. While I have organized the books published in 2007–2008 according to past, present, and past-present conversations, they all represent on-going conversations that proceed from a contemplative vision of the world into various aspects of postmodern life. While different in many ways, I sensed that the works selected for this bibliographic essay share something in common. What exactly that might be became clear to me while reading Luce Irigary's book entitled *Conversations*.[18] Lamenting the loss of conversation in the academy, Irigary recalls the model of dialogue offered by Plato, drawing our attention to the participants in the *Symposium* who threw themselves into their search of truth; a search that was never limited by logical reasoning but pressed the boundaries of personal experience in such a way that intellectual inquiry into sexual love was both "amorous and about love."[19] With this model in mind, Irigary advocates for scholarship that is essentially conversational in nature and design:

> Now truth results from who or what we are, from our experience(s), from our journey, among other things from our advancement in the recognition of the other as other and in our ability to exchange with such an other in mind. The quality of conversations, which are gathered in this book, could be assessed, not according to the degree of asepsis and disengagement, but according to the degree of attentive respect for the other. That is, according to the involvement of the persons who enter into dialogue in the exchange itself; instead of their neutralization for the benefit of a truth indifferent to the one and the other, a truth that they would attempt to reach in the name of a scientific asceticism beyond any personal involvement.[20]

What Irigary articulates here is evidenced in the books selected for this review, as well as, by those who reviewed the books whose voices now enter and extend conversations initiated by a monk who entered the silence of a monastic community and has been heard from ever since. Here we find a conversation grounded in Merton's life experience <u>and</u> the life experiences of those who choose to read Merton and write books in response to what Merton has shared. Consequently, we not only find in these books an analysis of Merton's work but, perhaps more importantly, a response to his insights and questions that continue to expand a truth that is sought by and shared with others. Here in practice we see what Merton articulated in theory with regard to the nature of religious thought which he stressed did not move from question to answer but from question to question with each new question opening a larger field of vision.[21]

Past Conversations

The first two books to be considered in this essay offer an opportunity to listen-in on two conversations that contributed significantly to Merton's life and work. The voices of Ad Reinhardt and Latin American poets intersect and converge in the voice of a monk who was able to find in an artist from New York and poets from the Southern hemisphere fellow monks with whom he shared a lucid awareness of Life, resistance to the present state-of-affairs, and a communion of silence.[22]

Even though Michael Corris' *Ad Reinhardt* is a book about the artist and the references to Merton are, while significant, limited to a few pages, it deserves attention if for no other reason than Merton's designation of Reinhardt as "Dean of the Great Silence."[23] As one might guess, the title of "dean" reflects a playful exchange between the two. In a letter written late in 1963, Reinhardt asks Merton if monks get promoted inside monasteries the way everyone does outside, especially in the art world where, if one endures long enough, one becomes a dean? Merton responded:

> Yes, as one dean to another. I am frequently promoted as dean, usually by myself as I get little cooperation in this matter from others. However, it is true that with your encouragement and assistance I am already the dean of small abstract calligraphy.[24]

The letter continues with Merton asking Reinhardt's appraisal of a few of his small abstract calligraphies and advice on printing methods and getting "the great brush into a small bottle of India ink." There was, however, a serious side to this playful relationship. As Roger Lipsey points out in *Angelic Mistakes; the Art of Thomas Merton*:

> The surface tone is humorous between two friends of long standing, but they were facing one another, and they knew it. Soon Merton stepped decisively toward the world of contemporary art—in his own way, by the light of spirituality—rather than away from it. "We have to be men of our time," he told the novices in 1964 in the course of a discussion of art. It was a hard-won conclusion, reaching past art into the fullness of his new perspective.[25]

As noted here, Reinhardt's influence on Merton is sufficiently significant to warrant serious attention. Lipsey sees Reinhardt as an agent of change in Merton's life whose gift of art supplies and advice on printing techniques were tokens of much more valuable offerings of friendship, letters, and conversation that opened the New York world of abstract art to Merton wherein he was able to discover a visual language that worked with his interest in zen and *via negativa*.[26] It becomes increasing clear that an understanding of Merton's art provides a new and alternative perspective on his spiritual formation and his writings on the contemplative experience. In order to fully appreciate this new perspective, a study of Reinhardt's life and work is essential. Merton was, as Lipsey points out, a "student of Reinhardt" as evidenced not only by Merton's "Reinhardt-like" style but in the way in which Reinhardt engaged Merton on the relationship between art and religion.[27]

So, as we now see, the title Merton bestowed on Reinhardt hints at something far more meaningful than mindless banter between friends. It indicates an important dimension of the relationship they shared. Merton recognized that Reinhardt understood something from his vantage point as a visual artist that he had not as yet fully clarified for himself; something that could be discovered in conversation with Reinhardt. While an avant-garde artist from New York and a hermit in Kentucky may at first glance appear to have little in common, in this case, appearances are deceptive. Reinhardt has been seen as a "black monk gliding in the corridors of an impregnable intellectual fortress"[28] and Merton could just as easily be seen as Beat poet and artist tramping across America hanging onto the side of box cars. Perhaps this should not surprise us when we remember that they were undergraduates together at Columbia and there formed a friendship that was shaped by a vision of the world presented to them by their Alma Mater. Even though their lives could be transposed, artist/monk and monk/artist, they were two very different men with different experiences emerging from different vocations. What made the relationship possible was a mutual respect for one another's differences <u>and</u> a shared desire to discover a truth together.

In order to get at the truth that they sought and the conversation that they shared, we only need to focus on the painting Reinhardt sent to Merton. It was a miniature version of a five-foot square painting of a black cross on black canvas with varying shades of black distinguishing the cross from the background. Merton describes the painting in a letter to Reinhardt:

> It has the following noble feature, namely its refusal to have anything else around it. It thinks that only one thing is necessary and this is time, but this one thing is by no means apparent to one who will not take the trouble to look. It is a most religious, devout, and latreutic small painting.[29]

It is his journal entry on the 17th of November 1957, however, that reveals how Merton viewed the painting:

> Reinhardt finally sent his "small" painting. Almost invisible cross on a black background. As though immersed in darkness and trying to emerge from it. Seen in relation to my other object the picture is meaningless—a black square "without purpose"—You have to look hard to see the cross. One must turn away from everything else and concentrate on the picture as though peering through a window into the night. The picture demands this—or is meaningless for I presume that someone might be unmoved by any such demand. I should say a very "holy" picture—helps prayer—an "image" without features to accustom the mind at once to the night of prayer—and to help one set aside trivial and useless images that wander into prayer and spoil it.[30]

In his review of *Ad Reinhardt* for this volume of *The Merton Annual*, Lipsey describes Merton's response to the dark cruciform painting, its effect on Merton and its use for mediation:

> It was pure abstraction—yet Merton could "read" it with unerring good judgement as a shy work of sacred art. In his comments Merton was not drawing on a body of established

criticism; there was scarcely any at the time. Yet even now, when Reinhardt is universally admired and the critical enterprise has looked long and hard at this work, Merton's comments— burning with sincerity, lucid, and felt—are among the most penetrating we shall have about the Black Paintings.

While the presence of this painting in the hermitage is a visible reminder of Reinhardt's influence on Merton, it also reflects Merton's influence on Reinhardt. Corris writes:

> Reinhardt's most private reflections on the 'black' paintings are indebted to Merton's writing on this discipline and to his lively correspondence with the artist. For Merton, contemplative practices are classed as 'beginnings', where the decisive moment is 'a sudden emptying of the soul in which images vanish, concepts and words are silent, and freedom and clarity suddenly open out within you until your whole being embraces wonder, the depth, the obviousness and yet the emptiness and unfathomable incomprehensibility of God'.[31]

Corris specifically focuses on Merton's reading of St. John of the Cross where "'dark contemplation' and 'the night of sense' does not necessarily signify a complete renunciation of sensation, but allows for another mode of being within a sensual life."[32] This connection between spiritual and sensual was a primary focus for the two men. As we will note later when considering Merton's interest in Latin American poets, Merton was particularly interested in the interconnection between these two dimensions of human experience for his own work and formation as a monk. This was no less true for Reinhardt. Throughout his friendship with Merton, Reinhardt found a valuable partner in conversation and a benchmark for the integration of spirituality into his art.[33]

Between Reinhardt's painting and Merton's looking, a conversation was taking place. And, I would say that this is a particularly useful way to think of the relationship. The painting is the place where the two, monk and artist, sit together. Even so, Corris believes that there is a place where they diverge:

> Yet the point of intersection of Merton's theological concerns and Reinhardt's aesthetic concerns is surely an uneasy place for the 'black' paintings to reside. While Reinhardt shared Merton's enthusiasm for these religious doctrines and precepts, the artist chose to consider them in terms of a matrix of social

and ideological concerns. In Reinhardt's mind this may have blunted the wayward spirituality that Merton was prepared to project onto the 'black' paintings.[34]

Lipsey, in his review responds to Corris:

> Undoubtedly true, the context should be broad and varied. But the term "wayward" sets off an alarm. Why should the negative theology, the rigorous path of Meister Eckhart, the notion of kenosis, the acknowledgment of the need to empty oneself of nonsense in order to know the truth, be in any sense "wayward?" All of these things were points of reference for Reinhardt as for Merton; Reinhardt drew on them in the dry but compelling poetry of his critical writings. Reinhardt belongs to art, not the Abbey, and the art world must and will fight its battles in its own terms. But so much in Reinhardt's writings from the period of the Black Paintings connects directly or obliquely with Merton's concerns. Reinhardt's aesthetic, social, and ideological positions, brilliantly and painstakingly set before the reader by Corris, do not erase his perfectly evident concern to explore in the Black Paintings a visual correlative or embodiment of the *via negativa*.

An interest in the dark path of Merton's spiritual journey inevitably leads now from Merton's relationship with Reinhardt to the conversation presently emerging between Corris and Lipsey. As with Reinhard and Merton so also with Corris and Lipsey, it may be through the engagement of opposite opinions that a deeper understanding of the truth they are seeking together may be found.

Michael Corris, Professor of Fine Art at the Art and Design Research Center, Sheffield Hallam University in Great Britain, digs beneath the surface of Reinhardt's life to reveal the spiritual dimensions not only of Reinhardt's art but also of the artist himself who approached his art with the intention of practicing values grounded in a process that, like that of a monk, seeks to transcend the artist's ego as the final or absolute subject and thereby experience the immediate moment of self-awareness as an un-visualizable void. Corris offers us a unique biography and an invaluable study of an artist with whom Merton shared a long and enduring inquiry into the illuminating darkness of humankind's search for meaning.

Malgorzata Poks turns our attention from the art scene of New York to the poets of Latin America in her *Thomas Merton and Latin*

America: a Consonance of Voices.[35] Poks inquires into Merton's interest in poets from the Southern hemisphere, his translations of their poetry, and his personal contacts with Latin American intellectuals. She does so in such a way that we are able to see how this interest is an essential aspect of Merton's ongoing inquiry into humanity's struggle to live authentically in the technological age. As we shall see, Poks opens for us a conversation of great significance. Initiated by Merton, the conversation eventually included the voices of Jorge Carrera Andrade, Carlos Drummond de Andrade, Ernesto Cardenal, Alfonso Cortes, Pablo Antonio Cuadra, Nicanor Parra, and Cesar Vallejo. And, then, of course, Poks' voice must now be added who extends and offers the conversation to us. As Patrick O'Connell notes in his review for this edition of *The Merton Annual*:

> It is a matter of some wonder, and a cause for much gratitude, that a young Central European scholar has explored in such breadth and depth these spiritual and cultural bonds uniting the Western hemisphere in the spirit and the writing of one monk-poet—at once a sign of Merton's own ability to transcend geographical, cultural and linguistic boundaries, and a salutary reminder that voices on what might seem to be the margins can often provide central insights for those willing and able to attend to them.

Poks, quoting Robert Daggy at the outset in her *Preliminary Remarks*, underscores an essential characteristic of Merton's approach to these poets: "Merton did not, as he did in other areas of interest, write *about* Latin America but *to* and *for* Latin Americans."[36] This difference of approach is one of importance. Merton's intention was to open a conversation with poets whom he believed had something important to say, something he was greatly interested in hearing and something he believed the North needed to consider. For Merton, this hearing went much deeper than merely listening. It was an effort to enter into a relationship with these poets at the deepest possible level and there to create something new together. Consequently, one might add *with* to Daggy's *to* and *for* especially when we are reminded by Poks that:

> Merton firmly believed that the contemplative experience must inevitably lead to dialogue and that the fruits of contemplation are shared. His meditations on the literary works of others,

therefore, resulted in the subsequent publication of numerous essays and highly praised translations, which, while remaining masterfully faithful to the original, reflect Merton's own lived and authentic experience as much as they do that of the authors. Merton's working definition of translation as "a new creation emerging from communion in the same silence" enables us to approach his English renditions of Ibero-American poetry as endowed with a life of its own, thanks to the translator's success in capturing what he calls a poem's "nativity or *natura*." It bears stressing that, according to this definition, a translation, no matter how faithful to the original, will always be "a new creation" in so far as the translator, a unique individual with a unique perspective, first has to enter into another person's experience so deeply as to make it his own ("connatural" with him), and then, reemerging from this "communion in silence," has to transliterate this experience in his own idiom. Far from detracting from faithfulness to the original poem, the newness Merton speaks of is a necessary condition if a translation is to be alive.[37]

The choice of *consonance* in the title and *resonance* throughout the book amplifies Merton's translations as far more than mere transliterations but a harmonizing of voices, his voice with the voices of the poets from the Southern continent and, in such a way, that they together echo "conversations carried over ages and across distances."[38] Perhaps more importantly, however, is the *voice* that they sought and found together.

His wholehearted embrace of Latin America confirms the seriousness of his dedication to understand and help bring forth the destiny of the New World, which was bound up with that of the entire world: the eschatological new creation was becoming manifest in Indian America, and it was the voice of the New Man that Merton heard in the poetry, written and unwritten, of that continent. The new American proclaimed by Carrera and Andrade and welcomed by Merton was a total poet, a compassionate revolutionary whose colors were those of life and hope. Merton's poetic vision was a prophetic anticipation of humankind's new morning and a proclamation of a new world beyond geography. Passionate about the things of the earth and knowing their being as rooted in the metaphysical ground, the new Americans would help redeem the time from despair on the one hand, and shallow positivistic optimism on the other. Through them the hemisphere was becoming conscious of its vocation to redeem the world.[39]

The voice of the New Man was the "secret" and "the ultimate truth of life" that they, Merton and the Latin American poets, "saw flashing in poetic intuition and the unpredictable wisdom of dreams."[40] This reference to the New Man suggests that it would not be wrong to think that Poks situates Merton's translations within the context of his book entitled *The New Man*. The book was written and published in and around the same time, 50s and 60s, as his translations of the poetry from Latin America. The two projects seem to share a common concern. Both explore the question of human identity, the obstacles to discovering our true identity, the consequences of failing to do so, and the possibilities offered in the contemplative life of poets and monks. There is a significant difference, however, between this book and the translations. While the language of *The New Man* is what one might expect of a Christian monk, biblical and theological, the translations are part of Merton's effort to discover another language; a language that speaks to persons outside his tradition but is nonetheless true to his tradition. Merton's mixed feelings with regard to this book of meditations, however, suggests that he might have been aware that something was missing; that he had something else in mind that was not fully accomplished with *The New Man*.[41] Poks helps us to see in the translations that Merton is doing something more than sharing his thoughts on the question of humankind's identity and destiny. With the translations he is invoking the voice of the New Man; a voice emerging from the voices of compassionate rebel-poets intent on creating an inclusive world[42] of diverse yet mutual understanding, a world of true peace and prosperity, a world that[43] counters the technological society noted at the outset of this essay. *Thomas Merton and Latin America; a Consonance of Voices* offers us far more than a study of Merton's translations of Cuadra, Andrade and others. Poks shows that:

Merton and his fellow "monks" affirm an alternative vision of life, based on the sophianic values of relatedness, compassion and solidarity. Renouncing hate, aggression, and other forms of violence, they revolt against the solipsistic consciousness that celebrates the unique self as the primary fact of existence. Their ethic of revolt consists in prophetically witnessing to a new reality, the seeds of which are already secretly present in the exhausted modern world, a reality that is based on truth and on resistance to the absurd.[44]

Thomas Merton and Latin America: a Consonance of Voices ends with appendix entitled *Thomas Merton and the Poets of North America: A Consonance of Sorts* that turns our attention Northward. Why the shift in direction? First of all, Poks wants to draw our attention to the fact that Merton was not as alone as he might have thought with regard to his interest in Ibero-American verses. There were other North American artists, poets, and thinkers who shared the "realization that the dark masculinity of the West was ready for a healing reintegration" with the sensuality of the feminine that was so apparent in the poetry from the South.[45] There is another reason for the appendix. Poks wants to point out that there was a blind side to Merton's understanding of poetry in North America. After providing a brief history of a tradition in American poetry that shared much in common with the poetry from the South, Poks writes:

> But since Merton had not been reading much American poetry, he was ignorant of most of these new trends, let alone of their resonance with his own poetic development and with the anti-poetry of Nicanor Parra. It was only in 1966 that he finally came to regret the "impossible and sweeping statements" he had once made about the contemporary poetry of English America. As late as 1965 he still believed Robert Lowell to be a notable exception on the North American poetic desert. A year later, though, when the Latin American impulse started to lose its momentum, he was beginning to make surprising discoveries on his very doorstep. With characteristic enthusiasm, Merton started tapping these new sources of poetic vitality.[46]

Ross Labrie agreeing with Poks and finding this section of particular interest, responds:

> Even if Merton was right in feeling, finally, that T.S. Eliot's poetry, in spite of that poet's eloquent interest in religion, was overly rational and a trifle dry, nevertheless there were other American poets who should have attracted him in a more particular way than they did. William Carlos Williams, for example, had in the 1920s expressed the sort of reservations about Eliot that Merton registered in the 1960s. Poks might have been helpful here in distinguishing high modernism (Eliot and

Pound) from low modernism, which included people like Williams. As a low modernist, as it were, Williams was experimental and yet not academically stuffy as Eliot and Pound were. With Williams' strong interest in the luminous innocence of the human and natural world and with his strong interest in social justice, he in many ways was a figure who would have grown in Merton's estimation even beyond the respect with which Merton held him in the late 1960s. The same might be said of e.e. cummings, another low modernist whose experimentalism with language, outrage at institutionalism, and Whitmanesque passion for a hidden and unrecognized America would have appealed to Merton.[47]

Poks recognizes that she has entered "unexplored territory" that required her to use "a wide angle lens and leave more detailed explorations of the topic to future research." Shifting metaphors, she describes her book as "a matter of opening a window, if not exactly a door, unto Thomas Merton's Latin American project."[48] Labrie's response indicates that Poks may very well have opened a door to the North as well as the South with regard to Merton's place as a poet. Beyond Merton's interest in poetry, Poks opens the door for a feast of conversations on related subjects. Merton's essays on Albert Camus would inevitably come to the table. Her references to the "rebel" resonate with Camus and the connections in Merton's thought between this French writer and Latin American poets; an intersection of inquiries that directions our attention to Merton's primary interest in discovering a way to re-integrate reason and wisdom.[49] The conversations would inevitably go East when Poks' passing references to Zen are noted.[50] Given my current reading of Merton's interest in yoga as a physical, mental and spiritual practice, I would inevitably draw our attention to the following lines:

All the poets discussed in this book attempt to overcome what Merton defined as "the psychic and spiritual cramp" of modern man. They also struggle to liberate the sphere of the sensuous, believing that human libido, released from the repressive influence of the performance principle, would enable us to experience the world with our whole self again, the rational and the sensual alike, as prehistoric people used to do. This event would make modern man and woman a more integrated and more authentic human being. It bears stressing that Merton's first intuition of the importance of the sensuous to a holistic development of the human person came during his stay in Cuba. There Merton experienced Catholic spirituality as conducive to a more complete experience of life, through the sensuous joy attendant on the sacramental life, than was possible to achieve in the rational and abstract Protestant culture of English America.[51]

I have little doubt that the reference to Cuba as Merton's first intuition of the sensuous would occupy most of the evening's conversation as we traced his life experiences from France to India. If someone at this table had read Corris' book on Ad Reinhardt, he or she might say something about Merton and Reinhardt's interest in the relation between the sensual and the spiritual. Of more immediate interest, however, is the way in which Poks sheds light on the trajectories of this essay, reminding us as she does that in the new world imagined by Merton and these poets the:

> ...irrational must be accepted as part of experiential reality, the Dionysian needs to be integrated with the Apollonian, and rational and empirical cognition needs to be integrated with the "heart of knowing" or *cardiognosis*, privileged by the "wisdom" approach to life and seeking to understand reality in the light of the ultimate causes.[52]

The new world that includes rather than excludes the heart is, as we earlier noted, the world imagined by Luce Iragary; a world that is explored in conversation where minds <u>and</u> hearts are openly shared and explored. To read Merton only with the mind, to respond to Merton only with the cutting edge of reason, is to misrepresent and misunderstand what it was that he had hoped to share with us. Merton scholarship, to be true to Merton, must strive toward the new world of which Poks writes; a world in which critical examination of Merton texts is a step towards, rather than away from, an intelligent reading of the heart.

Present Conversations

The following three books represent the new world sought by Merton and surveyed by Poks. Each author explores different territories and does so by entering into conversation with Merton. And, this may be just as Merton would have wanted it. William Shannon, in "The Future of Thomas Merton: A Progress Report," writes:

In short, Merton is a person who, through his writings, enters into conversation with you. He tells about himself and you see not only yourself, but every person. He writes autobiography and *we* find biography – our own. He digs so deeply into raw humanity that his words will reach women and men for ages to come.[53]

The important word here is *but*. Without *but every person*, I would be concerned that reading Merton could become a narcissistic exercise. The line, when read in its entirety, suggests something very different. Merton invokes within his reader an awareness of the true Self that is radically inclusive; the Self that sees oneself in every person. Perhaps Poks has something like this in mind when she positions *participation* over against *solipsism* when noting this essential distinction in Merton's mind as he sought an alternative model of inquiry to that of the Enlightenment.[54] While it is true that Merton draws us away from the maddening crowd to discover ourselves at the deepest possible level in silence and solitude, it is equally true that he calls us into solidarity with every person and into full participation in the life of the world. Consequently, we would not be wrong to think of the next three books as invitations to participate in a conversation with Merton, the authors of the books and those who have reviewed the books. As we read each book, we come to realize that Smock's meditation on Merton's poetry becomes our meditation, Porter's personal reflections on Merton's biography becomes our autobiography and Palmer's book on Merton's intellectual and spiritual experience of paradox becomes our experience. How does this happen? Each writer leans into Merton, listening with heart and mind, inquiring with an imagination that transcends, without eliminating, reason. Read alone or with a group, these books require the full participation of the reader, drawing us out of ourselves and into a fuller experience of Life.

Frederick Smock's *Pax Intrantibus: A Meditation on the Poetry of Thomas Merton* is, as the title indicates, a meditation on Merton's poetry. In the preface, Smock, poet-in-residence at Bellarmine University, identifies two characteristics of this meditation:

There have been many studies published about Merton's life and work, but relatively few about his poetry. Merton shares a great deal with the ancient Chinese poet-monks, and, in their fashion, I have been tempted to write lengthy chapter titles, such as, "Sitting on Cold Mountain During a Spring Rain-shower and Hearing the Monastery Call to Prayers, I Think About Merton's Imagery of the Bell." In the end, I let the prose stand alone. Associative as it is. Intuitive as it is. One poet to another.[55]

It is associative and intuitive. Smock identifies with Merton as a poet and from there feels his way through the poetry until some insight or impression shows itself. Note, for example, how he begins a meditation with the story of a visit to Merton's hermitage on a rainy Saturday in March with a small group of retreatants and one brother:

> Meditating at his hearth, browsing his bookshelves, we found ourselves in imaginary society with Merton. The quality of our contemplation might have been relatively poor. Still, we were breathing the same air, and walking barefoot up and down in the same pine needles. We also read a number of his poems that speak to the notion of retreat itself. I remember with particular clarity a stanza from his poem "In Silence."[56]

After writing out the stanza from this poem for us to read, Smock slowly weaves the meaning of the poem into his own experience as a "secular writer [who] shares a great deal with a poet-monk – the desire for some kind of transcendental affirmation, and the discovery of the self."[57] He is not, however, unaware of those with him. On the contrary, he is fully aware of them, a small group of pilgrims of which he is one. Nor is Smock unaware of the reader. Here, as elsewhere in *Pax Intrantibus*, Smock draws everyone together into a shared moment of affirmation and discovery:

> When the woods began to grow dark, near time for vespers, we closed up the cabin and trekked back. We were not quite the same people who had come out that noon, nor was it quite the same world to which we returned. We were more capacious. "Art pushes out the boundaries of our universe a little bit," Salman Rushdie said to me in conversation one day. And that is something of what we felt – that our boundaries had been pushed out a little bit. And if the change within us was incomplete, at least our new capacity had prepared us for it.[58]

It is perhaps Smock's appreciation of silence that makes him particularly attentive, receptive, and insightful with regard to Merton's poetry. He understands that it is the poet's job "to listen, so that things will speak through him." This book is in some ways an account of his listening to Merton and allowing Merton's poetry to speak through him and through him to us. Consequently, *Pax Intrantibus* is an invitation to us to listen. While in many ways Smock's personal meditation, it is none-the-less a meditation that seeks to engage us in a conversation. As noted by Kevin Griffith in his review for this volume of *The Merton Annual*:

> . . . [this] book is a meditation, not a critique. It is filled with insights to ponder. Merton's forays into Islam and his attempts to achieve a "radical ecumenism"; his disparagement of the materialism of the United States; his ceaseless humility as he became an important world figure – all are worthy of our consideration as we head into a century that looks to be marked by hardship, a century where superficial spirituality and mindless consumerism will not provide us with the answers that we need. *Pax Intrantibus* is the kind of book that tries to provide some answers we do need and, perhaps, are too afraid to confront.

That last line forewarns the reader that this book with such an inviting title is not for the fainthearted. Inevitably the meandering reflections that saunter through Merton's hermitage and poems stop us dead in our tracks with the harsh realities of our world, the world of Huxley and Postman, the world opposed by Merton, Reinhardt, and the poets from Latin America. Smock is no less aware of that world. The twelfth meditation begins:

> Denise Levertov, in her poem "Contraband," suggests that the "tree of knowledge was the tree of reason," but that it is "toxic in large quantities." Reason in excess, and the hubris that can come simply with knowing a lot, can become a tyranny of the mind, like a "dense cloud that harden[s] to steel." Or, as Gertrude Stein put it, in her 1959 essay *Reflections on the Atomic Bomb*, "Everybody gets so much information all day long that they lose their common sense," (And this was before the Internet!).[59]

From here, Smock draws our attention to a poem by Merton. *Psalm* brings to our attention that while reason and knowledge can wall us off from God, imagination provides an alternative route not only to God but to peace on earth. Throughout the book, the author provides this alternative route into a far broader inquiry than one might have expected at the outset. This route extends beyond Merton's life and work. It is a route that eventually finds its way into our lives and raises questions about our work for peace in the twenty-first century. The poems and prayerful meditations in this book are hidden questions that emerge out of the silence, doubt and faith of two poets, one to another, and, now, to us.

J. S. Porter's *Thomas Merton at the Heart of Things* presents the reader with an interesting biography. By interesting I do not mean a new biography that provides information from unpublished journals, letters and/or interviews. By interesting I mean the way in which Porter approaches Merton. As Ross Labrie in his review for this volume of *The Merton Annual* writes:

> This isn't the book for those who like linear and analytical stud-ies. It is more likely the sort of book for those who like personal and impressionistic accounts of writers who reach deep into the impressionist's psyche and won't let go. Dionysian rather than Apollonian if you like. On the one hand you are never quite sure, in spite of the table of contents, where you will be taken next. On the other hand there are fine moments of illumination as you journey through the book. The journey is Merton's in the first instance, but it is also Porter's as he retrospectively charts his own course from a family background in Ulster Protestant-ism to the universally human, spiritual consciousness that in Merton, the Roman Catholic monk, comes to engage him.

This somewhat unusual approach is not without justification. Porter bases his approach on the way Merton worked. Porter un-derstands Merton's way of thinking as "relational, personal and experiential." He shows how Merton moves from one encounter to another, reading and reflecting, and, perhaps most importantly, forming friendships from which new questions and insights even-tually surface.[60] And, this is what Porter does with Merton. It is also what he suggests the reader should do when reading Merton. When reading Merton, one is drawn into a *spiritual friendship*.[61] The Cistercian tradition understands friendship to be essential to the formation and health not only of the monk but the well-being of the monastic community.[62] *Thomas Merton at the Heart of Things* brings to our attention the need to take seriously this important aspect of Merton's work, i.e. his capacity for friendship and the ways in which friendship contributed to his life and work.[63] Porter rightly believes that we should read Merton as a friend listens to a friend because this is the way Merton writes. Merton offers us more than words. In a chapter entitled *Tone Meister*, Porter writes:

> Tone has to do with how one sounds, whether angry or pomp-ous or flippant. But it also has to do with where one stands when one speaks – whether one is above or below or beside the other. Middle to late Merton speaks friend to friend or brother to sister as if he were standing beside us, on ground neither more nor less elevated than the ground on which we stand. The power of his writing comes, in part, from his standing with us as he speaks, not as an authority or an expert but as a friend who is living through what we are living through as though his life were always co-temporaneous with ours.[64]

According to Porter, Merton writes *to* us. Or, since the correspon-dence is "co-temporaneous," we might say that Merton speaks *with* us. As Porter points out with regard to a journal entry:

> ... since it is published, it comes to us as an overheard mono-logue to which we are privy. The monologue projects beyond itself, reaches for the other, and hence calls us into dialogue. The "you" of the passage is both Merton and ourselves. When one soul opens fully, all souls open a little.[65]

This dialogue, to which the reader is called, is, according to Porter, *incarnate speech.*[66] In other words, the conversation, while address-ing spiritual concerns, is always and emphatically embodied in life experiences. Consequently, the opening of souls is the open-ing of biographies, i.e. the sharing of life stories. Inevitably this means an encounter with the most perplexing aspects of our lives. As Porter explains, when a reader comes to Merton, that person enters a world of ironies, ambivalences, and paradoxes and joins with Merton in his life and work of sorting out the tangled mess in which we presently find ourselves. With Merton, the reader searches the desert regions of the human heart and, with Merton, undergoes change and transformation.[67]

It is difficult not to question the classification of Porter's book as a biography. There is no question that just as Smock's book focuses on Merton's poetry, Porter focuses on Merton's life. The vantage point from which Porter focuses, however, is not that of a biographer. Porter is a poet and essayist whose perspective and interests are different than those of a biographer. He explores the possibility of entering into a literary friendship with Merton and one that transforms the reader. As we have noted above, the transformation has something to do with opening ourselves, as Merton opened himself, to the deeper dimensions of the Self. Porter understands, however, that this opening is more than a personal transformation. It is an opening intended for the salvation of the world. It is a transformation that has everything to do with how the reader will see the world, live in that world, and address the issues of the day. Consequently, it inevitably addresses our inability to communicate effectively across cultures. That inability, as noted by Porter, is seen by Merton to be rooted in our inability to communicate with something deep within ourselves that we have come to view from a great distance as strange, alien and hostile. In order to embrace this side of ourselves, we are required to accept ambiguity, contradictions, and paradox as an essential aspect of human existence.

The reissuing of Parker Palmer's *The Promise of Paradox; a Celebration of Contradictions in the Christian Life*[68] provides an opportunity to reconsider an old conversation in a new day. With regard to this particular book, it is appropriate to refer to it as a conversation. Perhaps it would be closer to the truth to say that the book echoes a number of conversations, most notably the one between Henri Nouwen and Parker Palmer. The reissued edition begins with memories of that conversation. Nouwen had written an introduction for the original 1980 edition. The reissued edition contains that introduction and a new introduction by Palmer. The two introductions, set side by side, remind readers of the friendship and conversation that shaped the book before them. Palmer recalls their first encounter at a meeting called by the Lilly Endowment for consultation on spirituality held at the Algonquin Hotel in New York city:

> When I met Henri, he was already a well-known and much-loved writer. His classic *Reaching Out: The Three Movements of the Spiritual Life* (1975) had touched me and many other readers. Henri was only seven years older than I, but to me, he seemed like a wise older brother, a virtuoso of the spiritual life with a genius for writing and teaching. He was also very funny, a requisite quality for any guru who hoped to win my trust.[69]

This friendship continued for the next twenty years until Nouwen's death in 1996. Nouwen remembers the many hours they enjoyed together: eating, playing, talking, reading, writing and praying; activities that provided the basis for what he describes as "a supportive, nurturing and creative friendship."[70]

While working on his first book, *The Promise of Paradox*, Palmer asked Nouwen to write the introduction. He was somewhat apprehensive about the request since the book seemed to Palmer to have fallen together in a series of unanticipated and unplanned happenstances; in what he would later describe as "a moment of satori worthy of a Zen wannabe."[71] This may very well explain not only the content but style of this book. Nouwen, however, straightaway recognized what was at the heart of Palmer's work:

> This friendship has allowed me to see the pages of this book being born from Parker's own direct struggles with life and its many options and possibilities. Parker has shown me how true it is that you don't think your way into a new kind of living but live your way into a new kind of thinking. Every part of this book is a reflection of a new kind of living in which Parker and his family have engaged.[72]

Nouwen continues the introduction by pointing out that Palmer's life story contains all the elements which contribute to making a well-known scholar. He does so only to highlight that *The Promise of Paradox* is not the direct fruit of all of his academic and social accomplishments. "On the contrary," Nouwen explains, "it is the fruit of the many questions with which Parker bracketed these accomplishments. It is born out of the courageous and often agonizing critique of his own social, educational, and religious development."[73]

The reissued edition situates Palmer's effort at *living into a new way of thinking* in a new context. This time he seeks to engage a formidable opponent in conversation. Since the publication of *The Promise of Paradox* in 1980, much has changed. During the intervening years, the Religious Right emerged as a significant presence in American culture. In the new introduction, Palmer, after expressing some reservation about the republishing of this book, turns his attention to theological fascists whose dominance of radio and television airwaves obscures the meaning of words he once used without hesitation.

> My squeamishness [with the reissuing of *The Promise of* Paradox] has little to do with any fundamental change in my beliefs.

I still understand myself as a Christian, and many traditional Christian understandings still shape my life. But in 2008, I find it hard to name my beliefs using traditional Christian language because that vocabulary has been taken hostage by theological terrorists and tortured beyond recognition. Of course, this is not the first time Christian rhetoric has been violated in public places.[74]

Recognizing that something serious has happened to the spiritual formation of religious life in America, Palmer, setting aside his reservation, sees the importance of *The Promise of Paradox* for readers today. By contextualizing the book in twenty-first century, he breathes new life into the book. An old conversation becomes a new conversation as relevant today as it was twenty-eight years ago. One might even say that the book was meant for today and has been on a kind of library hold until now. At a time in history marked by incredible change, diversity, and conflict, it is not difficult to understand the need for feelings of security that comes from the reassurance of unambiguous *truth*. Consequently, anyone who able to supply what is demanded, will find buyer. For this reason, the Religious Right has done well even though their product is seriously flawed. The flaw becomes most apparent when Life draws their most basic beliefs into the most puzzling of contradictions. Contradiction and paradoxes are problematic for persons seeking certainty and security. They are not, however, a problem for Palmer. As the title indicates, promise lies dormant in paradox.

It is no surprise that Palmer turns to Merton in the first chapter of the book. While reading Merton's *The Sign of Jonas*, he discovered a writer whose religious convictions, while sturdy, were "laced with wit and fresh images of the religious life." More importantly, here was a writer who embraced the contradictions of life and, in fact, understood "life as a whale of a paradox."[75] Palmer explores three contradictions in Merton's thought to see what might be discovered, not so much about Merton, but about the contradictions that we face today.[76] Of the many contradictions that could have been selected, Palmer focuses on Marxism, Taoism and the Cross to illustrate "how the tension among them open into a deeper truth."[77] For example, Palmer points out:

By allowing Christianity and Marxism to create their own dialectic, Merton was able to develop a critical perspective on monastic life – a perspective premised on principles within the

Christian tradition that Marxism helped Merton to reclaim. Such is the power of paradox: apparently alien points of view can remind us of the inner truth of our own![78]

What inner truth? While simple and in many ways obvious, it was an overlooked truth and one with serious consequences; consequences noted at the outset of this essay and earlier recognized by Huxley and more recently by Postman. Christianity, like Marxism, is against alienation. While Marx focused on the way in which capitalism alienates the worker from a meaningful life, Merton focused on the way in which the modern world of commerce alienates consumers from their hearts. Of course, alienation from one's heart extends beyond one's own well-being to the well-being of those who produce the goods that are purchased. Whether we begin with Marx or Jesus, Merton understood that we eventually come to the same conclusion, i.e. alienation is the problem.

Palmer recognizes that while Merton embraced the contradictions of our age, it was the paradox of the cross that provided Merton with the necessary perspective from which he could discern the promise hidden with contradictions:

> The cross is also a symbol of contradictions whose very structure suggests the oppositions of life. As its crossbar reaches left and right, the cross represents the way we are pulled between conflicting demands and obligations on life's "horizontal" plane. As its vertical member reaches up and down, the cross represents the way we are stretched in that dimension of life, pulled between heaven and earth. To walk the way of the cross is to be torn by opposition and contradiction, tension and conflict.[79]

As mentioned earlier, Palmer is less interested in telling us about Merton than in helping us get on with our own journey through life. So, eventually, he *gets to the point*, as we sometimes say, and writes:

> Thomas Merton understood that the way we respond to contradiction is pivotal to our spiritual lives. The moments when we meet and reckon with contradiction are turning points where we either enter or evade the mystery of God.... We embark on the spiritual journey in hopes of achieving wholeness, but long before we get there, the journey only sharpens and magnifies our sense of contradiction. The truth of the Spirit contradicts

the lies we are living. The light of the Spirit contradicts our inner shadow-life. The unity of the Spirit contradicts our brokenness.[80]

Eventually, after adding his own voice to Merton's, Palmer brings us back to Merton and concludes:

So in the manner of paradox, we come full circle. By living the contradictions, we will come to hope, and in hope will we be empowered to live life's contradictions. How do we break into this circle that goes round and round with no apparent point of entry? Someday, far out at sea, heading away from the place where God has called us, lost in contradiction, we will be swallowed by grace and find ourselves—with Jonah, with Merton, with all the saints—traveling toward our destiny in the belly of a paradox.[81]

Gray Matthews' review of *The Promise of Paradox* in this volume of *The Merton Annual* enters the conversation and concludes my thoughts on the book by drawing our attention to the reader's experience:

I did not expect this to happen. Reading Palmer's book for review purposes led me to approach it in a slightly more detached way than I normally would have (as a kind of devotee, like any other contemplative sympathizer). I did not expect, however, to reflect on my own inner turmoil. I came to realize that I have been living lately with three unrecognized paradoxes that until now I had not understood as such, let alone articulated even as problems. The beauty of Palmer's book, is in its capacity to reveal that the problems of the human heart are not private concerns but are paradoxically, hence intimately, connected to the lives of others.

Past-Present Conversations

The next two books indicate ways in which Merton's conversations from the past have continued into the present. The first book accomplishes this by reissuing a work that was begun by Merton during his school days in England. The underlying concerns that set the initial project in motion apparently remained with him throughout the rest of his life until the 1960s when he returned to the manuscript, added a brilliant introduction, and published it under the title of *Gandhi on Nonviolence*.[82] It is as timely now as it was when originally published. We find ourselves once again involved in wars that cause the death of innocent men, women and children. So again we look for an alternative solution to violence. This book is a clear and unambiguous reminder that there is one.

Merton selected and arranged quotations from Gandhi on nonviolence in five sections entitled: *Principles of Non-Violence, Non-Violence: True and False, The Spiritual Dimensions of Non-Violence, The Political Scope of Non-Violence,* and *The Purity of Non-Violence.* Each section begins with a brief yet insightful synopsis of what the reader will discover. For example:

SECTION ONE

Principles of Non-Violence

AHIMSA (non-violence) is for Gandhi the basic law of our being. That is why it can be used as the most effective principle for social action, since it is in deep accord with the truth of man's nature and corresponds to his innate desire for peace, justice, order, freedom, and personal dignity. Since *himsa* (violence) degrades and corrupts man, to meet force with force and hatred with hatred only increases man's progressive degeneration. Non-violence, on the contrary, heals and restores man's nature, while giving him a means to restore social order and justice. *Ahimsa* is not a policy for the seizure of power. It is a way of transforming relationships so as to bring about peaceful transfer of power, effected freely and without compulsion by all concerned, because all have come to recognize it as right.

The quotations follow. Most notable are the spaces between the quotations. A typical page looks and reads like this:

Non-violence is not a garment to be put on and off at will. Its seat is in the heart, and it must be an inseparable part of our very being.   I-61

The acquisition of the spirit of non-violence is a matter of long training in self-denial and appreciation of the hidden forces within ourselves. It changes one's outlook on life…. It is the greatest force because it is the highest expression of the soul. I-65

What are we to make of the space that follows each saying? In his preface to the new edition, Mark Kurlansky describes Merton's selection and arrangement as a catechism.

> Merton, the brilliant Catholic theologian and scholar of Eastern thought, seemed the perfect person to sort through the ninety volumes of Gandhi's writings, to analyze and interpret them. But instead he chose to create this brief anthology of one and two line observations. In its monk-like starkness it gives us an unusual insight into Gandhi's genius, and gift for consistently issuing short statements of such depth. Almost any of the quotes in this book makes a weighty epigraph. Merton did a Catholic thing; he took Gandhi's writings and cooked them down into a catechism, a clear, brief, and uncomplicated guide to the teachings of the Great Soul.[83]

Perhaps Kurlansky is correct, at least in part. Julie Adams, however, in her review of *Gandhi on Non-Violence* for this volume of *The Merton Annual*, read Merton's arrangement of quotations in a different light. Having recently read Patanjali's *Yoga Sutras*, she experienced her reading of the Gandhi quotes in much the same way. That is to say, she read the quotations as aphorisms from a guru, dispeller of darkness, that are to be memorized, ingested, and lived until at last the truth contained therein becomes one's own truth. Whether Merton had this in mind, is difficult to say at this time. Inquiry into Merton's arrangement of the quotations may reveal similarities with the form and function of sutras. We know that he was familiar with sutras. Furthermore, the practice associated with sutras is not unlike *lectio divina*. With both practices, reading is more than a process of gathering information. It is a process of formation. The reader is drawn into an interior conversation where the few lines are turned time again until at last the lesson is learned by heart and mind. And this is what Adams experienced and recognized as a new and valuable way of learning. Planning to enter the Peace Corp after graduating from college, she was aware that she needed something more than lessons on peacemaking. She needed something that would prepare her for the difficult work of peacemaking. She found it here. The spaces between the readings provided pauses where she was free to ponder the few lines shared by Merton from Gandhi until they became hers; opening and enriching her heart with ancient wisdom.

When Merton returned to the quotations in 1964, he added an introduction entitled *Gandhi and the One-Eyed Giant*. The title invokes images of the biblical story of a shepherd and giant on a battlefield. In the center of the field stands the One-Eyed Giant:

> . . . bringing with him the characteristic split and blindness which were at once his strength, his torment, and his ruin. With his self-isolated and self-scrutinizing individual mind, Western man was master of concepts and abstractions. He was king of quantity and the driver of those forces over which quantitative knowledge gave him supremacy without understanding.[84]

Approaching the battlefield, we see the small figure of Gandhi, the Noble Soul. For battle, he carries only the ancient wisdom of sages from India, philosophers from Greece, and the Gospel from Nazareth. Unlike the One-Eyed Giant, the Mahatma seeks not to destroy his opponent but to save him. Merton's essay reveals the heart and soul of this man who lived a noble life in obedience to the principle of non-violence. In doing so, Merton also reveals the universal truth of non-violence therein stressing the necessity for practicing non-violence within the tension of world affairs, clarifying the ways in which the principles of non-violence inform cross-cultural and inter-faith dialogue, and the possibilities of non-violence for overcoming the destructive tendencies of modern thought with an alternative way of thinking that affirms and fosters life. While Merton focuses on Gandhi's understanding of non-violence, the essay tells us as much about Merton as it does about Gandhi. It is difficult, if not impossible, to distinguish one from the other on this issue. As the essay unfolds, Merton weaves the wisdom of Upanishads with that of the Shepherd of Hermes without sacrificing the integrity of either tradition. Gradually the reader becomes aware that Gandhi's principle of non-violence is truly universal.

Even so, we are fully aware that non-violence remains suspect. Gandhi's way, while admired, has found few disciples. Kurlansky addresses this unfortunate fact and, in doing so, provides a valuable insight into Gandhi's legacy.

> I amuse myself speculating what Sigmund Freud would have made of Mohandas Karamchand Gandhi had he gotten him on his couch. The two lives did overlap in time if not in geographic or intellectual space. Gandhi seems like a Freudian

feast, starting with his life-long guilt over having been engaged in sex with his wife at the moment of his father's death. His life was a constant illustration of Freud's thesis that we cannot be happy because our inherent nature is contrary to the demands of our conscience or, as Freud put it, our ego is at war with our superego.[85]

Kurlansky moves from this provocative introduction to a description of Gandhi's engagement of the struggle between the ego and superego; an engagement to which Gandhi submitted himself by way of a simple diet, long fasts, celibacy, and adherence to the commandment to "Love thy neighbor as thyself." While Gandhi, like Freud, understood this to be an impossible undertaking, he nonetheless pressed on and not for his own salvation alone but for the salvation of India and the British. It is here that Gandhi's personal struggle takes on political and social significance. After carefully sketching out what could become notes for a stage production of a meeting between Freud and Gandhi, Kurlansky resolves the tension between the two:

> Freud believed that just as the human superego is a voice seeking to curb the unsocial urges of the ego, society has a superego that tries to curb its unsocial behavior. This societal superego, Freud maintained, came from "the impression left behind by the personalities of great leaders, people who were endowed with immense spiritual or intellectual power. . . ."[86]

The very next line in the text reads: "Mohandas K. Gandhi was such a person." In that one line, Kurlansky justifies the reissuing of *Gandhi on Non-Violence*. While the practice of non-violence will perhaps remain incomprehensible for many, Gandhi has left behind an impression on history that will remain a reminder of a truth hidden deep within the human conscience; a truth recognized by Merton while a school boy in England, returned to as a monk in Kentucky, and now shared with us in a book that will be read and re-read by many seeking an alternative way of living in the world.

The second book is fourth in a series of publications by Fons Vitae that provide readers an opportunity to benefit from papers and conversations at conferences that focus on interfaith dialogue. All of these publications have titles that begin with *Merton* thereby acknowledging the important role that he plays even now. *Merton and Buddhism; Wisdom, Emptiness and Everyday Mind* [87] like *Gan-*

dhi and Nonviolence is timely. Religious diversity has become the norm in the twenty-first century. Whether experienced online or next door, history now sets the difficult work of inter-religious dialogue before everyone. How we respond to this challenge will determine the future of human civilization. Failure to understand and sincerely appreciate the religious traditions of our neighbors will inevitably lead to the escalation of conflict, more human suffering, and further destruction of ancient cultures. Failure to meet this challenge will close the door on the new world imagined by Merton and the poets of Latin America; a world in which the voice of people everywhere is set free to resonate with the vast mystery that lies hidden deep within the human heart. Failure to find ways for religious traditions to engage in open and honest conversations may very well result in the victory of the One-Eyed Giant and the death of Wisdom. Those who gathered for a conference at the Louisville Presbyterian Seminary in Kentucky during the month of February in 2005, Buddhists and Christians, took on this challenge. And now, thanks to the work of Bonnie Bowman Thurston, we have the opportunity to read the papers presented at the conference and note the on-going nature of a conversation initiated by Merton. Several presenters at the conference remember Merton's *Mystics and Zen Masters* or *Zen and the Birds of Appetite* as their first encounter with Buddhism. Now, some forty odd years since the publication of those books, scholars gathered to assess Merton's knowledge of Theravada, Tibetan, and Zen Buddhism and the influence of Buddhism on his photography, art, and poetry.

If Merton were able to read the table of contents for this collection of articles, I imagine that it would be John Keenan's article that would catch his eye straight-away. *The Limits of Thomas Merton's Understanding of Buddhism* represents the kind of response to his work that Merton welcomed. As his correspondence indicates, he was open to the questions and criticism raised by others. While pleased to see that Keenan appreciated his contribution to Christian-Buddhist dialogue, Merton would most likely press onto the weightier parts of the paper to discover what was lacking in his understanding. And, of course, Keenan could very well have expected a letter from Merton; a letter that would continue the conversation. This "what if" yet believable scenario may help us clarify Merton's place within the history of Christian-Buddhist dialogue.

Pascaline Coff, summarizing Keenan's criticism of Merton, draws our attention to an obvious yet overlooked point regarding Merton and Buddhism in America.

> Keenan insists that "based as his works are on D. T. Suzuki's Zen teachings, we cannot look to Merton for any adequate understanding of Buddhism." For, as Keenan believes, Suzuki presented an "export Zen" tailored to the West without having Zen credentials or the weight of any Zen institution behind him. All so true. Suzuki influenced Merton, and Merton influenced many here in the West just as Buddhism was breaking into the West. Yet much has happened in the realms of teachers, writers, and translators in the Zen and Buddhist understanding and practice since then.[88]

The "since then" is important to note. Buddhism, like every tradition that finds itself relocated to North America, has gone through a process of rediscovering itself in a new culture. This relocation usually includes redefining essential beliefs and practices and, unfortunately, not always in ways that are true to the original tradition. Eastern traditions, like Zen and Yoga, entered the West through the underground, migrated into university courses and remained there until someone recognized that these practices could be sold at market in a popularized form. While this has resulted in the introduction of Eastern traditions to a Western audience, it has not done so without problems that rightly raise concern by persons like Keenan. This concern presses the issue of inter-religious dialogue at just the right place; the place where it is most vulnerable and in most need of attention. Keenan's brief description of this problem is, as they say, *right-on*.

> After forty years of conversation, people tire of dialogue, because it so often rehearses the same old ground about our common humanity, offering no new insight and no new approach. We bow to one another and cooperate on social issues. All well and good, but that does grow tedious…. All this goes without any delving into the actual teachings of these traditions, as if we had never trained ourselves to read scriptures and commentaries, to converse, argue, and enjoy the creative tension. All our creative trials and challenges are slipping into a numbing cup of soporific wine of dialogic oblivion. Perhaps

so afraid of past sectarianism, this age of ours seems to have become enamored of a new type of unitarian sameness.[89]

I have no difficulty imagining Merton highlighting these lines. He would have been in full agreement. Merton was opposed to syncretism and indifferentism. For example, look at what he said in his essay on Gandhi:

> There have of course been spurious attempts to bring East and West together. One need not review all the infatuated theoso-phies of the nineteenth century. Nor need one bother to criticize the laughable syncretisms which have occupied the talents of publicists (more often Eastern than Western) in which Jesus, Buddha, Confucius, Tolstoy, Marx, Nietzsche, and anyone else you like join in the cosmic dance which turns out to be not Shiva's but just anybody's.[90]

His deep respect for Buddhism, or for that matter any religious tradition, including the non-religious tradition of Albert Camus, would not allow him to overlook the distinctive differences be-tween traditions or attempt to blend them together into a colorless spirituality of universal consciousness and bliss. While he found himself in an age enamored with unitarian sameness, Merton was fully aware that this initial stage, where common ground was the primary concern, was giving way to a more serious consideration of the distinctive characteristics of each tradition. He welcomed this advanced stage of inquiry believing that within authentic inter-religious dialogue something hopeful would emerge.[91]

Merton's place within the history of Buddhist-Christian dia-logue is not as a Buddhist scholar but as a Christian monk who approached Buddhism with wide open curiosity, intuition, and moments of wonder that enriched his contemplative vision of the world. One could say the same about the way Merton approached the Latin American Poets, Ad Reinhardt, or many others with whom he entered a conversation in search of…what? That is the question that needs to be asked. It is difficult to believe that Merton simply meandered from one subject to another without a question or two in the back of his mind; a cognitive interest, or matrix of interests, that guided his journeys to the far corners of the world. Was it a desire to reconnect science and wisdom? Or, was it to recon-nect spirituality and sensuality? Whatever it was, it was always at play in the way he approached others. As we draw this essay to a close, we turn our attention to the way in which Merton engaged and continues to engage generations of *friends* in a conversation grounded in a contemplative vision of the world.

Conclusion

Merton was and remains through his writings a hermit at the center of the city. As noted earlier by Stone, this places Merton in a well established tradition. He stands in the tradition of Clement of Alexandria. Confessing his love for and affinity with Clement, Merton's admiration is more than apparent from the numerous references to this Alexandrian as a great Christian whose mind was noble and broad and, while belonging to antiquity, ever new. Therefore it should be no surprise to find Merton looking to Clement as a source for renewal of monastic spirituality in the twentieth century and doing so for the very reasons pointed out in this essay, i.e. the reconnecting of monastic silence with public discourse, ancient wisdom with modern science, and contemplative vision with political realities.[92] His essay on Clement's *The Protreptikos* clearly articulates what he had found of great value in this early Christian theologian.

> The voice of Clement is the voice of one who fully penetrates the mystery of the *pascha Christi*, the Christian exodus from this world in and with the Risen Christ. He has the full triumphant sense of victory which is authentically and perfectly Christian: a victory over death, over sin, over the confusion and dissensions of this world, with its raging cruelty and its futile concerns. A victory which leads not to contempt of man and of the world, but on the contrary to a true, pure, serene love, filled with compassion, able to discover and to "save" for Christ all that is good and noble in man, in society, in philosophy and in humanistic culture. This is the greatness and genius of Clement, who was no Desert Father. He lived in the midst of Alexandria, moved amid its crowds, knew its intellectual elite, and loved them all in Christ.[93]

Clement was able to live within the city, presenting the Christian faith in terms comprehensible to the world in which he lived because, as Merton explains, he was:

> ...a man of unlimited comprehension and compassion who did not fear to seek elements of truth wherever they could be

found. For truth, he said, is one. And consequently its partial and incomplete expression is already something of the great unity we all desire. The full expression is found most perfectly in the Divine Logos, the Incarnate Word, Jesus Christ.[94]

In order to fully understand and appreciate Merton's life and work, his admiration for Clement of Alexandria must always be kept in mind. While a hermit behind the walls of the Abbey of Gethsemani in the hills of Kentucky, he faithfully maintained his vow of conversation. He had one truth to share. It was the same truth that Clement shared in his day in the streets of Alexandria. And, it is this one truth, sought, discovered, and lived in the silence and solitude of a Trappist community, that Merton shared with Ad Reinhardt, Latin American poets, and Buddhist monks. It is this one truth that continues to be shared when an old book on Gandhi is republished and a young student reads it for the first time. It is this one truth that writers like Frederick Smock, J.S. Porter, and Parker Palmer turn and turn again to catch a glimpse of the multifaceted "great unity" that is at the center of our being; what Merton identified at Fourth and Walnut as *le point vierge*:

> At the center of our being is a point of nothingness which is untouched by sin and by illusion, a point of pure truth, a point or spark which belongs entirely to God, which is truth, a point or spark which belongs entirely to God, which is never at our disposal, from which God disposes of our lives, which is inaccessible to the fantasies of our own mind or the brutalities of our own will. This little point of nothingness and of *absolute poverty* is the pure glory of God in us. It is so to speak His name written in us, as our poverty, as our indigence, as our dependence, as our sonship. It is like a pure diamond, blazing with the invisible light of heaven. It is in everybody, and if we could see it we would see these billions of points of light coming together in the face and blaze of a sun that would make all the darkness and cruelty of life vanish completely…. I have no program for this seeing. It is only given. But the gate of heaven is everywhere.[95]

While Merton had no program for this seeing, he found in silence words that could awaken within readers what had been awakened within him. Robert Inchausti's *Echoing Silence; Thomas Merton on the Vocation of Writing*[96] provides a window through which to see how

Merton's worked with words to engage the world in a conversation with the Divine Logos. Inchausti's selection and arrangement of texts, brings to our attention, among other things, points relevant for this essay. For example, he explains that Merton became "a stylistic innovator who used language reflexively to construct a critique of itself" thereby exposing "the soulless tautologies of our systematically distorted, communication systems."[97] In the chapter entitled "The Christian Writer in the Modern World," we find a quote from *Camus and the Church*, one of seven essays by Merton on Camus, that underscores Merton's intentions with regard to his vow of conversation.

> Our task is not suddenly to burst out into the dazzle of utter unadulterated truth but laboriously to reshape an accurate and honest language that will permit communication between men on all social and intellectual levels, instead of multiplying a Babel of esoteric and technical tongues which isolate men in their specialties.[98]

The first word of this quote must not be passed over too quickly. The "our" is a reminder of Merton's expansion of his monastic community to include Camus and others to take on the difficult task of redeeming communication in the modern world that has become distorted, soulless, and destructive. To do this, he recognized the need to talk with persons outside his Christian tradition. So, as noted by Inchausti, Merton "translated the 'insider' speech of Catholic monasticism into the 'universal' language of personal and existential revelation" and thereby:

> ... brought contemplation into the twentieth century, divesting it of its antique scholasticism and ancient prejudices: making it efficient far beyond the inner circle of Christian initiates. He retained the best that was thought and said within the monastic counter culture—preserving its traditions while broadening its appeal and bringing it into dialogue with the contemporary world.[99]

Convinced that communication in depth, across the lines that have historically divided religious traditions, is now not only possible but essential for the future of humankind,[100] Merton sought to awaken the world to the contemplative life of silence and solitude where words once again will have the power to reveal and restore the deepest dimensions of the mystery from which the story of every person's life unfolds. When silence is echoing in the human heart, true words may be spoken and conversation will replace "intersecting monologues." Then, most honorable reader, we will discover that it is not as an author that Merton speaks to us, not as a story-teller, not as a philosopher, not as a friend only. He speaks to us in some way as our own true self, aware as he was of the One who lives and speaks in all of us.[101]

Endnotes

1. Stephen Miller, *Conversations: A History of a Declining Art* (New Haven and London: Yale University Press, 2006), p. x.

2. *Conversation: A History of a Declining Art*, p. xi.

3. Neil Postman, *Amusing Ourselves to Death; Public Discourse in an Age of Entertainment* (New York: Penquin Books, 1986).

4. *Amusing Ourselves to Death*, p. 157.

5. *Amusing Ourselves to Death*, p. viii.

6. *Amusing Ourselves to Death*, p. 156.

7. *Striving Towards Being; The Letters of Thomas Merton and Czeslaw Milosz*, ed. Robert Faggen (New York: Farrar, Straus and Giroux, 1997), p. 3.

8. *Striving Towards Being*, p. 56.

9. Thomas Merton, *Thomas Merton on Peace*, ed. Gordan C. Zahn (New York: McCall Publishing Company, 1971), p. 235.

10. Thomas Merton, *Mystics and Zen Masters* (New York: Farrar, Straus and Giroux, 1967), pp. 203-214.

11. *Mystics and Zen Masters*, p. 204.

12. *Mystics and Zen Masters*, p. 210.

13. Thomas Merton, *A Vow of Conversation*, ed. Naomi Burton Stone (New York: Farrar, Straus and Giroux, 1988), pp. vii-viii.

14. *A Vow of Conversation*, p. 156.

15. *A Vow of Conversation*, p. vii.

16. *Gandhi on Non-Violence*, edited with an Introduction by Thomas Merton and Preface by Mark Kurlansky (New York: New Directions, 2007), p. 10.

17. Thomas Merton, *The Asian Journal*, ed. Naomi Burton Stone, Patrick Hart and James Laughlin (New York: New Directions, 1973), p. 317.

18. Luce Irigaray, *Conversations* (New York: Continuum Books, 2008).

19. *Conversations*, p. xi.

20. *Conversations*, p. x-xi.

21. Thomas Merton, *Opening the Bible* (Collegeville, MN: Liturgical Press, 1970), pp. 19-20.

22. See "Message to Poets" in *The Literary Essays of Thomas Merton*,

ed. Patrick Hart (New York: New Directions, 1981), pp. 371-374.

23. Thomas Merton, *The Road to Joy; Letters to New and Old Friends*, ed. Robert E. Daggy (New York: Farrar, Straus and Giroux, 1989), p. 282.

24. *Road to Joy*, p. 282.

25. Roger Lipsey, *Angelic Mistakes; The Art of Thomas Merton* (Boston & London; New Seeds, 2006), p. 16.

26. *The Art of Thomas Merton*, p. 196.

27. *The Art of Thomas Merton*, p. 27.

28. Michael Corris, *Ad Reinhardt* (London: Reaktion Books, 2008), pp. 8, 90.

29. *Ad Reinhardt*, p. 88.

30. Thomas Merton, *A Search for Solitude; the Journals of Thomas Merton*, ed. Lawrence S. Cunningham (San Francisco: Harper Collins, 1996), pp. 139-140.

31. *Ad Reinhardt*, pp. 88-89.

32. *Ad Reinhardt*, p. 89.

33. *Ad Reinhardt*, p. 89.

34. *Ad Reinhardt*, p. 89-90.

35. Malgorzata Poks, *Thomas Merton and Latin America: a Consonance of Voices* (Katowice, Poland: Wyzsza Szkola Zarzadzania Marketingowego, 2007).

36. *Thomas Merton and Latin America*, p. 13 n. 2.

37. *Thomas Merton and Latin America*, p. 22.

38. *Thomas Merton and Latin America*, pp. 23-24.

39. *Thomas Merton and Latin America*, p. 258.

40. *Thomas Merton and Latin America*, pp. 25-26.

41. Thomas Merton, *Turning Toward the World*, ed. Victor A Kramer (San Francisco: Harper Collins, 1996), pp. 92, 96-97, 125.

42. *Thomas Merton and Latin America*, p. 18.

43. *Thomas Merton and Latin America*, p. 20.

44. *Thomas Merton and Latin America*, p. 254.

45. *Thomas Merton and Latin America*, p. 264.

46. *Thomas Merton and Latin America*, pp. 268-269.

47. Ross Labrie, "Explications of Explorations: Review of *Thomas Merton and Latin America: A Consonance of Voices* by Malgorzata Poks." *The Merton Seasonal* 33.2 (Summer 2008), p. 31.

48. *Thomas Merton and Latin America*, p. 14.

49. *Thomas Merton and Latin America*, p. 38.

50. *Thomas Merton and Latin America*, pp. 230, 270, 272.

51. *Thomas Merton and Latin America*, p. 254.

52. *Thomas Merton and Latin America*, p. 256.

53. William H. Shannon, "The Future of Thomas Merton: A Progress Report." *The Merton Seasonal* 33.4 (Winter 2008), p. 5.

54. *Thomas Merton and Latin America*, p. 275.

55. Frederick Smock, *Pax Intrantibus; A Meditation on the Poetry of Thomas Merton* (Frankfort, Kentucky: Broadstone Books, 2007), pp. 11-12.

56. *Pax Intrantibus*, p. 28.

57. *Pax Intrantibus*, p. 29.

58. *Pax Intrantibus*, p. 29.

59. *Pax Intrantibus*, p. 46.

60. J.S. Porter, *Thomas Merton; Hermit at the Heart of Things* (Ottawa: Novalis, 2008), pp. 14-15.

61. *Thomas Merton; Hermit at the Heart of Things*, p. 31.

62. Aelred of Rievaulx, *Spiritual Friendship* (Kalamazoo, Michigan: Cistercian Publications, 1977).

63. See James Harford, *Merton and Friends; A Joint Biography of Thomas Merton, Robert Lax, and Edward Rice* (New York: Continuum, 2006).

64. *Thomas Merton; Hermit at the Heart of Things*, p. 74.

65. *Thomas Merton; Hermit at the Heart of Things*, pp. 74, 173.

66. *Thomas Merton; Hermit at the Heart of Things*, p. 13.

67. *Thomas Merton; Hermit at the Heart of Things*, pp. 42-43.

68. Parker J. Palmer, *The Promise of Paradox; A Celebration of Contradictions in the Christian Life* (San Francisco: Jossey-Bass, 2008).

69. *Promise of Paradox*, p. xviii.

70. *Promise of Paradox*, p. ix.

71. *Promise of Paradox*, p. xvii.

72. *Promise of Paradox*, p. ix.

73. *Promise of Paradox*, p. x.

74. *Promise of Paradox*, p. xxi.

75. *Promise of Paradox*, pp. 1-2.

76. *Promise of Paradox*, p. 4.

77. *Promise of Paradox*, p. 8.

78. *Promise of Paradox*, p. 14.

79. *Promise of Paradox*, pp. 30-31.

80. *Promise of Paradox*, p. 5.

81. *Promise of Paradox*, p. 37.

82. *Gandhi on Non-Violence*, edited with an introduction by Thomas Merton and a preface by Mark Kurlansky (New York: New Directions, 2007).

83. *Gandhi on Non-Violence*, p. xvi.

84. *Gandhi on Non-Violence*, p. 3.

85. *Gandhi on Non-Violence*, p. xi.

86. *Gandhi on Non-Violence*, p. xvii.

87. *Merton and Buddhism; Wisdom, Emptiness and Everyday Mind*, edited by Bonnie Bowman Thurston and illustrated by Gray Henry (Louisville, Kentucky: Fons Vitae, 2007).

88. Pascaline Coff, Review of *Merton and Buddhism; Wisdom, Emptiness*

and Everyday Mind. Cistercian Studies Quarterly 43.2 (2008), pp. 240-244.

89. John P. Keenan, "The Limits of Thomas Merton's Understanding of Buddhism" in *Merton and Buddhism; Wisdom, Emptiness and Everyday Mind,* p. 129.

90. *Gandhi on Non-Violence,* p. 6.

91. *Gandhi on Non-Violence,* p. 6.

92. *Survival or Prophecy? The Letters of Thomas Merton and Jean Leclercq,* ed. Patrick Hart (New York: Farrar, Straus, and Giroux, 2002), p. 76.

93.*Clement of Alexandria; Selections from the Protreptikos,* translated, edited with an introduction by Thomas Merton (New York: New Directions, 1962), pp. 1-2.

94. *Clement of Alexandria; Selections from the Protreptikos,* p. 3.

95. Thomas Merton, *Conjectures of a Guilty Bystander* (New York: Doubleday, 1966). p. 142.

96. Thomas Merton, *Echoing Silence: Thomas Merton on the Vocation of Writing,* edited with an introduction by Robert Inchausti (Boston and London: New Seeds Books, 2007).

97. *Echoing Silence: Thomas Merton on the Vocation of Writing,* p. ix.

98. *Echoing Silence: Thomas Merton on the Vocation of Writing,* p. 64.

99. *Echoing Silence: Thomas Merton on the Vocation of Writing,* p. x.

100. *The Asian Journal,* pp. 312-313.

101. Thomas Merton, *Introductions East and West; the Foreign Prefaces,* ed. Robert E. Daggy (Greensboro: Unicorn Press, 1981), p. 47.

Reviews

CORRIS, Michael , *Ad Reinhardt* (London: Reaktion Books, 2008), pp. 240. ISBN 978-1-86189-356-7 (cloth). $39.95.

"Do I want a small painting?," Merton wrote to his friend, the painter Ad Reinhardt, in the fall of 1957. "You inquire if I want a small painting. What you wish to know: do I desire a small painting…. Well, it is clear at least to me that I desire a small painting since I am in point of fact crazy mad for a small painting. They have to keep me chained to the wall day and night and a gag in my mouth because I roar continuously that I am dying for lack of a small painting…. I am consumed with a most ardent thirst for a small painting." In due course the object of desire reached the Abbey. It was a perfect Black Painting, a miniature version of the five-foot by five-foot canvas which, by that time and for years to come, was Reinhardt's exclusive concern. Painted in tones of black only, the image was of an equal-armed cross. It was a pure abstraction—yet Merton could "read" it with unerring good judgment as a shy work of sacred art. "It has the following noble features," he soon wrote to Reinhardt, "namely its refusal to have anything to do with anything else around it, notably the furniture etc. It is a most recollected small painting. It thinks that only one thing is necessary and this is true, but this one thing is by no means apparent to one who will not take the trouble to look. It is a most religious, devout, and latreutic small painting." In his comments Merton was not drawing on a body of established art criticism; there was scarcely any at the time. Yet even now, when Reinhardt is universally admired and the critical enterprise has looked long and hard at his work, Merton's comments—burning with sincerity, lucid and felt—are among the most penetrating we shall have about the Black Paintings.

For us Merton people, stubbornly preserving the memory of Thomas Merton's life and works, his example of spirituality and engagement, his grand use of language to touch mind and heart, the exchange of letters between Merton and Reinhardt may be all we need or wish to know of his friend since college days, the painter Ad Reinhardt. It is a rich exchange, very much a part of the Merton legacy. But for students of art the situation is different.

For them the Reinhardt legacy—the works themselves, the artist's numerous intriguing writings, and the performance as artist turned in by Ad Reinhardt—calls for close attention.

Michael Corris, professor of fine art in Great Britain, greatly advances the understanding of Reinhardt's work and person through his new book. He explores and documents the heretofore least-known zone of Reinhardt's activity, as a political cartoonist in his youth and middle years supporting left-wing causes and publications in the United States. He guides us through the complex body of art commentary generated by Reinhardt's own writings on art and, more specifically, on his own art; by the perspectives of Reinhardt's contemporaries, artists and critics; and by critics active since Reinhardt's death in 1966, who have naturally contributed still more insights and puzzles. He clarifies Reinhardt's stance among his artist contemporaries as a severe critic, a polemicist, yet a loyal participant in art world forums where his wit and wisdom were anticipated and valued. He was the ultimate curmudgeon, the growl, the doubt—yet loved. Everyone knew he was unique. And behind the public performance, which was often entertaining in the way that Diogenes and the Cynics were entertaining, his peers recognized the utter seriousness of his engagement with art.

In his complex explorations, Corris moves well past Merton's relatively simple, heartfelt response to Reinhardt's art, and turns back to question it. "…The point of intersection," writes Corris (p. 89), "of Merton's theological concerns and Reinhardt's aesthetic concerns is surely an uneasy place for the 'black' paintings to reside. While Reinhardt shared Merton's enthusiasm for religious doctrines and precepts, the artist chose to consider them in terms of a matrix of social and ideological concerns. In Reinhardt's mind this may have blunted the wayward spirituality that Merton was prepared to project onto the 'black' paintings." Undoubtedly true, the context should be broad and varied. But the term "wayward" sets off an alarm. Why would the negative theology, the rigorous path of Meister Eckhart, the experiential reports of St. John of the Cross, the notion of kenosis, the acknowledgment of the need to empty oneself of nonsense in order to know the truth, be in any sense "wayward"? All of these things were points of reference for Reinhardt as for Merton; Reinhardt drew on them in the dry but compelling poetry of his critical writings. Reinhardt belongs to art, not to the Abbey, and the art world must and will fight its battles in its own terms. But so much in Reinhardt's writings from the period of the Black Paintings connects directly or obliquely with Merton's concerns. Reinhardt's aesthetic, social, and ideological positions, brilliantly and painstakingly set before the reader by Corris, do not erase his perfectly evident concern to explore in the Black Paintings a visual correlative or embodiment of the *via negativa*.

Reinhardt's paintings should be seen. Please do what you can to see one. Reinhardt's writings should be read in enough depth to know and remember their unique perspective and rhythm. The best are litanies inserted into our very modern world, which scarcely knows or cares what a litany might be. Under the combat conditions of the art world of his time—not so unlike the art world of our time—Reinhardt was a religious artist.

Roger Lipsey

POKS, Malgorzata, *Thomas Merton and Latin America: a Consonance of Voices* (Katowice: Wyzsza Szkola Zarzadzania Marketingowego, 2007), pp. 288. ISBN 978-83-61061-00-7. n.p. (paperback).

At this point in time, four decades after Thomas Merton's death, few studies of his work could be said to break new ground, but Malgorzata Poks' new book on Merton and Latin American poets, a revision of her doctoral dissertation, written, in English, at a Polish university, can legitimately lay claim to do precisely that. One might suppose that it is rather peripheral ground, but of course the later Merton emphasized that wisdom is often discovered at the margins, and Poks makes a strong case that Merton's determination to become "a man of the whole hemisphere" is a central aspect of his project to discover and participate in that hidden sapiential wholeness he so memorably describes in "Hagia Sophia."

Poks' opening chapter provides the most thorough account yet written of the importance of Latin America and its culture to Merton, and the reciprocal importance of Merton's interest in and support for the lively literary awakenings throughout Central and South America in the mid-twentieth century. Drawing on letters, journals, articles and poems, as well as on previous studies of Stefan Baciu and Robert Daggy, along with Christine Bochen's introduction to *The Courage for Truth: Letters to Writers*, the author makes the case that Merton found to the south a "more spiritual, concrete, hieratic, intuitive, affective" alternative to the "rationalistic, pragmatic, aggressive" European and North American post-Enlightenment culture, "isolated from the natural world and living by abstraction" (30). She traces Merton's fascination with the Hispanic world, both continental and American, from shortly after his baptism in 1938 through his 1940 visit to Cuba, which prompted both his epiphany in a Havana Church and the inspiration for his "first important poem" (39), "Song for Our Lady of Cobre," to the reawakening of interest largely catalyzed by the arrival of Ernesto Cardenal at Gethsemani as a novice in 1957. This renewed contact eventually led to an ever-widening network of contacts with Latin American poets and thinkers, particularly in Nicaragua but also in Cuba and throughout South America, to seminal writings such as "Day of a Stranger," "Letter to Pablo Antonio Cuadra Concerning Giants" and "Message to Poets," to Merton's deepening interest in indigenous cultures that would find its way into much of his later poetry, to his being recognized by many young, and not so young, literary figures as a mentor and a model, a bridge uniting the hemispheres, "the only living spiritual master in both Americas," as one admirer put it, respected "for his integrity as a writer and witness to truth" (55). This interest also led to Merton's translations of Latin American poets into English both as a way of immersing himself more deeply in a literary world he found so attractive and of exposing an English-speaking audience to some of the riches of that world.

The body of Poks' work that follows this introductory overview consists of chapters devoted to each of the seven poets whom Merton translated: the Ecuadorian Jorge Carrera Andrade, the Brazilian Carlos Drummond de Andrade, the Nicaraguans Alfonso Cortés, Ernesto Cardenal and Pablo Antonio Cuadra, the Chilean Nicanor Parra and the Peruvian César Vallejo, some of whom had become personal friends. (The discussion of Cardenal actually overflows into the following chapter on Cuadra, apparently because of the centrality of indigenous elements in both their work, a somewhat awkward break in the pattern that might have the unintended effect of diminishing the crucial significance for Merton of Cuadra and his work.) Each chapter provides background on the poet, relying not only on Merton's own comments on the five poets included in his 1963 volume *Emblems of a Season of Fury* but on Poks' own wide-ranging research, and offers sensitive and perceptive explications of each of the poems Merton translated, highlighting the points of intersection between translator and original poet. Thus Poks shows how Carrera Andrade's "inner journey" to the "secret country" which is "everywhere and nowhere because it is within ourselves" proves to be "exemplary . . . for 'monks' and 'ministers of silence'" (70-71). She notes the "Franciscan love of life" (99) characteristic of Brazilian poetry as exemplified by Carlos Drummond de Andrade, the "extraordinary ontological sense" (102) of the ostensibly deranged Alfonso Cortés, the iconoclastic antipoetry of Nicanor Parra, and Merton's "exceptional resonance" (230) with Vallejo, whose identification with the outcast and the persecuted in his *Poemas Humanas* he found prophetic. Merton's closest connections were to his erstwhile novice Cardenal and the latter's cousin Cuadra, with both of whom he shared a growing fascination for the indigenous cultures of the Americas; Merton translates excerpts from Cardenal's spare collection of short poems on his monastic experience, *Gethsemani, Ky*, three epigrams that are more political in tenor, and the longer "Drake in the Southern Sea," an ambiguous paradigm of the encounter between Anglo and Hispanic cultures in the Americas. The fourteen poems Merton translates from Cuadra's *El Jaguar y la Luna*, the most from any poet, testify to how powerful Merton found his Nicaraguan friend's efforts to express "contemporary aspirations in the language of ancient myth" (176), an effort he himself would make in *The Geography of Lograire* and other late writings.

Poks, who demonstrated her mastery of Merton's original poetic corpus in a lengthy and very impressive article in *The Merton Annual*, vol. 14 ("Thomas Merton's Poetry of Endless Inscription"), is very much aware of analogies and possible influences connecting these translations with Merton's own work, and intersperses detailed discussions of many of these links throughout the book. For example "Grace's House" is compared with Carlos Drummond's "Memories of the Ancient World," seen through the eyes of the young girl Clara; a lovely reading of Merton's French poem "Le Secret," dedicated to Cortés, is provided in the chapter on that poet; Merton's essay "The Sacred City," his short sequence in prose and verse "The Early Legend," and the Meso-American sections of the "South" canto of *Lograire* are discussed extensively in the Cardenal/Cuadra chapter (along with the "Letter to Che: Canto Bilingue" – Merton's one venture into Spanish verse); Merton's own experiments in antipoetry, such as *Original Child Bomb* and *Cables to the Ace*, are considered in relation to Parra. Along the way, Poks also manages to incorporate at least brief notices of virtually every Merton prose work that has an explicit connection to Latin America, as well as a significant number that do not. An added bonus is Poks' Appendix, "Thomas Merton and the Poets of North America: A Consonance of Sorts," in which she shows that Merton was not alone in his mid-century appreciation for Hispanic poetry and traces Merton's growing awareness, particularly through Louis Zukofsky, of the Objectivists and Black Mountain poets, as well as his contacts with the Beat movement through Lawrence Ferlinghetti, connections that she suggests would have modified Merton's expressed alienation from anglophone poetry and preference for those writing in Spanish and Portuguese – a suggestive if sketchy discussion that one hopes she will explore in more detail in the future.

There are a couple of somewhat problematic aspects to the methodology of this impressive study. One is the fact that for the most part Poks simply follows the alphabetical arrangement of the *Collected Poems*, which has no authorial warrant, both in the order in which she presents the poets and in her close readings of the individual translations of each writer. Since much of her argument is based on the gradually unfolding development of Merton's contacts with Latin America, it would seem to be more useful, and more logical, to consider the poets in the order in which he encountered them rather than in the arbitrary arrangement of the alphabet, which places Carlos Drummond and Nicanor Parra, both translated subsequent to the 1963 appearance of *Emblems*, in the second and sixth of the seven chapters devoted to individual writers. Likewise, to consider the translations neither in the order in which the original poems were written nor in the order in which Merton arranged them himself (for those poets and poems that appeared in *Emblems*), tends somewhat toward treating each translation in isolation from both the poet's own artistic development and from Merton's aesthetic response to the poet and his work. At times Poks even seems to suggest a kind of progression as she moves through her explications, though she is aware of the non-authorial character of the order (cf. 244); when she does make an exception to this approach, as with Cuadra's "The Jaguar Myth" (191 ff.), her exposition is strengthened significantly.

The other problematic aspect of the work is that the translations are never considered precisely as translations, that is, never compared to the originals. Except for a couple of footnotes in which Poks points out an absent simile in one of Merton's translations from Cardenal and Cardenal himself notes a mistranslation in one of the epigrams (148-49), there is virtually no attention given to

Merton's particular word choices, to the music his new language creates, which of course are what determine whether, and how, a translation becomes a genuine poem in its own right. Poks recognizes this missing dimension at the very outset of her work (13), and rightly points out that attempting to provide detailed comparisons of originals and translations would swell the book beyond reasonable bounds; but it would have been helpful to focus on the qualities of the translation *qua* translation for at least a few key passages, or perhaps for a single poem, for each of the poets discussed. It is telling in this regard that the one bilingual collection of Merton's translations, the ten poems and translations of Pablo Antonio Cuadra included in *The Jaguar and the Moon* (1971), published posthumously but planned by Merton himself, is not mentioned at all by Poks.

Notwithstanding these undeveloped aspects of Merton's translation work, Poks' volume makes a major contribution to elucidating Merton's enthusiastic response to the wisdom of Latin America as articulated by these poets, and to situating this response in relationship to other aspects of his maturing vision in the final decade of his life. She makes a convincing case that in listening to, and enabling others to listen to, "the voice of the New Man . . . in the poetry, written and unwritten," of Latin America, Merton was experiencing a prefiguring of "the eschatological new creation" and sharing in the process by which "the hemisphere was becoming conscious of its vocation to redeem the world" (258). It is a matter of some wonder, and a cause for much gratitude, that a young Central European scholar has explored in such breadth and depth these spiritual and cultural bonds uniting the Western hemisphere in the spirit and the writing of one monk-poet – at once a sign of Merton's own ability to transcend geographical, cultural and linguistic boundaries, and a salutary reminder that voices on what might seem to be the margins can often provide central insights for those willing and able to attend to them.

Patrick F. O'Connell

SMOCK, Frederick, *Pax Intrantibus: A Meditation on the Poetry of Thomas Merton* (Frankfurt, Kentucky: Broadstone Books, 2007), pp. 91. ISBN-13: 978-0-9721144-6-2 (cloth). $25.00.

These days, it seems that people tend to have three reactions to poetry: They ignore it (most people); they ridicule it (see Jim Berhle's website Americanpoetry.biz); or, in rare occasions, they deeply appreciate its power to lift the human soul. Frederick Smock, a poet himself, falls firmly into the last camp, and it is refreshing to read his serious and moving ruminations on the poetry of Thomas Merton.

Smock's book is a short one, yet it is one that the reader can amble through slowly, stopping to ponder both Smock's and Merton's insights along the way. Smock allows both his and Merton's life to intersect, but *Pax Intrantibus* is, thankfully, not a self-indulgent memoir or an attempt to spin off of Merton's fame. We have all read those brands of books, and they are, unfortunately, becoming increasingly more popular. Smock's book is both humble and revealing.

Smock begins with the profound realization that both he, as a boy, and Merton heard the same artillery shells exploding as troops practiced firing at Fort Knox, near both Louisville and the abbey of Gethsemani. The horror of war surrounds us, he points out, and it is the poet's job to articulate the name for that particular horror. Smock points out how Merton's poetry was, like any serious poet's, a struggle "to give a name to the nameless" (14-15). Merton strove during his whole brief life to particularize abstractions like silence, spirit, violence, and love. Many poets fail quickly in their endeavors to do so and descend into shallow irony or cynicism. Merton did not, but he also did not achieve the greatness of those he chose to emulate.

And that point is one thing that sticks with me as consider Smock's book. Merton was a great man. A major spiritual figure, obviously. As Smock points out, he was named a "Catholic Geshe" by the Dalai Lama (57). Such a title is "conferred not on the basis of intellect, or training, but on the basis of character" (57). But was he a great poet? As a reader, and a poet myself, I cannot help but feel a little uneasy when Smock chooses to put excerpts from Merton's poetry up against lines from Auden, Milosz, and Basho, among others. When juxtaposed with that of his betters, Merton's poetry often comes off as, well, facile. For instance, the point of the stanza from Merton's poem "In Silence" (28) could be easily boiled down to the old cliche, "just be yourself." Merton the poet strikes me at times as a poor man's Robert Bly, a deep image poet who just can't seem to find the right deep image. There's no shame in this, and Merton himself understood how hard it was to get a poem right. And his best poetry is rewarding. Smock never questions Merton's abilities, though. Generally, he takes a "I-am-not-worthy" attitude toward Merton's poetic output.

But, in fairness to Smock, his book is a mediation, not a critique. It is filled with insights to ponder. Merton's forays into Islam and his attempts to achieve a "radical ecumenism" (69); his disparagement of the materialism of the United States; his ceaseless humility as he became an important world figure—all are worthy of our consideration as we head into a century that looks to be marked by hardship, a century where superficial spirituality and mindless consumerism will not provide us with the answers we need. *Pax Intrantibus* is the kind of book that tries to provide some answers we do need and, perhaps, are too afraid to confront. It is well worth reading.

Kevin Griffith

PORTER, J.S. *Thomas Merton: Hermit at the Heart of Things* (Ottowa, Canada: Novalis, 2008), PP. 215. ISBN 978-2-89646-008-3. $24.95.

This isn't the book for those who like linear and analytical studies. It is more likely the sort of book for those who like personal and impressionistic accounts of writers who reach deep into the impressionist's psyche and won't let go. Dionysian rather than Apollonian if you like. On the one hand you are never quite sure, in spite of the table of contents, where you will be taken next. On the other hand there are fine moments of illumination as you journey through the book. The journey is Merton's in the first instance, but it is also Porter's as he retrospectively charts his own course from a family background in Ulster Protestantism to the universally human, spiritual consciousness that in Merton, the Roman Catholic monk, comes to engage him. The labels of course slip away as both Porter and Merton are depicted moving towards an inclusive but certainly not a reductive spirituality.

Here are a few examples of the gold in the ore. Writing about Merton's handwriting, Porter observes that the early script is "tight," reflective of a "linear, moralistic, serious," monk and writer. Later, in the case of the *Asian Journal*, for example, the writing becomes a "hen-scratch," reflective of a man who had become "looser, more tolerant, funnier, less sure of himself." Another point of illumination occurs when Porter brings out the precise influence of Hannah Arendt on Merton's writing about Eichmann. There is a spray of light too when Porter notices the unexpected and yet convincing similarities in the journal keeping of Merton and Anais Nin, whom Merton happened to be reading on his Asian journey in 1968. Or sometimes Porter, who inveterately remembers and praises those who have influenced his thinking, recalls the penetrating thoughts of others as in his recalling of John Howard Griffin's observation about Merton's love affair in 1966 that to be "moderate in matters of love is simply not to love."

In some ways this is a study of self-imposed exorcism in which Porter attempts, unsuccessfully one may conclude, to free himself at last from Merton's haunting of him. And here is where the insights into Merton offered by Porter correspond to the personal narrative in which Porter shadowboxes with his ubiquitous Trappist demon. It is in fact Merton's gifts as a writer that enable this possession to occur, especially Merton's openness about himself that so contagiously opens the selves of those who read him. This was the same openness that led Merton to identify almost completely with those he was reading. Merton speaks to the reader, Porter suggests, as if "he were you or you were he or you and he were one." Furthermore, Porter adds, one is stuck by the apparent ease with which Merton as a letter writer reveals himself to strangers." To Boris Pasternak, he reveals his fantasy life; to a Sufi scholar, his working day. . . . and to a girl in grade six, some of his deepest convictions concerning monastic life."

While Porter explores the many Mertons—the monk, poet, social critic, letter writer, and journal keeper—in an effort to show the unifying presence underlying these various kinds of writing, his focus is on Merton's approach to the reader. For Porter, Merton is a writer whose presence and intimacy cause those at conferences to tell each other stories about their first encounters with him. Porter does not go in for stylistic or rhetorical analysis and, indeed, one would like to see a closer reading of Merton's prose and poetry than one finds in the book although he does pay some attention to a few of Merton's major symbols. Porter is more concerned, though, and rightly so perhaps, with Merton's voice. It is of course voice that we hear in important artists, whether literary, musical or otherwise. Who can mistake Mozart's voice, for example, for say, that of Brahms? Through voice, Porter suggests, when you meet Merton on the page, you feel as if you have met him "in the flesh." In an effort to develop his discussion of voice in writing, Porter pursues the topic of tone. Here, although the discussion is somewhat tenuous, Porter shows an unerring sense of what allows us to recognize the voice of a particular writer. Part of Merton's voice and tone is his way, Porter points out, of always presenting himself as a beginner, someone "who comes to life as if he were a stranger to it and is beginning to find his way in it for the first time."

Another of Porter's themes, although one not articulated as explicitly as one perhaps might have liked, is Merton's existentialism, which Porter cites in concrete instances rather than in abstract commentary. Merton's way of dealing with questions or problems, Porter maintains, is to "live them." In this way Merton came to an awareness of the value of Latin American writing through his contact with Latin American poets. Similarly, in his quest to understand Buddhism he made contact with those like D.T. Suzuki, who lived Buddhism.

As I have intimated, while this book is about Merton, it is also about Porter, and this is especially evident in the last chapter which is entitled "Hello, Goodbye, Hello Again." Perhaps surprising, given Merton's hold on Porter's imagination, are the trailing thoughts about Merton. Porter confesses to being "dumbfounded" by his loss of interest in the prominent biographical issues about Merton. These include the romance with M., the fathering of an illegitimate child in the U.K. prior to his Columbia and Gethsemani years, and the so-called epiphanies that occurred at Fourth and Walnut in Louisville and at Polonnarawa in what was then Ceylon. I couldn't agree more. Although these matters have preoccupied critics and biographers for some time, somehow they seem secondary at last, rather like those "inessential houses" on Long Island mentioned by the narrator at the ending of Fitzgerald's *Great Gatsby*. What remains behind is the presence of Merton *essentially* to be encountered in the narratives, poems, essays, journals, and letters in which he lives as vividly as ever. Although the experiences that went into the making of Merton shaped the man, they do not equal him.

Ross Labrie

PALMER, Parker J., *The Promise of Paradox: A Celebration of Contradictions in the Christian Life* (San Francisco: Jossey-Bass, 1980, 2008), pp. 175. ISBN 9780787996963 (cloth). $18.95.

Reviewing a book can sometimes lead to reviewing one's own life. This may be most apt to happen, I suppose, when the book under review has been crafted by its author from an intense review of their own life. A double viewing, in other words, can occur. You see yourself in what the other has seen. Hence, one re-views more than a book. In *The Promise of Paradox*, contemplative educator Parker Palmer celebrates the evolving role of contradictions as they are experienced in the spiritual life, and even re-views his own book in a new Introduction.

The present work is actually the third edition of Palmer's first book, *The Promise of Paradox*. First published in 1980 by Ave Maria Press, but later having fallen oddly out of print, it was picked up in 1993 by the Servant Leadership School affiliated with the Church of the Saviour in Washington, DC (Palmer has donated all proceeds of *Paradox* to the School). The reappearance of *Paradox* in 1993 was joined by the second edition of Palmer's splendid contemporary classic on education as a spiritual journey, *To Know As We Are Known*. Palmer's work is of interest to Merton readers for at least three reasons: He quotes Merton extensively in all his works, he writes from and promotes a contemplative perspective of life, love and learning, and he has participated in a conference commemorating the 25th anniversary of the Merton Center at Bellarmine, which led to the publication of his keynote address, "Contemplation Reconsidered: The Human Way In," in Volume 8 of *The Merton Annual* (1996).

The essential change to the 2008 edition of Paradox is the addition of a substantial 24 page Introduction by Palmer, which I will focus on for this review. The rest of the book remains virtually untouched. Still intact is the 1980 Introduction by Henri Nouwen. Chapter one frames the entire work in light of Merton's writings and experiences about life "in the belly of a paradox" (*The Sign of Jonas*). Subsequent chapters creatively explore the paradox of outer and inner stations of the cross, the relationship between individual and community, scarcity and abundance in society, and finally the paradoxical way of spirit in the life of the mind (education). Palmer writes simply, clearly and humbly, which is why one will not find common experiences or ideas treated with clichés, automatic dogma or even the hint of omniscience.

In his provocative, new Introduction, he acknowledges two reactions upon rereading his first book: There is much that he would not change, and much that he would not say today. Thus Palmer found himself wrapped in another paradox rooted in his own words and thoughts. He admits, too, to finding it increasingly difficult today "to name my beliefs using the traditional Christian language because that vocabulary has been taken hostage by theological terrorists and tortured beyond recognition" (xxi). His faith is still strong, but he recognizes, as did Merton, many problems in trying to communicate amidst the constraints of language and the tyranny of (mis)interpretation. Yet he realizes that he still can, nevertheless, certainly speak with uncertainty, for "when you are traveling toward your destiny in the belly of a paradox, as we all are, there are no certainties. But the creative opportunities are boundless. Resist the fact, and life can get brutal. Embrace it, and life becomes one whale of a ride" (xxxvii). Such an understanding clearly informs Palmer's powerful ecumenism that also runs throughout his writing.

Palmer's thesis in *Paradox* is simply and not so simply this: The promise that apparent opposites can cohere in a life lived with a both/and perspective instead of an either/or point of view. Running through the heart of human experience, one might say, is an ever abiding *seemingness*, which means that anything and everything can seem one way or another depending on how you are looking. There always seems to be a relationship between what and how we see, as well as an ever-growing relationship between vision and understanding. One pair of traditional terms for this are *appearance* (or illusion because not total) and *reality*. Contemplation, for Palmer, is defined in general as any way that one can penetrate illusion and touch reality, a perspective that weaves throughout his writings about the unresolved tensions of life—the paradoxes. Thus spirituality, for Palmer, is essentially contemplative rather than moralistic, and is rooted in the paradox of the whole, which naturally assumes there is always more to reality than what we can see, say or do.

Those who may be long on the spiritual journey will already know about living with paradoxes, but Palmer's book does not merely re-explain timeless truths, but rather cultivates deepening insights into one's own paradoxes. As Christians, we are very familiar with such enduring paradoxes such as losing your life to find it, dying to self to live, the first shall be last, in the world but not of it. The value of *The Promise of Paradox*, however, is that it helps the reader come to see one's own contradictions—in terms of the daily tensions, battles and embittered choices that often threaten to tear us apart—and the wondrous possibility of their becoming paradoxes through which we can come to find rest and a little closer to understanding our own quizzical lives.

I did not expect this to happen. Reading Palmer's book for review purposes led me to approach it in a slightly more detached way than I normally would have (as a kind of devotee, like any other contemplative sympathizer). I did not expect, however, to reflect on my own inner turmoil. I came to realize that I have been living lately with three unrecognized paradoxes that until now I had not understood as such, let alone articulated even as problems. The beauty of Palmer's book, is in its capacity to reveal that the problems of the human heart are not private concerns but are paradoxically, hence intimately, connected to the lives of others. Or as Palmer uses Merton's phrasing to make the case: We and the world interpenetrate each other. Thus the same quest for certainty that torments and twists an individual life into a private bureaucracy is also related to the collective illusions involved in the forceful construction of a world steeped in nationalistic interests in opposition to those of other nations, other cultures, other ways of life, other children of God. Palmer does not fall into the trap of relativism, however, because he is keenly aware that paradoxes do not require the neglect of critical faculties but rather their sharpening. Thomas Merton stands as a model for Palmer as someone who lived through paradoxes, who did not try to escape or evade them. By living the contradictions, Palmer advises, we are "swallowed by grace" and allowed to travel with Merton and all the saints in the luminescent belly of a paradox (37).

Gray Matthews

Merton, Thomas, *Gandhi on Non-Violence* : *Selected Texts from Gandhi's Non-Violence in Peace and War*. Edited with an Introduction by Thomas Merton. Preface by Mark Kurlansky. (New York: New Directions Publishing Corporation, 2007), pp. xi + 96. ISBN 978-0-8112-1686-9 (paperback). $13.95.

It has often been noted that the twentieth century, though rife with scientific achievements, also claims the title for the most devastating wars, the most brutal genocides, and the most widespread violations of human rights. In the first few years of the twenty-first century, not much has improved and has perhaps even worsened. Imperialism, oppression, and violence still characterize both the international and domestic policies of the world's most powerful nations and are becoming more and more acceptable by modern standards. This trend of violence and moral degradation became

clear to L.L. Whyte in the years immediately following World War
II, though he viewed the future with optimism. In his eyes, the
"uninhibited perversions" of society, such as its "relentless passion
for quantity," "uncontrolled industrialism and excess of analytical
thought" would experience only "a brief period of dominance"
(2). Despite his hopefulness, however, he admits that "one more
dark decade would disprove my judgment, revealing a rot deeper
than I have seen" (2).

In his 1964 essay "Gandhi and the One-Eyed Giant," Thomas
Merton looks to this very quotation as an observation that demands
attention, particularly in light of the fact that the "rot" most certainly
did lie deeper than Whyte had perceived. Merton's contemporary
America was one of the Vietnam War, the civil rights movement,
and of a nation emerging as one of the world's superpowers. It is
not surprising, then, that Merton would return to one of his earliest
works, a selection from the writings of Mohandas Gandhi, in this
time of sociopolitical upheaval. The struggles facing Gandhi and
Merton differed in specifics, but reflected each other in the most
fundamental of ways. Both men challenged the existing definition of a contemplative life by considering social action essential
to their spiritual wholeness. The similarities in the way these two
influential men perceived the world and their role as contemplatives in such a world make Merton the perfect candidate to provide
insight on Gandhi's writings and lifework.

At first glance, Thomas Merton may seem to be in many ways
of the opposite of Gandhi. Drawn to a monastery at a young age,
it is easy to characterize his personal inclination as one to seclusion
or isolation. Mark Kurlansky remarks in his preface to the newly
released edition that Merton, "unlike Gandhi, had a strong urge to
withdraw from the world" and was even "considered a recluse" to
the other members of the monastery (xv). This analysis, however,
simplifies Merton's perspective on monastic life by focusing on his
physical isolation and disregarding his obvious desire and ability to
affect change through writing. The more important aspect of Merton's and Gandhi's lives is their shared "obligation to speak out"
(xv). Both men responded to injustice with consistent yet patient
fervor, recognizing the necessity for change but also realizing that
the resistance of force that had so often been used in the past would
only perpetuate the cycle of violence. "Freedom won through
bloodshed or fraud," Gandhi writes, "is no freedom" (66).

Because Merton's ideas on social justice in many ways re-sembled Gandhi's, his careful selection of quotations exhibits an insightful understanding of Gandhi's approach to non-violence. Though compiled during Merton's youth, this collection shows a mature grasp on Gandhi's ability to masterfully balance a life of both activism and contemplation, a challenge Merton would have to overcome later in life. Divided into five different sections, "Principles of Non-Violence," "Non-Violence: True and False," "The Spiritual Dimensions of Non-Violence," "The Political Scope of Non-Violence," and "The Purity of Nonviolence," Merton suc-cinctly highlights the fundamental characteristics of Gandhi's views on non-violence by including only the most illuminating quotations, which creates a sort of sutra-like feel to the book. Through this compilation, we see Gandhi's unwavering commit-ment to justice and, perhaps more importantly, his unshakeable foundation in *ahimsa*. Non-violence, he writes, cannot simply be viewed as a means to reach a political end, but instead "has to be all-pervasive. I cannot be non-violent about one activity of mine and violent about others. That would be a policy, not a life force" (66).

Merton's selection of quotations also enforces the ideal of non-violent activism as vastly superior to passivity. The distinc-tion between non-violence of the strong and non-violence of "the weak and impotent" is clearly a recurring theme and an important element of *ahimsa* (56). Cowardice, Gandhi argues, often disguises itself as non-violence when in reality it merely contributes to a system of violence by accepting oppression without any active resistance. Remaining a victim of oppression denotes participation in that system and often results in the expansion of oppression.

In addition to his careful selection of passages, Merton further deepens his portrait of Gandhi through the opening essay, writ-ten years after the original compilation of quotations. This essay is important not only in terms of understanding Gandhi himself, but also in terms of appreciating the universal, timeless applica-tions of *ahimsa*. Both Gandhi and Merton experienced the horror of imperialism firsthand—Gandhi as the victim of imperialism and Merton as the beneficiary. The injustice that had become commonplace in both of their nations, however, tormented each equally. Gandhi could no longer bear to see his nation oppressed and demeaned by the British Empire, while Merton was unable to live in complicity with a United States rooted in militarism, materialism, and racism.

It is in their similar reactions to injustice that Merton and Gandhi are most alike and why Merton's essay so successfully expands our understanding of Gandhi's experiences and teachings. Merton sees a world that, like Whyte suggested over fifty years ago, has to a great extent lost its sense of spiritual depth and integrity. Instead of finding a balance between the "science" of the West and the "wisdom" of the East, "the one-eyed giant" of "science without wisdom" (3) has prevailed, resulting in "a schizoid society, schizoid national structures, schizoid military and business complexes, and, need one add, schizoid religious sects" (6). The tools of oppression have developed into subtler forms, but perhaps with greater consequences. The tools of reform, however, remain the same. Today, in the first decade of the twenty-first century, it may be easy to look back on Gandhi's experiences and attribute his success to simpler times, to an isolated situation, maybe even to luck. On the contrary, Merton's explanation of Gandhi's life proves that non-violent strategies have never been more relevant or even less relevant because they are rooted in timeless truth. Only through internal commitment to non-violence and a clear, spiritual devotion as strong as Gandhi's can true change be achieved. This is the lesson Merton learned through his upbringing in western culture and his studies of eastern culture, as well as the lesson Gandhi learned through his upbringing in eastern culture and studies of western culture. This is the balance between science and wisdom that eradicates the spiritual and social crisis in the contemporary world.

Gandhi's incredible wisdom and achievements can often mistakenly lead to idolization, to seeing his work as something godlike and therefore unreachable. In reality, however, that perspective destroys the very core of non-violent action. While the ideals of non-violence are perhaps divinely-inspired, it is imperfect humans, each as flawed as the next, who comprise its implementation and realization. In the final section of the book, we see a glimpse of Gandhi's confessions of doubt, his recognition of his own faults, and his disappointment in the fallibility of human action. Strangely enough, these quotations struck me as the most hopeful of the entire text, confirming that perfection is not a requirement and victory is not an expectation of non-violence.

As society continues to stubbornly invest in the impermanent power of money and violence, an individual's attempts to counteract that system can seem worthless, empty—even naïve. Through its simple, straight-forward style, this book reveals the fallacy in that myth of individual impotency. Gandhi's life serves as inspiration for the most average, seemingly voice-less individuals. His example enforces that we are the critical element to non-violence, the only avenue through which non-violence can be achieved. Only through our influence, individual by individual, can the cycle of violence be broken. Moreover, Gandhi and Merton confirm the essentiality of non-violence to our own spiritual health and the necessity of non-violence in guiding both our external and internal realities back to their natural, peaceful state.

Julie Frazier

Merton & Buddhism: Wisdom, Emptiness & Everyday Mind. Edited by Bonnie Bowman Thurston. Illustrated by Gray Henry. (Louisville, Kentucky: Fons Vitae, 2007), pp. xvii + 271. ISBN 1-887752-84-6 (paperback). $26.95.

This is the fourth volume of The Fons Vitae Thomas Merton Series that focuses upon Merton's contributions to inter-religious dialogue. Earlier editions included *Merton & Sufism, Merton & Hesychasm, and Merton & Judaism.* The latest edition, *Merton & Buddhism,* is a collection of scholarly essays that not only examines Merton's interest in Buddhism, but also its influence on his artistic contemplations in poetry, photography and brushwork. The book is lavishly illustrated, with almost one hundred black and white photos of Merton, places he visited, people he met, Buddhist iconography and art, and Merton's photography and brushwork. There is also a stunning sixteen page full-color centerfold of Buddha figures.

The essays in this volume are divided into three sections. The first section includes a succinct overview of Buddhism by Rodger Corless and an overview of Merton's acquaintance with Buddhism and Buddhists by Bonnie B. Thurston. While this material will not be new to Merton scholars, it will be essential to those who have a more limited background in Merton studies. The second section contains four essays that examine Merton's experience with different Buddhist traditions. There are essays by James A. Wiseman on Theravada Buddhism, Judith Simmer-Brown on Tibetan Buddhism and two essays on Zen Buddhism by Ruben L.F. Habito and John P. Keenan respectively. The third section of essays examines the Zen influence and themes in Merton's artistic contemplations. Roger Lipsey's essay looks at Merton's brushwork, while Paul Pearson takes his photography and Bonnie B. Thurston takes his poetry. There is a fourth, "bonus" section, edited by Thurston, titled "Footnotes to the Asian Journey of Thomas Merton," that includes interviews with some of the principle players in Merton's visit to India. While some of this material has been published elsewhere, there is some new material to be found.

Aside from its interest to those in Merton studies, this book would be very useful for anyone interested in inter religious dialogue or the history of Buddhism in America. It certainly belongs in the library of those interested in comparative religion and contemplative practice. Students of either Buddhism or Christianity will certainly be stimulated to investigate the parallels that Merton was already exploring decades ago.

Most readers of Merton, when they think of Merton and Buddhism, usually think in terms of Zen and Suzuki, perhaps rightly so. However, I think the essays by Wiseman and Simmer-Brown do a fine job of demonstrating the importance of Merton's contact with Theravada and Tibetan Buddhism leaders, practitioners and teachers. The week Merton spent in Sri Lanka is poorly documented and represents a significant gap in the historical record that could be further explored. The Tibetan journey is simply astounding. The importance of Merton's meetings with H.H. Dalai Lama and Kyabje Chadral Rinpoche cannot be overstated. Both recognized Merton as a fellow spiritual traveler who had attained great spiritual wisdom. Merton received advanced teaching and transmissions from these lineage holders that significantly expanded his experience an understanding of Tibetan Buddhism. The fact that Merton declared Chadral Rinpoche would be his Dzogchen teacher suggests that this was a turning point in his path toward Buddhism.

The essays by Habito and Keenan take up Merton's engagement with Zen Buddhism from opposite sides of the looking glass. The interesting ways in which the essays contrast and complement each other underscores the editor's skillful pairing. Keenan's essay takes on the issue of Merton's long engagement with D.T. Suzuki in light of contemporary criticism of Suzuki's Zen credentials and scholarship. In brief, Suzuki's Zen is a popularized Zen that under-represents the tradition's rich texture of scripture and religious practice. Of course, it could not be otherwise, Merton was a spiritual explorer, and he, like Suzuki, opened up passages that western students of Buddhism will long be wandering. Habito's essay avoids the well-trod path through Merton's academic and intellectual engagement with Buddhism. Turning the glass around, Habito looks at Merton's spiritual journey through the lens of the Sanbo Kyodan Lineage that combines elements of both Soto and Rinzai Zen traditions. From this perspective, Merton's becomes an exemplary Zen life, from his experience of *dukha,* the dissatisfaction or suffering resulting in the abandonment of ordinary life for a life of contemplation, to his experience of shared suffering of the epiphany at Fourth & Walnut, Merton's life is revealed as *nothing* but *ordinary.*

The third section of essays is concerned with Merton's art. Essays by Lipsey and Pearson explore the development of his spare visual style in both brushwork and photography. Thurston's essay on his poetry reveals that same light touch in his poetry. Together, the three essays may provide the most telling portrait of Merton. There is such a haunted, ethereal quality to his work, as if it is always pointing to something just the other side of the visible world. Merton's poetry and artwork seem to draw us to a place beyond sign and language, toward an immediacy of the spirit.

This collection of essays is a wonderful celebration of Merton's years of thought and experience with Buddhism. The editor, Bonnie B. Thurston, has done an excellent job of putting together a compelling portrait of a spiritual master. It should be required reading for anyone interested in this aspect of Merton's spiritual journey. The book could also function as an excellent introduction to the history of Buddhism in America. It is a truly beautiful book, both for its lush illustrations and the vision of Merton it evokes.

Craig Burgdof

Thomas Merton., *Echoing Silence: Thomas Merton on the Vocation of Writing.* Edited with an Introduction by Robert Inchausti (Boston & London: New Seeds Books, 2007), pp, xiii + 215. ISBN 978-1-59030-348-1. $14.00 (paperback).

The book's title and cover photo serve the reader well. "Echoing Silence" evokes Merton's paradoxical embrace of two vocations – that of a contemplative *and* that of a writer – while the picture of Merton's hermitage worktable, standing against a backdrop of full bookshelves, invites the viewer to imagine Thomas Merton reading and writing in a space cleared by solitude and silence yet resonant with the wisdom and witness of countless saints, sages and fellow writers that together comprised the "living balance of spirits" of which Merton wrote in *Day of a Stranger*.

In a brief introduction, Robert Inchausti traces in broad strokes Merton's growth as a writer from the teenager wanting "to discover who he was and what he believed" to the "culture critic" in dialogue with an intellectually and religiously diverse and divided world. Inchausti's selections enable the reader to glimpse what Glenn Hinson once termed "the many faces of Thomas Merton" and witness the development of his thought as well as its breadth. Merton was a man of many interests as evidenced in the topics addressed in these pages: art, Buddhism, Camus, communication, creativity, culture, God, Pasternak, peace, poetry, religion, silence, truth, war, wisdom – to name just a few. Although, as Inchausti reminds us, Merton "moved in and out of particular interests, phases, roles and theories, what is most consistent – what defines his attitude, orientation, style and contribution is his perennial return to origins, to emptiness, and to God." The monk grew as a writer and the writer's growth was informed by his being a monk.

While focused on Merton the writer, the selections allow the reader to glimpse something of the young convert of *Seven Story Mountain*, the earnest monk, the explorer of the inner life, the courageous prophet, the life-long student and critic of literature, and the hermit in dialogue with writers and religious leaders all over the world. What comes through in this volume, as in all of Merton's writing, is something Merton himself realized when he wrote in *The Sign of Jonas*: "Every book I write is a mirror of my own character and conscience." Reading *Echoing Silence*, one might dare to say that almost every line Merton wrote was such a mirror.

The book is divided into six parts: "Writing as a Spiritual Calling," The Christian Writer in the Modern World," "On Poetry," "On Other Writers" "On His Own Writing," and "Advice to Writers." Each part consists of selections, ranging from a few lines to a page or two in length. The selections are drawn from the many different genres in which Merton wrote – essays and books, letters and journals, autobiography and poetry. Time wise, the selections span three decades from the forties to the sixties. A closer look at several parts of the book will serve to illustrate the depth and breadth of selections, skillfully selected by Inchausti.

The first part, which explores "Writing as a Spiritual Calling" includes selections from texts written between 1941 and 1966 – in journals, in *The Seven Storey Mountain*, and a host of essays. In these pages, we are reminded of Merton's life-long desire to be a writer, his struggle with being a monk *and* a writer, and his eventual coming to terms with the fact that he was called to be both and that these two vocations were interrelated. Perhaps Merton had this eventual resolution in mind when he wrote to Robert Menchin on January 15, 1966: "I have never for a moment questioned the vocation to be a monk, but I have had to settle many other questions about ways and means, the where and the how of being a monk… For me the monastery has not been a mere refuge. It has meant facing responsibility on the deepest level, and it has meant giving an account of myself to others…" And Merton gave such an account in what he wrote. "Silence," Merton observed in *No Man Is an Island (1951)*, "does not exist in our lives for its own sake… silence is the mother of speech." The ultimate speech Merton had in mind was the life lived in Christ but it was through his writing that Merton gave voice to the life and to the silence.

The selections excerpted in the second part, entitled "The Christian Writer in the Modern World," show Merton grappling with the role of writers and poets. His reflections range widely; he speaks of the "Christian dimensions of creativity"; the freedom of the artist; and the responsibility of the writer to speak out against injustice, falsehood, totalitarianism, political ideology and expediency. The Christian writer cannot be "a bystander" in the face of "the illness of political language," the rhetoric of "war makers" and the "war machine" itself. "Our task," Merton writes, "is not suddenly to burst out into the dazzle of utter unadulterated truth but laboriously to reshape an accurate and honest language that will permit communication between men on all social and intellectual levels, instead of multiplying a Babel of esoteric and technical tongues which isolate men in their specialties" ("Camus and the Church" [1966]). As a Christian writer, Merton also felt himself called not only to engage the issues of the world around him but also to speak of the reality within. Thus, in responding to a request from Pope Paul VI for a "message of contemplatives to the world," Merton wrote: "My brother, perhaps in my solitude I have become as it were an explorer for you, a searcher in realms which you are not able to visit… I have been summoned to explore a desert area of man's heart…." This part of the book ends, and appropriately so, with several passages from the talks Merton gave in Asia shortly before he died.

In subsequent parts of the book, Merton writes about the role of the poet, his solidarity with poets, and his hope for poetry as "a kind of recovery of paradise." As Merton put it in a review of *The Legend of Tucker Caliban*, "There is no revolution without prophetic sages." We read selections from Merton's letters to fellow writers, including Mark Van Doren, Boris Pasternak, Czeslaw Milosz, Napolean Chow, James Baldwin, Henry Miller and Walker Percy as well as excerpts from Merton's literary essays particularly those pertaining to Pasternak and Camus. We read Merton's reflections "On His Own Writing," drawn from letters to monastic superiors and fellow monks that record Merton's struggles with censors and superiors, as well as from letters to working writers like himself whom he encourages and by whom he himself is encouraged.

The book ends with a short section of "Advice to Writers," gleaned from sources as varied as *The Inner Experience* and *The Way of Chuang Tzu*. Merton's advice is well summed up in a few lines in a letter to Ernesto Cardenal: "Basically our first duty today it to human truth in its existential reality, and this sooner or later brings us into confrontations with systems and power." Meant for writers, Merton's words offer advice to readers and a challenge as well.

Echoing Silence is "a keeper"—one of those books that invites a reader to return to its pages—again and again—to enjoy Merton's insight and wisdom. And like all good anthologies, it is likely motivate many a reader, as it does this one, to return to the sources from which these selections were so carefully drawn.

Christine M. Bochen

Soul Searching: The Journey of Thomas Merton. A Film by Morgan Atkinson

Virtually all of the images chronicling Thomas Merton's short but rich life belong to the genre of photography and not film. Other than a poor quality 8mm film of an October 10, 1968 address that Merton presented on Marxism in Bangkok, Thailand—shortly before his tragic and untimely death—we have been left with no other known archival film of any period in the life of the man who many agree was the greatest spiritual master to grace the North American continent in the twentieth century. There are indeed prodigious biographical accounts, along with now voluminous works on and about Merton's philosophical, literary and spiritual writings. These are in the form of scholarly works, written narrative, poetry, music, art, and theatre. Moreover, the Thomas Merton Center has dutifully digitized the well-prepared lectures Merton gave as novice master at Gethsemane—but here too, the listener must project his or her imagination to achieve any semblance of what it must have been like to be in the presence of a being of such immense spiritual light and wisdom.

Soul Searching is one such projection. Producer-director Morgan Atkinson has employed what has now become recognized as the Ken Burns style of documentary filmmaking: an interweaving of narration, montage, and interviews with accompanying musical support, all toward the end of evoking in our minds and imaginations Merton's unorthodox presence and charismatic appeal. Atkinson makes the directorial choice of beginning the film with Merton's infamous Asian journey; an event scholars suggest was, in profoundly unfathomable ways, the denouement of his existential and eremitical lives. We see in the Thomas Merton gazing toward the east, an ebullient seeker of truth and love. There can be no doubt that Merton's decision to travel to Asia, as well as his openness to Eastern spiritualities, brought about great confusion and consternation in the minds of those who perceived him to be a bastion of Cistercian monastic tradition and holiness. In *Soul Searching* we are reminded that Merton's more ripened spirituality (by his own admission) was rooted not in the dogma or ritual of Catholicism, but in a preternaturally direct experience of truth whose center can only be characterized (as it is in Taoism) as consistently fluid and formless. Thus, Merton's soul searching was born not entirely in the theatre of his mind, but in his embodiment as a human being, and in the moment- to- moment I-Thou encounter with other souls and the miraculous grace and numinosity of God's creation.

The film's initial musings around Merton's Asian journey seem short lived, morphing abruptly and somewhat awkwardly into a biographical perspective that asks the viewer to consider the young Thomas' profligate excesses in a context of speakeasies and galvanizing jazz music. It is within this transition that *Soul Searching* begins unfolding the existential narrative of Merton's ineffable conversion from a life of debauchery to his heart-centered epiphany of Christ as his Savior and lifeblood. If we consider that documentaries are produced primarily to educate, then *Soul Searching* has made a valuable contribution to its audience by portraying

Merton's tumultuous psychospiritual odyssey through the Scylla and Charybdis of his own mind and emotions. Lost, yet indefatigable, Merton's soul plunges into the depths of his own angst and despair, rising only momentarily before resuming its place in the wilderness of his loveless existence. The humiliation that Merton experienced as he contacted his inner demons, catalyzed him toward the realization and somewhat prophetic voice declaring, "It is time to stop being sick and be really well. It is time to be full of peace and silence." On his first visit to Gethsemane Merton was deeply affected by the Cistercian rhythms of prayer that seemed to him to contribute greatly in creating "a world of peace and silence." He perceived the incontrovertible importance of the monks' daily life of devotional prayer as critical to the survival of the world.

Merton's experiences of monastic life and Gethsemane's paradisiacal landscape corroborated what was already germinating in his psyche and soul as a result of the suffering he had encountered in his downtrodden secular life. While Merton came face to face with the dark and delusional forces that constitute the false self, his awareness penetrated into the ways ideologies and social structures fixated upon the meaningless and futile shibboleths of modern consumerist existence. Echoed in *Soul Searching* is the stentorian voice of John the Baptist in Merton's admonishment that the self-made man and unbridled freedom of corporations does not, in any real sense, constitute the "good life"—rather these phenomena are expressions of the spiritual ills of contemporary American society.

Merton seemed to be intent on awakening us to what is real, disabusing us of our everyday notions of what we assume to be implicitly valuable. Perhaps the greatest of these self-deceptions is the notion of becoming "someone." There are a number of interview segments in *Soul Searching* that present Merton's development as a contemplative more as a radical disidentification with his biographical self than, as many would imagine, an integrated coalescence of his former worldly incarnations. Moreover, he seemed intensely devoted to situating himself as an experiential witness to what was ontologically true. Complacency, for Merton, was the near enemy, and the somnambulant state of Heidegger's Das Man was, for him, an anathema of cosmic proportions, by dint of fact that such unconsciousness brings with it the obscuration of the existential and divine uniqueness that God imprints in each soul. *Soul Searching* provides us with more than ample justification to reframe Merton's restlessness and dissatisfaction in his pursuit of the truth, not as an exercise in neurosis, but as a continual foun-taining of renewals that were ultimately in the service of a higher ordering of his consciousness and infilling him with a bodhisattva -like compassion for the welfare of all sentient beings.

The leitmotif of death for the sake of love occupies an important perspective in the film. To undertake the death of the self is based unequivocally on the passion and desire to live one's life for God; which is tantamount to saying: to do things for love and love alone. It would come to be the mantra that Merton lived by: to act out of a love for God and our brothers and sisters.

Contrary to popular conceptions associated with monastic life as an enclave of blissfully pure souls anticipating union with God, through Merton's writings we become aware of the all too human realities of coenobitic life. Merton was able to articulate with great clarity the paradoxes that confronted the monks un-dertaking monastic ascesis. The juggernaut of dying to one's own personal identity in deference to a transcendent will, must have concerned Merton deeply, for there were novices who, to begin with, had entered cloistered life with poorly formed egos. There was a freedom waiting those who could give up their will to have God's will live within them, but this was problematic for the monks whose existential identities had not yet reached a level of development to allow for a relinquishing of the self to take place in a psychologically healthy way.

There are moments in which the film is able to capture some of the inner peace that is potentially available to the aspirant of contemplative life. Structurally however, *Soul Searching* is less compelling than the actual content of the film. There are too many narrators and, at times, the voiceover of Merton quotes is overdone and only adds to the aesthetic weaknesses of the montage. There are many scenes that appear rushed in the making and not very well thought through. While it is not always the case, the images seem incongruous with the selection of music.

Soul Searching can serve as an inspiring introduction to the life and spirituality of Thomas Merton. For those already familiar with Merton's writings there are pockets of revelation in the film that might not have been considered in a general perusal of his written works. One example involves the intermittent adversarial relationship Merton experienced with those who were in a posi-tion of authority to censor his writings. Merton's journal entries leave the reader sympathetic to his point of view, especially in regard to his objection to being asked to cease writing about highly politicized topics such as war and nuclear arms. Abbot Frederick Dunn, who was responsible for reining in Merton's zeal, is cast in a more compassionate light for supporting Merton's writing as a form of spiritual practice.

In the end *Soul Searching* succeeds in communicating an idea that Merton embodied throughout the course of his life. Through the film we come closer to ascertaining what Merton—as a contemplative in thought, action and within the deeper realities of his heart—realized through direct experience of spiritual life: which is to say, "the mystical journey is profoundly human."

Arthur Giacalone

MERTON, Thomas. *In My Own Words*, ed. Jonathan Montaldo (Liguori, MO: Liguori, 2007), pp. xi + 112. ISBN 978-0-7648-1671-0. $14.95.

Yes, Thomas Merton in his own words, but in a curiously narrow selection of those words, one that I find puzzling. I say narrow rather than focused; because although the book is designed as a selection of statements about what Merton saw as his "core task: to realize union with God by prayer and monastic contemplative living" (x), it provides in my view a very limited take on what "monastic contemplative living" as lived out by Merton actually was.

The selections taken together overwhelmingly emphasize Merton's identity as a Catholic Christian, and the place of Christ in his life as a monk.

I have not the slightest desire to contest these points; indeed, with the editor, I affirm them. But the book's overall effect is one that made me wonder whether it might not have been edited the way it was to prove to the editors of the recent American Catholic catechism, the one from which Merton was excised, that they had been mistaken in their decision to exclude him. The Merton of this anthology would never have become an interfaith pioneer, an outspoken peace activist, a practitioner of Zen calligraphy or printmaking, or the author of "Day of a Stranger." In one excerpt from *Contemplation in a World of Action*, it is true, Merton does say that the monastic life is "not only contemplative but prophetic"

(99); but there is virtually nothing in the rest of the book to support or develop this thought.

Of particular note is the way that the issue of solitude repeatedly appears. Merton wants "an even more solitary life than we have here in the monastery" (4). What grows on him most (this was written in 1947) "is the desire for solitude—to vanish completely ... and never be heard of again" (33). He would like to go "into solitude for good" (35). "Without solitude of some sort there is and can be no maturity" (72), he says—not surprisingly as a worshipper of a "Solitary God" (72)—no reference here to the community of Persons in the Trinity. Again I freely acknowledge that solitude is a major theme in Merton's spirituality; but there is something lopsided about how prominent a place it holds in the book. It does not hold up for us the paradoxical character of Thomas Merton who at the same time hungered for solitude and corresponded with hundreds in his return from solitude, indeed who saw his actions in the larger world to proceed from his experience of solitude.

Admittedly, Merton was a monk *sui generis*, monastic "in his own way," to use a phrase which has been applied to Leonard Cohen--like Merton a poet, a dissenting voice, and a cultural icon. But he combined his wide-ranging thoughts, readings, writings and relationships, zaniness/Zenniness and mischievousness with a solid commitment to his identity as Christian, monk and priest. I am unable to believe, in fact, that the Merton of "Day of a Stranger" would have wanted to hang out, so to speak, with the Merton of the limited dimensions which this book offers to its readers. I would recommend to its readers that they read it in company with either Lawrence S. Cunningham's *Thomas Merton, Spiritual Master* or by Christine Bochen's *Thomas Merton: Essential Writings*, either of which offers continuity between the essentially early Merton and the later, socially engaged and transcultural figure which he became.

Donald Grayston

MERTON, Thomas, *Lent and Easter Wisdom*. Compiled by Jonathan Montaldo for The Merton Institute for Contemplative Living. (Liguori, MO: Liguori Publications, 2006), pp. xii + 115 pages. $9.95 (paperback).

Each year, on Ash Wednesday, millions of Christians, begin the Lenten journey, hearing Jesus' instruction from the Gospel according to Matthew, "But when you pray, go to your inner room, close the door, and pray to your Father in secret. And your Father who sees in secret will repay you." Where do they go to find that "inner room?" Pastors, spiritual directors, catechists, adult-faith formation directors, music ministers, and liturgists seek means to open passageways through the clutter of multitasking lives for the persons they serve. Jonathan Montaldo, Associate Director of the Merton Institute for Contemplative Living, has compiled daily reflections for the journey to conversion through Lent, Triduum, and the First Week of Easter. Each day, access to the inner room of the reader's heart, is opened by a passage from the Scriptures, an excerpt from Thomas Merton's collection of essays, *Seasons of Celebration*, a prayer, and a question to prompt journaling by the reader.

The forty-days preparation for Easter, since its origin in the late fourth century, has always imitated Jesus' sojourn in the wilderness. Through a great variety of dietary and devotional practices, it has reflected the three pillars of Judaeo-Christian tradition: fasting, prayer, and almsgiving. Christian life, rooted in the Paschal Mystery, is always a journey of conversion through these three channels. The restoration of the catechumenate through the Rite of Christian Initiation has provided in most Catholic parishes a visible reminder to the baptized members, that life in Christ is, as stated by Montaldo, "a movement from one state of being to another."

Cistercian monk, Thomas Merton, has charted his movement from one state of being to another through thousands of pages of journaling. Those familiar with his extraordinary gift of naming the utterances of his own soul in language that spoke kinship to the souls of millions of readers, will find in this compilation, nuggets that will bring fresh sight to each day of the journey. Drawn from fifteen essays written by Merton from 1950-1964, later published in *Seasons of Celebration*, each day's entry is adjoined to a related passage from the lectionary readings for the day, a prayer, and a question or consideration that invites journaling.

Journaling provides a framework for the "inner room," because it is a place of conversation between the person journaling and God alone. Thomas Merton, through his many pages of journaling has provided a model that neither intimidates those of us less articulate, nor substitutes for our own words, but leads us to an increasing freedom to speak our truth with God. It is apparent throughout Merton's journals, that the inner dialogue is prayer and not diary.

These are never conversations with himself. The critique often directed against contemplative practice, including journaling, is that it is navel-gazing. Merton's most interior experiences of God deepened his consciousness of his relationship with the entire human family and his relationship with all creation.

Montaldo's use of the lectionary as the guide for the journey unites the focus for the reflections and prayers of the individual with that of the whole Church. Before the liturgical reform of the Second Vatican Council, Lenten piety was, most often, individualistic and not anchored in the communal and ecclesial fonts of Scripture and liturgy. *Lent and Easter Wisdom from Thomas Merton* effectively helps those raised in the piety of the pre-Vatican II Catholic Church grow into a more ecclesial paschal consciousness. The Church fathers decreed in the Constitution on the Sacred Liturgy, Sacrosanctum Concilium, "the spiritual life, however, is not limited solely to participation in the liturgy. The Christian is indeed called to pray with his brethren, but he must also enter into his chamber to pray to the Father in secret; yet more, according to the teaching of the Apostle, he should 'pray without ceasing'." (1Thessalonians 5:17) These devotions should be so drawn up that they harmonize with the liturgical seasons." (Paragraph 12). For those whose prayer life is only in community, this book may serve as a guide to a deeper interior life. For those in the catechumenate, this book is a valuable companion during those final steps toward the dying and birthing of Baptism, Confirmation, and Eucharist.

The daily reflections for the first week of Lent call us into the desert with insights about asceticism and fasting. Merton instructs the reader "all Christian asceticism is characterized by wholeness and balance." The practices of fast and abstinence from food that are part of the Church's Lenten regimen, as well as those personally chosen "giving up for Lent" disciplines, must be rooted in the dying and rising of the Paschal Mystery. Through the second week, Merton directs the reader to look within. He comments on the wrestling with illusions that keep persons from true freedom. It is in the communal celebration of the mystery of Christ that "the Christian discovers the secret of his own inviolable solitude." Maturing through this season of redeemed time is the process toward union with Christ, as Merton describes: "Time does not limit freedom, but gives it scope for its exercise and choice." Since conversion is the goal of the Lenten journey, forgiveness and reconciliation are the seed and the fruit of the season. Merton's trust in God's mercy inspires the freedom to forgive. During that holiest season of the year, the Triduum, Merton focuses on two central words of the Scriptures: *"Hesed"*—the "loving kindness" constant in the covenant of the Hebrew Scriptures and *"metanoia"*—the "change of heart" response to the Gospel by the faithful disciple. These are the source and consequence of the dying and rising of Jesus Christ celebrated in Easter. "This gift, this mercy, this unbounded love for God for us has been lavished upon us as a result of Christ's victory." The Second Sunday of Easter, concludes this journey with Scripture and Merton. The light of Christ that flickered in darkened churches to announce the Resurrection is experienced in the inner room of the reader.

In reading one's own daily journaling of this season of prayer, the Christian can recognize his or her maturing into union with Christ and can say with St. Paul, "I regard everything as loss because of the surpassing value of knowing Christ Jesus my Lord." This compilation of readings and reflections provides the reader with small seeds of contemplation that will grow into a greater knowledge of the Risen Lord.

Fr. Ron Atwood

WALDRON, Robert, *Thomas Merton: Master of Attention* (London: Darton, Longman, & Todd, Ltd, 2007), pp. 101 ISBN 0-232-52714-8 (paperback). $16.95.

Those with an artistic temperament will love this book. Those who want to explore time-tested or new insights into contemplation as an act of *attention* will also love this book. Basing his work on Thomas Merton's experience with and love for art, Robert Waldron has created a gem of a treatise on prayer--from the original poem, "Attention," to the final chapter on love. The reader will be captivated by Waldron's graceful prose, his ability to insert biographical data at just the right moment, and his fresh insights into Merton's transformative experiences. As long-time English teacher, reader of psychology and of Merton, Waldron is aptly equipped to delve into Merton's life and writing. His opening chapter, devoted to a biography of Merton, is both full and lean: full enough for the neophyte and lean enough for the seasoned Merton reader.

In "The Connoisseur of Beauty," Waldron traces Merton's fascination with art during his pre-monastic days. With skill, he juxtaposes the "pictures of little irate Byzantine-looking saints"

(14) that Owen Merton was drawing in his last illness with Tom's fascination with the Byzantine mosaics in the churches in Rome. He also describes Merton's vision of his dead father as a mystical experience. When Merton writes in *Seven Storey Mountain* that during this eerie event he was "pierced deeply with a light," Waldron deftly reminds us of a similar piercing: Bernini's famous statue of *The Ecstasy of St. Teresa* (17-18).

Waldron spends considerable time discussing Merton's visit to the 1939 World's Fair in New York and his critique of paintings by Fra Angelico, Bruegel, Bosch, and El Greco. What Merton discovers about art and what is important for contemplation is the necessity of *seeing*. Merton's ability to see the unique *haecceitas* of each being enables him to later write about the importance of seeing rightly: "The first step in the interior life" is to unlearn "our wrong ways of seeing, tasting, feeling…" (quoted 24).

To underscore how *attention* is a pre-requisite for prayer, Waldron highlights similarities between the life and writing of Merton and Simone Weil, allowing the reader to understand how a theory of beauty involves *seeing*. "Every true artist," Weil comments, "has had real, direct, and immediate contact with the beauty of the world, contact that is of the nature of a sacrament" and "Looking is what saves us" (20). Merton echoes this same belief in many of his journals and published writing. In his commentary on the works of Fra Angelico, Merton declares: "Looking at this picture is exactly the same sort of thing as praying" (quoted 20). Whereas Weil sees all types of beauty as the bait God uses to win the soul and "open it to the breath from on high" (17), Waldron suggests that for Merton, the bait was the captivating beauty of Rome's churches.

These key ideas of Chapter 1 lay the foundation for all the subsequent chapters. In "The Close Reader of *Logos*," Waldron explains how, after his entrance into the monastery, Merton's love of art was transferred to Gregorian chant and *lectio divina*. Using carefully sifted biographical facts and tantalizing vignettes from Merton's journals to support his thesis, Waldron details how Merton's original attitude of *contemptus mundi* --with its rejection of the visual arts--was gradually modified to a more incarnational view of nature. Chapter 3 outlines the role Czeslaw Milosz played in introducing Merton to the writing of Simone Weil and offers a solid interpretation, by two recognized literary scholars, of the George Herbert poem cherished by Weil. These pages alone make interesting reflective reading for the contemporary seeker.

"Alone With the Alone," Chapter 4, focuses primarily on *A Vow of Conversation* and how Merton's study of Zen enhanced his ability to see. Indeed, Waldron considers this text as a kind of documentary on "learning to see" (49). He describes Merton's frequent journal jottings about the weather as new and fresh examples of his increased ability for "direct seeing" (61). They are, Waldron maintains, not Western but Eastern descriptions (50), akin to a Japanese pen and ink drawing, or the piercing poetry of Wallace Stevens and Robinson Jeffers (50). Such dabbling with Zen and seeing as no-seeing (59) sets the stage for two chapters on specific art forms Merton enjoyed in his later years: calligraphy and photography. Delightful as these two chapters are, I suspect there is meat here for separate book-length studies of the relationship between seeing/contemplation and Merton's art.

The final chapter, "Love and Do What You Will," investigates Merton relationship with "M" against the backdrop of T.S.Eliot's Prufrock, that quintessential victim of modernism paralyzed by fear and his own vulnerability. Waldron's take on the events of Merton's last years is to see how an inner gaze toward the ego is transformed into an outer gaze (91) that embraces a new gentleness (82-3). He regards Merton's relationship with "M" as a necessary prelude to his healing experience at Polonnaruwa. "Gazing upon the Polonnaruwa Buddhas," writes Waldron about the famous epiphany, " is simultaneously an aesthetic experience as well as a deeply religious one" (88). Great art always takes your breath away, but when you have the power of *attention*, another level of reality can be experienced. Waldron is convinced (and is convincing) that Merton's ability to *see* becomes a living out of Weil's concept that "absolutely unmixed attention is prayer" (quoted 90). Indeed, in Waldron's view, Merton's life from the 1939 World's Fair, with its prophetic critique of Bruegel's *The Wedding Dance,* to the great Buddhas at Polonnaruwa is a spiritual journey of increasing attention, culminating in a "numinous mystical experience" of wholeness (91).

Two brief quibbles, however: the author several times alludes to the importance of the doors of perception being cleansed without noting the source: William Blake's *The Marriage of Heaven and Hell,* and refers to "The Panther" by Rilke and "The Snowman" by Wallace Stevens without quoting lines of the poem for non-literary scholars. True, a bibliographic reference is provided, but having at least a stanza of each poem would help most readers.

Nevertheless, this focused study of art as a vehicle for learning-to-see is a solid contribution to Merton studies. *Master of Attention* is Waldron's fourth book on Merton. After studies of Merton from a Jungian perspective, an examination of his poetry, and an analysis of his poetry, essays, and journals, Waldron is admittedly a seeker of Merton's secret spark. He suspects the spark—the way to deeper prayer—is *attention*. I suspect he has it right this time.

Monica Weis

Contributors

William Apel is professor of religious studies at Linfield College, McMinnville, Oregon, and author of *Signs of Peace: The Interfaith Letters of Thomas Merton* (2006).

Fr. Ron Atwood, ordained in 1969 for the Diocese of Columbus, Ohio, is pastor of St. Francis of Assisi parish in Victorian Village. Since ordination, he has been involved in parish ministry, retreat work, youth ministry, hospital chaplaincy, spiritual direction, secondary school and college education, lay ministry formation and social justice work.

David Belcastro is Professor of Religious Studies and Chair of the Department of Religion and Philosophy at Capital University in Bexley, Ohio. A long-time contributor to ITMS conferences and publications, he currently serves as co-editor of *The Merton Annual*.

Christine M. Bochen is professor of Religious Studies and holds the Shannon Chair in Catholic Studies at Nazareth College. Her most recent publications are Merton's *Cold War Letters* (2006) and *Thomas Merton: A Life in Letters (2008)*, both edited with William H. Shannon. Together with William Shannon and Patrick O'Connell, she is co-author of *The Thomas Merton Encyclopedia (2002)*. She is a founding member and past president of the International Thomas Merton Society.

Craig Burgdof is Professor of World Religion and Chair of the Department of Religion and Philosophy at Capital University in Bexley, Ohio.

Nass Cannon is a practicing physician, Clinical Professor of Medicine at the University of Alabama at Birmingham and Chief of Staff at Cooper Green Mercy Hospital for the past decade, Nass explores the relationship between medicine and spirituality. A *Broken Healer,* he has sought Merton's guidance since the early seventies in the pursuit of wholeness, which Nass perceives as Health.

John P. Collins is a faculty member of the International Education Program, Inc. and former Lecturer at The College of the Holy

Cross has been a past contributor to *The Merton Seasonal, The Merton Annual , Cistercian Studies Quarterly*. He writes a monthly Thomas Merton column for The Catholic Free Press, Worcester, MA. For the past seven years he has been a discussion leader for the Thomas Merton Study Group at St. Mary's Parish in Shrewsbury, MA.

John D. Dadosky is an associate professor at Regis College/University of Toronto where he teaches philosophy and theology. He is author of *The Structure of Religious Knowing: Encountering the Sacred in Eliade and Lonergan* (SUNY Press, 2004). Recent essays include: "Towards a Fundamental RE-Interpretation of Vatican II" in *The Heythrop Journal* (September, 2008), "Merton's Dialogue with Zen: Pioneering or Passé?" in *Fu Jen International Religious Studies* (Taiwan—Summer, 2008) and "Sacralization, Secularization and Religious Fundamentalism" in *Studies in Religion/Sciences Religeuses* (Fall, 2007). He is currently working on a manuscript on the philosophy of beauty using Lonergan's philosophy of consciousness. He is also interested in post-Vatican II ecclesiology as well as method in interreligious dialogue.

Julie Frazier is currently a senior English Literature major at Capital University in Bexley, Ohio. Julie and her husband will be entering the Peace Corp after graduation.

Arthur Giacalone, Ph.D. is a Clinical/Consulting Psychologist in private practice in Walnut Creek, California. He is co-founder and current Director of the Institute of Contemplative Studies. In July 2004 Dr. Giacalone was awarded a William Shannon Fellowship by the International Thomas Merton Society in support of his proposal to produce a documentary on Thomas Merton's views on contemplation and contemplative life, entitled, Silent Lamp: Thomas Merton on Contemplative Life and the Spiritual Mysteries of the Heart (currently in production) www.silentlamp-merton.org.

Donald Grayston retired in 2004 from teaching Religious Studies at Simon Fraser University, in Vancouver, British Columbia. Currently, he is president of the International Thomas Merton Society, and director of the Pacific Jubilee Program in Spiritual Formation and Spiritual Direction.

Kevin Griffith, Professor of English at Capital University in Bexley, Ohio, has published three books of poetry, the latest of which is *Denmark, Kangaroo, Orange* (Pearl Editions, 2008). His poem "Love Your Enemy" was an honorable mention in the 2008 Thomas Merton Poetry of the Sacred Competition.

Fred Herron is a member of the Department of Theology and Religious Studies at St. John's University, Staten Island, Chairperson of the Religious Studies Department at Fontbonne Hall Academy, Brooklyn, Director of Adult Faith Formation at St. Clare parish, Staten Island and Program Director at Mount Manresa Jesuit Retreat House, Staten Island. Author of six books including *Combing the Tradition: Catholic Schools in the Era of Baptismal Consciousness, No Abiding Place: Thomas Merton and the Search for God* and *Wood, Waterfalls and Stars: Catholic Schools and the Catholic Imagination,* his articles have appeared in *Review for Religious, Momentum* and *The National Catholic Reporter.* He has spoken nationally and internationally in the areas of spirituality and Catholic education.

Daniel P. Horan, OFM is a Franciscan friar of Holy Name Province (NY) and a graduate student at the Washington Theological Union (DC). In addition to his work on Thomas Merton, he has written extensively on Franciscan theology, philosophy and spirituality, with particular interest in the authentic retrieval of medieval Franciscan thought for application in contemporary contexts. His articles have appeared or are forthcoming in several journals including *America, Spiritual Life, Seminary Journal, Review for Religious, The Cord, The Other Journal, The Merton Journal* (UK) and others. You can contact Dan or learn more about him and his work at www.danhoran.com.

Dewey Weiss Kramer is Professor Emerita of German and Humanities. Her teaching and research have gravitate increasingly toward subjects with a spiritual dimension, with current focus on Hildegard of Bingen. She has had Benedictine connections for decades, going back to her grade-school years and recently gave the Community Retreat for the Benedictine Sisters of Holy Name Monastery in Florida. She is founding editor of The Merton Annual; author of Open to the Spirit, the history of the Cistercian monastery of the Holy Spirit in Georgia; Oblate of St. benedict's Monastery in Minnesota and an avid performer on the recorder. She also happily shares home, interests, and activities scholarly and otherwise, with Victor A. Kramer.

Victor A. Kramer, founding editor of The Merton Annual, has seen some fifty books through the press. At present he gives days of recollection and retreats and is a spiritual director (CSD, 2006).

Ross Labrie is President of the Thomas Merton Society of Canada. He is the author of two books on Thomas Merton, *The Art of Thomas Merton* (1979) and *Thomas Merton and the Inclusive Imagination* (2001) as well as *The Catholic Imagination in American Literature* and *The Writings of Daniel Berrigan*. He has also served as an international advisor to the International Thomas Merton Society.

Roger Lipsey is the author of *Angelic Mistakes: The Art of Thomas Merton* (2006), recipient of the 'Louie' award from the International Thomas Merton Society. Roger is now working on a book about the mind and methods of Dag Hammarskjöld.

Gray Matthews is an Assistant Professor of Communication at the University of Memphis. He has served the ITMS a member of the board and membership committee, site coordinator for the 2007 conference, and coordinator for the Memphis ITMS chapter since 2001; he has contributed essays to *The Merton Annual* and currently serves as co-editor. He also teaches courses on Merton, mysticism and contemplative spirituality for the Catholic Diocese of West Tennessee and the Memphis Theological Seminary.

Patrick F. O'Connell teaches English and Theology at Gannon University, Erie, PA. A founding member and former president of the International Thomas Merton Society, he serves as editor of The Merton Seasonal. He is co-author of *The Thomas Merton Encyclopedia* (2002), and editor of *The Vision of Thomas Merton* (2003), *Cassian and the Fathers* (2005), *Pre-Benedictine Monasticism* (2006), and *Introduction to Christian Mysticism*, the first three volumes of Merton's novitiate conferences.

Pamela Werrbach Proietti has been a member of the Memphis chapter of ITMS since 2002 and is today a member of the Chicago chapter of ITMS. She has taught political philosophy for many years, most recently at the University of Memphis; she is currently studying pastoral counseling at Loyola University—Chicago, Institute for Pastoral Studies.

Albert J. Raboteau teaches in the Religion Department at Princeton. He offers courses in American Religious History, African-American Religion, Religion and Literature, and occasionally a seminar on Thomas Merton. His publications include *Slave Religion*; *Canaan Land*; *A Fire in the Bones*; and *A Sorrowful Joy*.

Timothy J. Shaffer is a doctoral student at Cornell University studying the role of education in democracy and citizen politics. He holds both an MTS and MPA from the University of Dayton, writing his MTS thesis on the Franciscan influence on Merton. He has published and spoken about this influence as well as issues of war and peace. He is a past Daggy Scholar and served as a Youth Representative to the ITMS Board of Directors.

Monica Weis SSJ, Professor of English at Nazareth College, Rochester NY, has been a past Vice President of ITMS and currently serves on the Board of Directors, the Publications Committee, and the Program Committee for ITMS - 11. She has written and lectured widely on Thomas Merton and nature.

Index

9239